THE MANITOUS

ALSO BY BASIL JOHNSTON

Ojibway Heritage
Ojibway Ceremonies
Indian School Days

THE MANITOUS

THE SPIRITUAL WORLD OF THE OJIBWAY

BASIL JOHNSTON

HarperCollins*Publishers*

HarperCollins books may be purchased for educational, business, or sales promotional use. For information please write: Special Markets Department, HarperCollins Publishers, Inc., 10 East 53rd Street, New York, NY 10022.

FIRST EDITION

Designed by Alma Hochhauser Orenstein

Illustrations by David Johnson

Library of Congress Cataloging-in-Publication Data
Johnston, Basil.
    The Manitous : the spiritual world of the Ojibway / Basil Johnston ; illustrations by David Johnson. — 1st ed.
        p.   cm.
    ISBN 0-06-017199-5
    1. Ojibwa Indians—Religion.   2. Ojibwa mythology.   3. Ojibwa Indians—Folklore.
I. Title.
E99.C6J636 1995
299'.783—dc20   95-9274

95 96 97 98 99 ❖/HC 10 9 8 7 6 5 4 3 2 1

I dedicate *The Manitous* to the recovery of the
Anishinaubae language and the restoration
of spiritual and cultural traditions in
Anishinaubae family and community life.

I am indebted to Sam Ozawamik and Alex McKay,
friends as well as tutors, for their persistent challenge
in asking, "What does it mean?"
I owe no less to my wife and love, Lucie,
for graciously giving her time and place to a muse.

CONTENTS

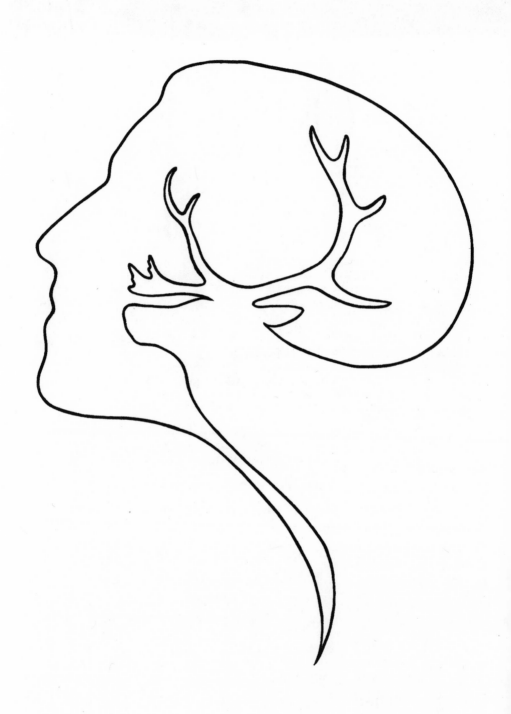

PREFACE

My awareness and interest in manitous began a long time ago on the Cape Croker Indian Reserve, located on the Georgian Bay side of Bruce Peninsula in Ontario. To keep me from wandering too far from her sight, my mother, Mary, told me about Weendigoes (Giant Cannibals) and maemaegawaehnssiwuk (little people), who lurked in the woods waiting to seize and carry off disobedient children. I was then about six. By the time I was nine, I learned from tribal storytellers that there were other manitous, such as Kitchi-Manitou and Nana'b'oozoo. These storytellers no longer narrated stories every night during the winter as they once had but now did so only on special occasions, such as during the communal celebration of Christmas in the village. They presented these manitous as good beings, more benevolent than the Giant Cannibals or little people.

During my teenage years, my teachers at public school and the Spanish Indian Residential School, along with history texts and other learned books, made it clear that our Anishinaubae cultural beliefs and myths were superstitious, pagan, and childish and that to believe in the presence and animation of all things with spirits was pantheism. Hearing that our stories and manitous were foolish and unchristian may have cast many doubts about the actuality of our supernatural figures, but it did not prevent our storytellers from telling stories or diminish our fascination and delight in them.

Like many other North American Indian people, I became drawn even more closely into North American affairs, especially into the cultural and educational spheres, by the continentwide American Indian awakening and rediscovery of the "Indian" in the early 1960s.

It was as a parent and an American Indian that I was invited to take in an "Indian Display" at the Churchill Avenue Public School in North York, Ontario, that was mounted by the fifth- and sixth-grade students after they had studied American Indians "in-depth" for five weeks. One of the students, referring to the substance and content of the five-week unit, asked, "Is that all there is?" To furnish that youngster and countless others like him, as well as their teachers, with what they could not derive from the available texts, I wrote *Ojibway Heritage* and *Ojibway Ceremonies,* along with other books and articles.

By the late 1970s, as an author and storyteller, I was invited to tell stories to native and nonnative audiences alike. Following these presentations, I was frequently asked to explain the meaning of the stories and of the manitous. Fortunately, I met Alex McKay of Big Trout Lake, Ontario, and Sam Ozawamik (Brown Beaver) of Manitoulin Island, Ontario, who taught me how to elicit meaning from the stories and from our native language. Elders such as Sam were more than willing to tell me what they knew about other manitous.

The questions, "Who are the manitous? What do the stories mean?" persisted wherever I went in Ojibway territory, whether in Canada or the United States. Native people had forgotten not only their language, but much of their heritage. I searched, but no texts were available that could furnish the information that students and others sought. There were only sketchy references here and there, not enough to settle questions or doubts, or to further understanding.

My interest in the manitous was no longer casual; it had now become fascination. Stories about the manitous allow native people to understand their cultural and spiritual heritage and enable them to see the worth and relevance of their ideas, institutions, perceptions, and values. Once they see the worth and relevance of their heritage, they may be inspired to restore it in their lives. Perhaps other people will find worth in our understandings as well.

I have ordered the chapters in this book according to the sequence in which the manitous appeared and performed services in the development and growth of the nation. After Kitchi-Manitou, the Creator, and Muzzu-Kummik-Quae, Mother Earth, follow the four brothers, Maudjee-kawiss, Pukawiss, Cheeby-aub-oozoo, Nana'b'oozoo; the manitous of the forests and meadows; the personal manitous; Nebaunaubaewuk; the Manitoussiwuk; the auttissookaunuk; Pauguk; and lastly, Weendigo. These chapters are, of course, brief, and represent only a portion of what each manitou deserves. The longest chapter is devoted to Nana'b'oozoo because he is the prototype of humankind and the center of human interest.

I have tried to keep with the practice of setting the stories down as they were told in the old days, allowing the stories to tell themselves, so to speak. But since many readers are unfamiliar with the old traditions and the allegorical nature of many Indian stories, I have added commentaries at the end of chapters, when necessary, to clarify the stories.

The glossary contains definitions and explanations of Ojibway words and terms that appear throughout the text.

INTRODUCTION

According to tradition, Kitchi-Manitou (the Great Mystery) created the world, plants, birds, animals, fish, and the other manitous in fulfillment of a vision. This world was flooded. But while the earth was under water and life was coming to an end, a new life was beginning in the skies. Geezhigo-Quae (Sky Woman) was espoused to a manitou in the skies, and she conceived.

The surviving animals and birds observed the changes taking place in Sky Woman's condition as they clung to life on the surface of the flood waters. They set aside whatever concerns they might have had about their own fates and asked one of their fellow survivors, the Giant Turtle, to offer his back as a place of rest for Sky Woman, who they then invited to come down.

Upon settling on the turtle's back, Sky Woman asked for a moiety of soil. Only the muskrat, the least of the animals, was able to retrieve the soil from beneath the flood waters, and Sky Woman took the pawful of soil and etched it around the rim of the turtle's back. She then breathed the breath of life, growth, and abundance into the soil and infused into the soil and earth the attributes of womanhood and motherhood, that of giving life, nourishment, shelter, instruction, and inspiration for the heart, mind, and spirit. Only after she had done these things did

Sky Woman give birth to twins, whose descendants took the name Anishinaubaek, meaning the Good Beings. In time, other nations labeled their fellow Anishinaubaek with other names, such as Ojibway (Chippewa), Ottawa, Pottawatomi, Algonquin, and Mississauga.

The island where the Anishinaubae people were born continued to grow until it became a continent, the Land of the Great Turtle, as North America is commonly known to many North American Indians. By virtue of Sky Woman's creation of an island that grew into a continent and then her giving birth to her children on it, the Anishinaubae people and other North American Indians believed that the continent was given to the first-born natives of this land. Kitchi-Manitou and Sky Woman granted ownership and stewardship of the land to the natives in joint tenancy with the manitous, the birds, animals, insects, and generations still to be born.

The Anishinaubaek believe that their people were born on this continent while it was still in its infancy, a conviction that differs from that of conservative scholars, who maintain that the North American Indians' place of origin is somewhere in Asia and that the Indians came to this continent via the Bering Strait anywhere from 10,000 to 25,000 years ago. The theory that the North American Indians originally came from Asia is at odds with more recent scholarly studies and discoveries that have suggested that humans have inhabited this continent far longer than was first believed, from as long as 250,000 years ago.

The new people born of Sky Woman grew slowly in number from a single family to a village. While the fledgling nation was still only a village, weak and backward, five manitous from another world came to them by sea and showed them how to develop their human talent and labor to provide for five basic necessities of survival: life, guardianship, healing, leading, and teaching. After these beings returned to their own spheres, the Anishinaubae people organized their families and communities according to these divisions and adopted symbols, which they called totems, to commemorate the benefits they received.

After the adoption of these five principles, which promoted progress, growth, and order, the new nation grew and expanded north, east, south, and west until it came to rank as one of the two largest North American Indian nations north of the Mexican border, extending eastward well into what is now the province of Quebec; south into Ontario, Michigan, Wisconsin, and Minnesota; west into Manitoba and parts of Saskatchewan; and north to a point roughly corresponding to the fiftieth parallel in northern Ontario. For the most part, the expansion was relatively peaceful, except for one battle that ended only when the Catbird People, who opposed the Anishinaubaek, were wiped from the face of the earth.

If the Anishinaubae nation lived in relative peace while occupying such a large territory, such good fortune may be attributed to the size of its population and the preoccupation of all its neighbors with survival, the primary goal of life, and in having neighbors who were kin in language and in many cultural respects: the Cree to the north; the Naskapi and Addikumaek to the east; and the Shawnee, Kickapoo, Sauk and Fox, and Menominees to the south and southwest. As neighbors, and sometimes as foes, were also people of different stock and culture, such as the Huron, Mohawk, Seneca, Onondaga, Oneida, Cayuga, and Tuscarora to the east and the Winnebago and Dakota to the west.

From youth to old age, the Anishinaubae people were hunters; fishers; harvesters; homemakers; healers; storytellers; and, only as a last resort, warriors. Their major purpose in life was to survive as individuals and communities. Survival was the need and first reality that governed their dreams, hopes, aspirations, and outlook and the kind of training and discipline that would best prepare their offspring to cope and be equal to the demands and challenges of primal life.

With but the most primitive, crudest tools, utensils, and weapons—bows and arrows of limited range and accuracy, clubs, spears, nets, stone knives, and digging sticks—the new people faced formidable odds and impediments. Despite the rugged lands, vast distances, blizzards and winds, mosquitoes and black flies, personal weaknesses and failings, these early Anishinaubae people roamed the land and plied the lakes and rivers in quest of food and medicine to nourish themselves.

Such a simple life, whose needs were restricted to the provision of food, clothing, and shelter; the maintenance of health; and self-protection, may seem unfulfilling and even stultifying, but to the men and women who had to survive under these conditions, life was rewarding and filled them with pride. Without exception, every man and woman had to master the practical skills: archery; spearing; setting nets and traps; making canoes, tools, shelters, and medicines; curing meat and vegetables; tanning hides and making clothing; understanding animals; and knowing the properties of plants and their parts. There was so much to master, so much beyond human knowledge and understanding.

It has long been assumed that people who were preoccupied with material needs and wants would have little interest in matters of the spirit and the mind. On the contrary, it was this very mode of life, this simple way of meeting simple needs, that awakened in man and woman a consciousness that there were realities and presences in life other than the corporeal and the material. The spirit, the manitou, the mystery, were part of life and could not be separated from it. Who and what made the laws that govern the Earth? Who and what gave the birds and the animals the sense of knowing about coming changes? Who and what governed success and failure? It was the grass at one's feet, the thunder and lightning above, the bleat of a deer as it struggled for life after it was shot, that evoked the sense that there was more to life than physical existence.

Men and woman wondered about the first paradox in life that confirmed their suspicions about the existence of other realities in life. Mother Earth was bountiful, producing more than enough for every living being, yet she did not yield her harvest easily or even handily. Men and woman had to glean what they could. Yet even though they had the same skills or weapons, some men and women seldom returned home from a hunting expedition empty-handed, whereas others came back home far too often with little or nothing to show for their efforts.

To keep from starving before winter was over and to avoid having to hunt and thereby putting oneself at risk of death at the hands of the Weendigoes, men and women labored mightily throughout the summer and fall to store enough food to last them until spring. Work was the chief ethic.

Gleaning life from the land and the lakes bound them to their community, much more closely than today. They moved as one, hunted and fished as one, celebrated triumphs as one, and mourned losses as one. They shared beliefs, customs, risks, rewards, and hopes.

Yet despite the traditional communal spirit and mode of life, the Anishinaubae people championed and upheld the importance of individuality and personal independence on the promise that the more self-reliant and free the individual, the stronger and better the well-being of the community. Both the individual and the community were best served by nurturing men and women who were resourceful, independent masters of their own time, space, and spirit, the equals of all other men and women in the community.

By the same token, men and women were also instilled with a sense of obligation to the community that required them to give something back to the people for all the benefits and favors they received. That which made men and women Anishinaubae was considered to be owed to the entire heritage of the community and the nation, and each person was bound to return something to his or her heritage and so add to its worth.

The belief in the influence of individuals bore upon the nation's choice of leadership and authority as well. Men and women chose the foremost among them, usually a hunter or a medicine man or woman, to lead them so as to derive the benefit of that person's continued success and kinship with the manitous. The person was chosen to lead a particular project or enterprise, to accept the first risks without the means of enforcing his or her wishes on any of his or her followers. This chosen leader was *ogimauh,* the foremost person for that one project or enterprise, which, when concluded, ended the tenure of the leader.

In the Anishinaubae nation there was no central authority or government, divinely appointed or humanly seized, to issue and enforce laws, dispense favors to friends, impose fines on enemies, declare war against other nations, or demand homage and tributes from its subjects. Yet there was order. The only authority was the collective of elders who adjudicated disputes put before them, counseled observance of the laws that governed the seasons, fostered friendship and goodwill within the community, and deferred to the manitous and the mystery of life by performing rituals and ceremonies and making offerings as prescribed by custom and tradition.

Traditionally, Anishinaubae history and heritage were taught by the elders and others, who instructed the people in everything from history, geography, and botany to astronomy, language, and spiritual heritage, at family and community gatherings during the winter months. But this was not the only time that lessons were given. Learned elders conducted special training programs during the year for those who were considered gifted and caring of the cultural and spiritual heritage. Young men and women who were chosen to receive special tutelage would be the learned elders when their time came, accredited to interpret and to adjudicate. The nightly winter gatherings were lessons, not simply storytelling sessions as so many people refer to them today.

It was during these lessons that youths came to learn about the manitous—their origin; presence; dwelling places; services and purposes; and kinship with all living beings, including plants, Mother Earth, animals, and human beings. The manitous were just as much a reality as were trees, valleys, hills, and winds. It was in these sessions that young people learned that Kitchi-Manitou infused everything and everyone with manitoulike attributes and principles that imparted growth, healing, character, individuality, and identity.

As guardians of the wards over which they were appointed, the manitous could withhold from hunters permission or opportunity to kill and even exact revenge if one of their flock was maltreated. Among the manitous there were two to be feared, two who granted no favors but sought and stalked human beings to destroy them: the Weendigoes, the Giant Cannibals, and the Matchi-auwishuk, the Evil Ones. These were man-hunting manitous that preyed upon evil-doing humans, as well as those who gave in to excesses. The threat of the Weendigoes and Matchi-auwish was usually enough to bring about compliance with the perceived laws and established customs. Except for these two there was nothing to fear of the manitous, but it was nevertheless deemed prudent to court them with deference and offerings.

Men and women felt the presence of the manitous all around them. Human beings had to comply with the natural laws of the world, and although they were subject to no other men or women, they had to abide by everything else and could not make anything comply or conform to their wishes. They were among the least of the creatures of the Earth and were dependent on the manitous' goodwill.

In their lessons the old storytellers tried to explain how life, being, and the world originated. They told of the creation of the world; life; order; the seasons; and phenomena in the skies, on Earth, and deep in the Underworld of the afterlife. They explained that "no man or woman can do this. Only a manitou."

For the Anishinaubae people, only Kitchi-Manitou could create the world and all that is in it; separate the seasons; set the cycle of birth, growth, decline, and death into motion; instill sense and an inner being in all living creatures; and give form and time to everything. Kitchi-Manitou was the creator, the Great Mystery. By combining *kitchi,* a prefix meaning immense and preeminent, and *manitou,* the Anishinaubae people coined a word for the creator.

Mystery is but one of the connotations of the word *manitou.* The word has other meanings as well: spiritual, mystical, supernatural, godlike or spiritlike, quiddity, essence. It is in these other senses that the term is often used and is to be understood, not just in the context of manitou beings.

Manitou refers to realities other than the physical ones of

rock, fire, water, air, wood, and flesh—to the unseen realities of individual beings and places and events that are beyond human understanding but are still clearly real.

Kitchi-Manitou created the manitou beings and forces and infused them, to various degrees, into beings and objects.

In creating Sky Woman and other manitous that dwell among the stars and beyond the Earth, Kitchi-Manitou endowed them with immortality, virtue, and wisdom. It is to them that men and women turn in their vision quests and purification rites for the betterment of their inner beings.

Cohabiting the Earth with human beings and other creatures are a range of other manitous. There are those whose mandate is to preside over plant and animal species. There are also those who dwell at the four cardinal points (North, East, South and West); these muses have jurisdiction over creative talent and over the accuracy of stories, laws, insights, wisdom, and the beauty of language. Calling on the muses to assist in the creation of a story was a sacred act. Cohabiting the cardinal points were other manitous that presided over human destinies, well-being, youth, and old age.

As benefactors, the manitous were welcome. Men and women were not afraid of the proximate manitous, addressing them and soliciting their favors as friends.

Although there are many fascinating manitous in the Anishinaubae heritage, I have chosen to write about the manitous who lived among the Anishinaubae people in human form in the early formative age of the people. The first two chapters are devoted to Kitchi-Manitou and Muzzu-Kummik-Quae, the Creator and Mother Earth. These manitous represent the origin of the Earth and humankind. The remaining chapters tell the stories, the legends, of the other manitous.

The accounts of the manitous that were human or half human in form begin with the story of Ae-pungishimook, the West, who lusted for Winonah, a human woman. This manitou possessed her once every generation, begetting four sons—Maudjee-kawiss, Pukawiss, Cheeby-aub-oozoo, and Nana'b'oo-zoo—who became the cornerstones of the Anishinaubae heritage and brought lasting tradition to the Anishinaubae people. The sons' gifts were strength and a sense of history; drama and costume; chanting, music, and dream-vision quests; and the pipe of peace, as well as a living sense of human potentials and shortcomings. Winonah acquired certain manitoulike attributes that enabled her to bear children a generation apart in age, but she is said to have died shortly after giving birth to her fourth and last son, Nana'b'oozoo.

The following chapters tell the stories of a range of other manitous who left an indelible mark on Anishinaubae tradition. Although hundreds of stories have been told and dozens of manitous have been witnessed and recorded in varying degrees, the stories that are retold here are the basic ones that can begin to preserve the heritage of the people.

A storyteller once depicted the alienation of the Anishinaubae people from their cultural heritage and their espousal of Western European civilization as a repudiation of their figurehead, Nana'b'oozoo. In the last story concerning him, Nana'-b'oozoo, spurned and scorned, hurt and humiliated by the people who he had loved and served for so many years, gathers all his worldly possessions, stows them into his canoe, and then helps his aged grandmother, N'okomiss, board. He does not want to leave, but he must, for he is no longer welcome in his ancestral home. Still, he tarries and looks longingly in hopes that someone will notice and bid them to stay. But no one gives Nana'b'oozoo and his grandmother a second glance, and they pass beyond the horizon and out of the lives of their kin.

No one in the village misses them; no one mourns their passing. No one cares enough. Perhaps, no one will ever care enough to call them back.

But should enough people care and recall Nana'b'oozoo into their midst by learning their ancestral language and espousing their old traditions, giving them new meanings and applications in the modern age, the spirit of Nana'b'oozoo and the Anishinaubae people will be restored to its rightful place in the lives of the Anishinaubae nation.

CHAPTER ONE

KITCHI-MANITOU
THE GREAT MYSTERY

When the North American Indians saw the Western European wayfarers and missionaries erect crosses, they were scandalized by an act they regarded as profane. For them, the erection of wooden memorials, called totemic staffs (*dodaem-wautik*), was conducted only as part of a funeral ceremony. These monuments were symbols of death, reminders of the afterlife and the afterworld, and tokens of the survivors' love and respect for the departed. Hence, for the strangers and their missionaries to implant a monument of death on an occasion other than a funeral and in a place other than a burial ground was a mockery of the dead.

The wayfarers' and missionaries' misconceptions about Anishinaubae life were drawn from their observations of aboriginal ceremonies and language. One such major misconception was related to the Anishinaubae notion of God. The chief cause of the misunderstanding was the term *manitou,* which from the beginning was interpreted to mean only spirit. Naturally, this narrow interpretation of the term distorted the essential truth of what the Anishinaubae people meant. The inference that fol-

lowed was to be expected—that the aboriginal mind was incapable of conceiving or expressing any but the simplest of the
abstract.

Thereafter, whenever an aboriginal person uttered the word
manitou, Western Europeans thought it meant spirit. When a
medicine person uttered the term *manitouwun* to refer to some
curative or healing property in a tree or plant, they took it to
mean spirit. When a person said the word *manitouwut* to refer to
the sacrosanct mood or atmosphere of a place, they assumed it
meant spirit. And when a person spoke the word *manitouwih* to
allude to a medicine person with miraculous healing powers,
they construed it to mean spirit.

Western Europeans took it for granted that aboriginal people, being of simple heart and mind, believed in the presence of
little spirits in rocks, trees, groves, and waterfalls, much as the
primitive peoples of Europe believed in goblins, trolls, and leprechauns. Men and women who addressed the manitous were
believed to worship spirits, idols.

But most aboriginal people understood their respective languages well enough to know from the context the precise sense
and meaning intended by the word manitou or any of its other
derivatives. Depending on the context, they knew that in addition to spirit, the term also meant property, essence, transcendental, mystical, muse, patron, and divine.

Therefore, when the Anishinaubae people predicated the
term manitou of God, they added the prefix "Kitchi," meaning
great. By this term they meant "The Great Mystery of the
supernatural order, one beyond human grasp, beyond words,
neither male nor female, not of the flesh." As a being of the
supernatural, transcendental order, Kitchi-Manitou cannot be
known or described in human corporeal terms. What little is
known of Kitchi-Manitou is known through the universe, the
cosmos, and the world. Kitchi-Manitou is the creator of all
things, all beings, including manitous.

According to the creation story, Kitchi-Manitou had a vision,
seeing, hearing, touching, tasting, smelling, sensing, and know-

ing the universe, the world, the manitous, plants, animals, and human beings, and brought them into existence. The story represents a belief in God and in creation, an explanation of the origin of things; it also serves as an example for men and women to emulate.

Following the example set by Kitchi-Manitou, every person is to seek a dream or vision within the expanse of his or her soul-spirit being and, having attained it, bring it into fulfillment and reality. Otherwise the dream or vision will be nullified. Furthermore, every person is endowed with the gift of a measure of talent or aptitude to enable him or her to bring the vision or dream to reality, to shape his or her own being, as it were, and to fashion an immediate world and destiny. But finding this substance deep within one's innermost being is not an easy task. One must descend to the depths or ascend to the very heights of one's soul-spirit being, by means of a vision or a dream, to discover and to retrieve that morsel of talent or aptitude. Sky Woman, the mother of the people who called themselves Anishinaubae, used her talents to re-create her world and that of her descendants from a morsel of mud obtained from the bottom of the flood waters. Nana'b'oozoo, the central figure in Anishinaubae mythology who also symbolizes human potential, re-created an island, his world, from a clutch of soil retrieved from the bottom of the sea. Had he not done so, he would have perished.

With the creation of the physical world and the beings in it, the work of Kitchi-Manitou was complete. Kitchi-Manitou had done all that needed to be done. From that moment on, the onus was on men and women and their cotenants on the Earth—the animals, birds, insects, fish, and plants—to continue the work put into motion by the Creator. Kitchi-Manitou had furnished them with all they required to fulfill their visions and purposes.

Kitchi-Manitou had done everything that needed to be done and had provided all the means for humankind's well-being, growth, and accomplishment, so Kitchi-Manitou was finished with the world and would take no further part in humankind's affairs.

But was Kitchi-Manitou's abdication from the world and its affairs an act of disinterest? On the contrary, creation was seen as the highest act of selflessness, of generosity, that anyone, manitou or other, can perform—the sharing of one's gifts. And Kitchi-Manitou's grant of freedom to human beings to seek and fulfill their visions and dreams according to their individual abilities was an act not only of generosity but of trust.

And what obligation do the recipients and beneficiaries owe their benefactor for the abundance and variety of benefits received? What would be the most fitting gift to tender to Kitchi-Manitou in recompense for all the things they received? Nothing. There was not a thing that human beings could offer Kitchi-Manitou in return, other than to imitate Kitchi-Manitou in the exercise of selflessness and generosity. By giving and sharing one's goods, knowledge, experience, and abilities with the less fortunate of their kin and neighbors—the elderly, sick, widows, and orphans—human beings could emulate Kitchi-Manitou.

From the innate sense of gratitude felt by most men and women sprang the practice of offering thanksgiving on public occasions and in private.

At the commencement of grand council conferences, at the assemblies of the Medaewaewin (Grand Medicine Society), at negotiations for peace, and at the beginning of festivals, the Pipe of Peace Smoking Ceremony was performed with the prefatory words, "Let us conjoin all our thoughts, intentions, dreams, and aspirations and all our petitions and prayers in thanksgiving to Kitchi-Manitou for having bestowed upon us such bounty and beauty beyond imagination . . . and for granting us such increase in our days as to enable us to gather together in communion as in days of old . . . to enable us to see our children's children." The words were formal, addressed to Kitchi-Manitou as if the Great Benefactor was distant.

For men and women, who often lived on the margin of existence and worked on the border of hardship and danger in the midst of plenty, the presence of Kitchi-Manitou and other manitous was immediate. Their experiences as hunters, fishers, and harvesters constantly reminded them that the success of their expeditions and the yield of their crops depended not so much on their skills or experience as on such intangibles as chance, the goodwill or ill will of the manitous, and the efficacy of their medicine. If success depended solely on skill or patience, the outcome of every expedition would have been assured, but human experience taught them that this was not so. Some hunters consistently returned from the forest empty-handed, while others came back with more meat than they could carry or consume. How were these outcomes to be explained? What did the one hunter possess that the other did not? Both used similar weapons and had similar skills and opportunities, yet one emerged from the woods with his back bent under the weight of meat, whereas the other returned with nothing for his children.

How could one account for such occurrences except in terms of the sanction and will of the manitou guardian who presided over the well-being of his hunted-animal victim? The successful hunter had gained the goodwill of the manitous and ultimately of Kitchi-Manitou by petition, the performance of rituals, and the exercise of due respect for the remains of the victim.

The expression of thanksgiving in words and in the offering of tobacco represented not only the hunter's gratitude but an admission of his dependence on the goodwill of the manitous and Kitchi-Manitou. The victim, whether a deer or another being, was humankind's cotenant on Earth, with its own purpose, existence, time, and right of place and life. Neither men nor women had the right to take it and had to ask permission of the manitous and of Kitchi-Manitou to take it on behalf of the needy. And when the deer drew within range of the hunter's arrow, it was a sign that Kitchi-Manitou had granted the hunter leave to take the victim's life. When the victim fell, the hunter apologized, but the words and sentiments went beyond the expression of remorse; the hunter was declaring a universal truth and reality, that of human beings' utter dependence on their cotenants on Earth for life, growth, and well-being.

If survival and dependence did not serve as reminders of the presence of Kitchi-Manitou, then humankind's disposition to learn and question would not allow anyone to forget. The young wanted to know what it was that called from the depth of the woods in the middle of the night, where babies came from, and where the dead went. And the answer to the inevitable question of the origin of things was Kitchi-Manitou.

The questions posed in youth lingered into manhood or womanhood, evoked by other phenomena, miracles: the annual dissolution and regeneration of the earth; the emergence of a caterpillar, plain and palling, and its transformation into a butterfly, a being of beauty and grace; the metamorphosis of a blossom into an apple; the growth and self-healing of a tree stricken by lightning; and hundreds of other wonders, occurring and recurring every day, year after year.

Whether they were stalking their quarry or estimating the quality and quantity of the harvest, men and women had to open their senses to the motions, sounds, and smells of the forests, mountains, winds, and skies by day and by night and in so doing opened their minds to an even greater degree to the works and presence of Kitchi-Manitou.

With their senses, nay their entire beings, awake and alive to the world, men and women discovered the presence of Kitchi-Manitou. Certain precipices, recesses in the woods, ravines, waterfalls, caves, or valleys were infused with a greater presence of Kitchi-Manitou than were others. It was to such places that men and women went in quest of a dream or a vision and wayfarers went to offer tobacco out of deference and reverence. Some men and women believed that such places were the abodes of manitous who shared in the mystery and sacredness of Kitchi-Manitou. Perhaps this was one of the reasons that the natives regarded the Earth as sacred and deserving of honor and respect.

Even if a bay or meadow or stream did not have enough presence of the mystery of Kitchi-Manitou to earn it the designation manitouwun, it had another attribute: beauty. Men and women gazed in wonder on the dance of the aurora borealis, a forest shimmering in the morning sun after freezing rain, and the pale wash of the moonlight on a lake. Such scenes instilled joy in the heart, mind, soul, and spirit. Men and women then declared that Kitchi-Manitou created goodness and beauty.

When the Western Europeans arrived on this continent and met the natives, they at once believed them to be heathens who, without a true religion, were in need of Christianity and civilized knowledge and technology. In refusing a missionary's invitation to renounce their beliefs and to espouse the beliefs contained in the Bible, Red Jacket, the celebrated Seneca orator, replied on behalf of his people: "Kitchi-Manitou has given us a different understanding." He meant in substance that Kitchi-Manitou had given the Red People a different understanding of the nature and attributes of God and a different sense of the nature of humankind and the world. Kitchi-Manitou had already provided occasion for revelation and the enlightenment of humankind.

CHAPTER TWO

MUZZU-KUMMIK-QUAE

MOTHER EARTH

In the Pipe of Peace Smoking Ceremony, the second whiff of tobacco is offered to the Earth with the prefatory words "To you, Mother, we give thanks." What the celebrant then says may be summarized as follows: "When I am hungry, you feed me; when I am cold and wet, you shelter me; when I am downcast, you comfort me. For this am I grateful. I am indebted to you."

By using the term Muzzu-Kummik-Quae, meaning Earth Woman and, by extension, Mother Earth, the celebrant equates the Earth with motherhood, womanhood. At the same time, the celebrant compares humankind to children. The words spoken in thanksgiving to the Earth are adult, but they express the same sentiments that children feel but cannot articulate. So instead of words, infants and children show gratitude and love to their mothers with smiles, hugs, a sparkle in their eyes. For the mothers, these expressions of love and gratitude are as eloquent and full of meaning as are those uttered by men or women.

It is fitting that the Anishinaubae people and all the North American Indian nations should express their indebtedness and gratitude to the Earth and to motherhood as often as they performed the Pipe of Peace Smoking Ceremony and many more times in private. Despite the fecundity of the Earth and their efforts, men and women sometimes trod on the edge of famine and courted sickness, especially in winter. That they often had to eat bark and lichens to survive and suffered illnesses reminded them of their utter dependence on the Earth. They could not take the Earth for granted. It would not allow them to forget.

And when the Anishinaubaek gave thanks to the Earth, they reflected on the land and the waters, the forests and the fields, the mountains and the valleys, the winds and colors, and all their animal cotenants on the Earth. Mother Earth in all her forms and conditions was what the celebrants meant when they offered the second whiff of tobacco incense. It was the Earth in its entirety, not just a portion of it, that men and women considered when they thought of Mother Earth.

Human beings' dependence on Mother Earth was not only ritualized with tobacco offerings, it was dramatized, as in the following story. Nana'b'oozoo, the Anishinaubae, was camped on the bank of a river when the waters inexplicably began to rise. The waters rose slowly and steadily, forcing him to retreat higher and higher up the mountain until, having reached the summit, he could retreat no farther.

From this perch Nana'b'oozoo looked around for land, for an island where he could take refuge, but as far as he could see there was nothing but water. At last, before the water covered what remained of the mountain that he stood on, Nana'b'oozoo caught two logs that were drifting nearby and lashed them together with his loincloth to form a crude raft.

Only after he had straddled his raft and was safely on board did Nana'b'oozoo grasp the gravity of his plight and that he was not alone. As far as he could see in every direction there were animals of every species—bears, deer, raccoons, mice, sparrows, snakes, and turtles—many out of their element in water, their eyes wide and rolling in terror, thrashing about desperately to keep from sinking. Screams and cries filled the air from those nearby who were pleading to be taken on board the raft. "Nana'-b'oozoo! Brother! Let me on" was repeated again and again.

To have to turn away his neighbors and to beat them off as they tried to scramble aboard pricked Nana'b'oozoo's conscience. He felt as if he were sending them to their deaths by turning them away. A mixture of pity and guilt tormented him, but he could not possibly take another creature on board his raft without endangering his own life.

In the midst of this pandemonium, Nana'b'oozoo turned his thoughts to himself and his own situation. He was safe for the present, but what good was safety if it would only prolong the kind and manner of his end?

He looked for some sign that the waters were receding, but there was none. All he could see as he looked about him was death staring him in the face, shouting at him, grinning at him. If he did not die by drowning, then surely he would perish by starvation. STARVATION! Was he now clinging to his raft and holding on to life only to give in to starvation, the form of death that he had always regarded as the worst possible: to grow weaker and slowly waste away in flesh and in spirit, to feel the end coming? Equally horrible to contemplate was the indignity that was to follow: his remains to be eaten by turtles, fish, and other flesh-eating creatures, his bones scattered by the current or by a Weendigo, to stave off its own starvation.

In this extremity Nana'b'oozoo called on the manitous to restore the waters to their proper levels; he prayed with all the sincerity that desperation inspires, but nothing happened. The waters did not subside, nor did a heavenly voice bid him to do something dramatic or miraculous.

While Nana'b'oozoo waited for deliverance, his mind was working. He remembered.

Once before the Earth had been flooded. On that occasion Geezhigo-Quae (Sky Woman) had restored and re-created the Earth from a small clutch of soil salvaged from the bottom of the sea. Could this not be imitated? Absurd! For such a deed was the act of a manitou, not a mere mortal. But Nana'b'oozoo had no other recourse.

"Needjee! [My friends]," he hailed the birds and animals swimming nearby, "Would you fetch some soil, so I can try to restore the Earth? You and I cannot last much longer in the water and without food. I do not know if I can restore the Earth, but there is no other way."

One after another, the swift, the strong, the fearless, and the resourceful animals all willingly made the attempt, but came back with nothing but excuses that the water was too deep, too cold, and too dark, and that farther down were evil manitous with long, slender tentacles ready to seize any trespasser who dared venture too near.

It was not the strong or the gifted, as might be expected, who retrieved the soil. Rather it was the least of their kin, the muskrat, who brought back the small bit of soil.

Into this knot of soil, no bigger than a chestnut, Nana'-b'oozoo breathed, in imitation of Geezhigo-Quae, who had breathed into a small pawful of soil, and a miracle took place. The tiny ball of mud grew in his hand until it became too heavy and too large for Nana'b'oozoo to hold. He set it down on his raft, where it continued to expand, burying the raft and forming a small island. And as the ball of mud became an island, the swimming birds and animals went ashore for refuge. It was not until much later that Nana'b'oozoo discovered that the knot of soil that he had held in the palm of his hand had grown into a mass greater than an island, with valleys and hills, forests and meadows, and that the waters had returned to their former levels and places in lakes and rivers.

Nana'b'oozoo had done what Geezhigo-Quae had done; he had created his island and his world. He had done what everyone is supposed to do, to quest for that tiny knot of soil, the gift of talent, and to make from it one's being and world.

Until the crisis of the flood, Nana'b'oozoo had taken the Earth for granted, as most people do. Only when he faced starvation and death had Nana'b'oozoo remembered it. It was then that he prayed to the manitous for the restoration of the land and the subsidence of the seas. Ignored by the manitous, Nana'b'oozoo appealed to the immediate and the corporeal world, calling on the birds and animals to bring him some soil.

The story may be pure fancy, but it does represent reality, the state of things for humankind. Without the logs, a species of vegetation, Nana'b'oozoo would have drowned, and without the assistance of the creatures of the animal world, he would not have obtained the morsel of soil necessary for the restoration of the Earth and his own survival.

From the beginning, men and women of all races and nations have borne out the reality of their dependence upon plants and animals represented in the Anishinaubae story of the great flood by constructing their dwellings and villages in or on the fringes of those areas where there is vegetation in the form of forests, oases, or plains and where birds and animals abide. Most peoples who have survived the melting of glacial ice or experienced the periodic overflow of great rivers in the spring have their own versions of the great flood.

Just as food is meant for every living being, human and animal, so Kitchi-Manitou set aside and appointed a place and a time for all beings to make homes for themselves and their offspring wherein they could seek shelter from the wind, rain, and snow and take refuge from their enemies. No one was granted primacy or dominion over the Earth or another species.

Indeed, if there is a primacy of any kind, it may well be that birds, animals, insects, fish, and even plants possess a primacy to a greater degree than do human beings, by virtue of their capacity to fend for themselves without assistance from other beings, human or otherwise. With the exception of corn (maize) and perhaps dogs, no animal or plant needs anything from humankind. No such claim can be made of human beings.

Having no need of human beings and endowed with their own natures, attributes, and independence, eagles, bears, butterflies, and whitefish, representing various species of the Earth, are humankind's cotenants upon the land, sharing the yield and fruit of Mother Earth. Such was the order of life that Kitchi-Manitou's vision intended and ordained.

But the Earth did much more than serve and fulfill humans' and animals' physical needs and appetites. Through all its stages and seasons, Mother Earth inspired and evoked in men and women a sense and appreciation of beauty, curiosity, and wonder and stirred in their souls joy and sometimes gloom. Old men and women often paused to gaze on the sun rising on the horizon as if from the depths of the sea in the morning or to watch it decline in the west in a shroud of crimson to gratify their sense and need for beauty, saying in wonder, "Only Kitchi-Manitou can do that." In their travels over their lands, the Anishinaubae people saw many spectacles, such as a rainbow at the foot of a waterfall or the dance of thousands of wavelets in a moonlit lake, that entranced them and made them long for time to stand still and make the vision last forever. Mother Earth was beautiful beyond words, for all time.

Besides beauty, Mother Earth also had a spiritual presence, an aura of mystery that imparted a sacred character to certain places. What conferred this sacredness on a pinnacle of rocks or a glade in the forest where one ought not to be was the presence of manitous. For the most part, men and women, as bidden, left these places undisturbed as much out of fear of offending the manitous and suffering some form of vengeance as out of a profound respect for the privacy of the supernatural beings. But it was in these places or nearby that men and women came to quest for visions and dreams and to talk to the manitous directly, to gain entry into their world or have them enter into the beings of men and women through dreams. Where but near the dwelling place of the manitous was there a better place from which to address the manitous and to be addressed by them?

Finally, the last sense in which the Earth was mother was as a teacher. It was through the changes and beauty of the Earth that the Anishinaubaek discovered the existence of Kitchi-Manitou and reasoned that the Great Mystery was the creator of all things and beings. Mother Earth revealed, by means of her transformations, that there is a Kitchi-Manitou, and some believed that other manitous were created by the First Mystery and set in the world to preside over the destinies and well-being of every species of living, sensate beings. By observing the relationship of plants, animals, and themselves to the Earth, the Anishinaubae people deduced that every eagle, bear, or blade of grass had its own place and time on Mother Earth and in the order of creation and the cosmos. From the order of dependence on other beings, the Anishinaubaek determined and accepted their place in relation to the natural order of Mother Earth.

CHAPTER THREE

MAUDJEE-KAWISS

THE FIRST SON

Within a month of Winonah becoming pregnant, her mother knew of her daughter's condition. She questioned her daughter until the girl told her who the father was and the manner in which Ae-pungishimook had taken her. Her mother was scandalized to learn that a manitou would be the father of Winonah's unborn child. But nothing could be done except to wish that things weren't so and that Winonah had not forgotten what she had been told.

One day, she had been out picking berries in the fields and had become separated from her companions when she had to urinate. Winonah forgot the ancient taboo never to face the west when performing the act and squatted directly toward the west.

When Ae-pungishimook saw Winonah's little moss-covered cleft, the coals of lust glowed in his loins, and without pro-longed foreplay or the recitation of sweet nothings, he cast his loincloth aside and humped the girl then and there. When his fire had petered out, Ae-pungishimook put his loincloth back on and staggered away, leaving poor Winonah to manage for herself and to face the future alone. Winonah rued the day that she had ever seen the manitou and never expected to see him again.

But soon after she gave birth to a boy, Ae-pungishimook arrived, anxious to see what the child he had sired looked like— not so much to see Winonah as to see whether the child was a boy or a girl. Seeing that the child was a boy, robust and lusty, Ae-pungishimook was as pleased as any father could be. As he looked years into the future, he foresaw in a dream that his son would be a hunter, fisherman, trapper, and defender without equal in the entire nation—a provider who made sure that the food racks were always amply stocked and a warrior who kept the villages safe.

As soon as the little boy was strong enough to hold objects in his grasp, Ae-pungishimook put toy clubs and lances in his hands, and not long after the boy had taken his first steps, he was firing arrows at targets, striking stumps with his club, and uttering war cries. Ae-pungishimook's dream was being fulfilled. By the time the boy was running, he was hunting, not little birds and chipmunks, as did other boys his age, but partridges and rabbits, and he even was spearing fish for his own dinner.

Even before the boy was of an age to go on a vision quest, he had outgrown every boy and man in the village and was so great in stature that it was difficult to imagine a bigger specimen any-where—anyone who could be compared to him in size and strength or in the ability to hunt and fish.

The fact was that although men and women felt safe having such a man in their midst and as one of their nation, they were uneasy because of his volatile temper. As yet, no one had seen what Ae-pungishimook's son could do if provoked, but no one desired a demonstration, either. It didn't require much to deduce what the boy could do.

To have to guard their words and even their facial expressions in the young man's presence did not sit well with the Anishin-aubae people, who considered themselves, both as individuals and as a people, the equals of all other men, women, and nations. They did not defer readily to power or leadership or to any kind of preeminence.

Fortunately, the boy often accompanied his father on extended fishing and hunting expeditions that became ever more frequent the older he grew, so life in the village was bearable without the threat of his constant presence.

Just what this boy's birth name was before his brother Pukawiss was born was soon forgotten and replaced by another, Maudjee-kawiss, meaning "the beginning son," the name by which he was thereafter known. In bestowing the name Maudjee-kawiss on the eldest child of Ae-pungishimook and Winonah, the people set a precedent that their descendants followed, calling their firstborn sons Maudjee-kawiss and their firstborn daughters Maudjee-quaewiss.

The names Maudjee-kawiss and Maudjee-quaewiss are more than commemorative. They illustrate the fact that the eldest child, regardless of his or her gender, enters the world ahead of his or her brothers or sisters. They also illustrate the propensity of younger children to follow and even imitate their elder brothers and sisters, in act and in speech, until such time as they no longer need guardianship and can look after themselves and pursue their own interests and conduct their own affairs. The eldest sons and daughters, regardless of whether they welcome the responsibility, are expected to safeguard and care for their younger brothers and sisters until their younger siblings can care for themselves.

When the boy who later came to be known as Pukawiss was born to Winonah and Ae-pungishimook, Maudjee-kawiss was expected to take his brother in hand and to keep him from harm for as long as his younger brother needed his companionship and protection. But, for one as advanced and mature as Maudjee-kawiss, the care of his younger brother was a nuisance made more burdensome by Pukawiss's frivolous character, a chore that lasted for three years until Pukawiss was old enough to go his own way. Until that day, Maudjee-kawiss had to listen to his mother demand, "Where's your brother? Why is your brother crying? Why aren't you playing with your brother?" No longer having anyone dogging his footsteps or threatening to tell on him for misdeeds real or imagined must have been an immense relief to Maudjee-kawiss. Now he could play his own games, accompany his own friends, and go with his father as often as he pleased. He had passed through a phase in life during which he lived up to his eldest-child name.

Once Maudjee-kawiss was relieved of the responsibility of looking after Pukawiss, he was free to accompany his father whenever, wherever, and for as long as it pleased him. Eventually he left his mother to live with his father somewhere in the west, exactly where no one could say.

From time to time, he came back to visit his mother and to check that his ancestral village was safe, but these visits decreased in frequency as the years went by. Maudjee-kawiss was much too busy patrolling the boundary of the Anishinaubae homeland, keeping the assorted enemies at bay.

With his reputation as a warrior, no one dared enter the homeland of his people to challenge Maudjee-kawiss or to risk incurring his wrath. Though keeping the borders safe was a full- time occupation, patrolling gave Maudjee-kawiss an opportunity to see the peoples who lived on lands that adjoined the Land of the Anishinaubaek, learning about their customs, traditions, and practices.

It took some time, but eventually Maudjee-kawiss saw all there was to see of the peoples and the lands to the east, the south, and the west. He had not yet gone north.

In his first venture north, he traveled until he came to a land where the trees were thin and scarce and the sun never set. He didn't know it, but he was in the Land of the Bear Nation and had arrived just when the nation's leaders were gathered in a conference. At least the gathering appeared to be a conference to Maudjee-kawiss, who observed the proceedings from his vantage point among some rushes near the water's edge. An immense crowd was seated upon the ground, but it was the speaker who aroused Maudjee-kawiss's interest and attention. Over the speaker's left forearm was draped a sash that was embroidered with numerous symbols to which he pointed many times during the course of his long speech. When the speaker sat down, the audience said "How! How!" to show its agreement. All the speakers who followed had sashes that they used in the same way. Maudjee-kawiss was curious to know what purpose the sashes served. He had never seen such a device used by his own people.

When the conference was terminated at the end of the day,

Maudjee-kawiss emerged from his observation place behind the bushes. In a loud voice, he hailed the spectators and the speakers, whom he took as the principal men and women of the nation. At the same time, he held up his right hand to indicate that he was there as a stranger on a peaceful, friendly visit and that he was alone. After a brief consultation among themselves, the Bear spokesmen beckoned him to come toward them. Maudjee-kawiss crossed the river.

On the other side, Maudjee-kawiss, an accomplished linguist, explained why he was in the Land of the Bear Nation and asked the leading men and women for permission to visit their land and to hunt and fish to feed himself while he was in their country. He hoped that the Bear Nation would grant him permission and extend to him the same kind of welcome and hospitality that people of other nations had shown him. While in their land, Maudjee-kawiss would respect and abide by all their customs and laws and act as a guest.

Never having received such a request, much less having heard of "sightseeing," the leaders of the Bear Nation were uncertain how to respond to it. They were suspicious, naturally, of all strangers, especially ones who offered explanations for their presence and purposes as questionable as "sightseeing." In their experience, the strangers they had encountered were often spies in disguise. They didn't say this to Maudjee-kawiss, of course, for they were too polite.

Before deciding what to do, the elders wanted to know more about Maudjee-kawiss and how long he intended to stay. They gathered what information they could from Maudjee-kawiss and sent scouts to check the countryside for enemy warriors. Then the elders retired to confer in private.

While the elders were consulting, Maudjee-kawiss sat down with some of the principal men and women to talk. Almost the first question he asked his hosts was about the purpose of the sashes they carried and referred to during their speeches in the council.

An old man, whom Maudjee-kawiss took as the principal spokesman, explained that the beaded and quilled sashes were historical records of the Bear Nation and that the symbols engraved on the sashes reminded the speakers of everything that was important to the people: ideas, beliefs, stories, rituals, codes, festivals, and the succession of events. To illustrate, the old man explained the meaning of the symbols on his sash to the spellbound Maudjee-kawiss. When he finished his explanation, he asked Maudjee-kawiss if his people had a similar device for recording their heritage. Maudjee-kawiss shook his head no.

All of a sudden Maudjee-kawiss wrenched the sash from the old man's grasp and bolted away, catching everyone unawares. The Bear headmen, couriers, and their warriors were caught off guard by the unexpected action, but they soon recovered their senses and ran in pursuit. They howled and shrieked as they ran.

One of the pursuing warriors, swifter than his companions, swifter than even Maudjee-kawiss, gained slowly on the fleeing Anishinaubae until he was just steps behind. Maudjee-kawiss thought he could feel the warrior's hot breath. At the last moment, Maudjee-kawiss turned and struck out blindly in self-defense. By luck, he struck his pursuer directly on the head, killing him before he fell to the ground.

To see their champion slain before their very eyes shocked the warriors and leaders of the Bear Nation, all of whom had witnessed the blow struck by Maudjee-kawiss. They had never seen one of their warriors defeated in battle. The stranger had killed their champion with one swing of his war club. In one instant, the Bear Nation was next to leaderless. They stopped in their tracks.

As the other Bear warriors, hunting and fishing chiefs, and elders caught up and joined those who had been at the scene, the crowd soon surrounded Maudjee-kawiss. The Anishinaubae warrior set himself for the charge. He closed and reclosed his hand around the handle of his war club. He circled, ready to meet any charge, ready to fight to the death and to take as many of the enemy with him as he could before being overpowered by the sheer force of their numbers.

The cries of the Bear people were sharp, deafening. "Kill him! Cut him up! Who'll be the first?!" And they closed in, slowly, not rushing.

But louder, shriller still was the cry "Kegoh! [Don't!] Kegoh!" uttered by the elders and repeated by the rest. The advancing warriors stopped, and the calls for the death of Maudjee-kawiss ended.

Instead of killing the stranger, even though he had wronged the family of the warrior and deserved death, the eldest elder proposed that the family of the deceased adopt Maudjee-kawiss. With the reluctant consent of the slain warrior's family to adopt the Anishinaubae warrior, the elders and leaders officially invited Maudjee-kawiss to be their new war leader, their new champion, and a member of their nation.

It was a great honor to be invited to be an *ogimauh* (a man or woman who counted many followers, and one on whom many people relied), but it was also a heavy burden to be responsible for others. Maudjee-kawiss wasn't sure he wanted to be one.

In practice, being an ogimauh meant that the leader was in the forefront of everything and everyone. These leaders broke the trail for their followers through the forest, across swamps and in water, in summer as well as in winter. They preceded their warriors into battle, risking their lives and health for their people, and provided an example and inspiration for others. They had to persuade people who were proud, individualistic, and headstrong to do their will, while not infringing on the people's sense of worth and place. These were not easy things to do. As long as a war chief was successful, the warriors would follow him and uphold his leadership, but if he lost too many followers in battle and took too many risks with his people's lives, he lost not only their support but his good name.

Because this was a difficult matter to settle and it meant that he would have to sacrifice some of his freedom, Maudjee-kawiss asked the elders of the Bear Nation for time to think about their proposal. In asking for time, he assured his hosts that he was not rejecting their invitation. But he wanted to go home first to discuss the duties with his family and the elders, since acceptance would entail even longer absences from his mother, grandmother, and ancestral home. Even if he were to accept leadership of the Bear Nation, he would not sever his ties with his people.

The Bear people understood. He asked the Bear elders if he

could borrow the sash that he had wrested from their champion to take home to show to his people. Not only did the old people agree to lend the sash to Maudjee-kawiss, but they gave it to him, as was customary for Indians to offer their prized possessions to those who coveted them.

At home, Maudjee-kawiss told his mother and grandmother about his encounter with the Bear Nation and their offer of chieftainship, but what he talked about more than anything else was the sash. His greatest wish, his dream for his people and their descendants, was for them to adopt the sash on which to record their heritage and history.

As Maudjee-kawiss recommended, the Anishinaubaek adopted the sash and called it *waubumaubeeyauk,* meaning "the sight of events as they occur in succession" and "events made clear by their place in the progression of time." To have such a history made the Anishinaubae leaders proud to recite their deeds from these "waumpum belts" at the commencement of meetings and important festivals.

Medicine men and women, members of the Medaewaewin and Waubunowin societies, imitated the political and war leaders by setting down their chants, dreams, visions, and prophecies on birch scrolls. Learned elders inscribed symbols on stones that the Anishinaubaek called teaching rocks, *kikinoomaukae-assin* (also *kikinoomaukae waubik*), telling stories that illustrated the nation's knowledge, beliefs, and institutions.

The elders set their teachings on these rocks in places that were remote from villages and kept the engraved images covered when not in use. The sites of these teaching rocks became places of higher learning to which the elders brought youths, especially chosen for their strength of character, to prepare and instruct them as future custodians and stewards of the spiritual and intellectual heritage of the Anishinaubae people. These old people sensed that the people's accumulated knowledge was much too valuable to be entrusted to chance, memory, and individual rediscovery. They understood that if this wisdom was to grow, they would have to entrust its keep to promising youths, to perpetuate and add to.

Since so much, even everything, depended on the preservation and development of the people's wisdom, the elders took great care in choosing as their successors only those with a strong interest in and respect for knowledge; who lived in harmony with their neighbors, Mother Earth, the manitous, animals, birds, fish, and insects; and who had both an abiding sense of truth and a disposition toward honesty. Few could be entrusted with this crucial responsibility, since there is a kinship between knowledge and wisdom, the teacher, and the teacher's reverence for the people's heritage in deed and in speech.

Another reason for choosing trustworthy youths to safeguard the people's heritage was that those who came to the elders for advice, information, and enlightenment were often skeptical and suspicious. They had to see, hear, and sense the truth before they would accept it as accurate. They were as difficult to convince as any other people in creation. None except children readily credited another with *w'daeb-wae* (meaning he or she is right and may be believed), but when they did, they meant it and in so doing paid the highest compliment they could pay another human being. Only men and women whose integrity elicited belief and trust were deemed worthy of being appointed keepers and interpreters of the spiritual, cultural, and intellectual traditions of the people.

The legacy of Maudjee-kawiss was the practice of recording the people's heritage on sashes, scrolls, and stones: deeds, dreams, visions, chants, prophecies, stories, myths, and legends that related to the people's existence on Earth. Maudjee-kawiss might not have seen the sense in recording anything that was not of practical value, since men and women of deed and action have little use and time for things of the mind and the spirit. But he did see the importance of recording history.

Maudjee-kawiss typifies men and women of deed and accomplishment, evidence of the worth of the people. He serves both to inspire and to instill pride; he is the national symbol, a superhero.

CHAPTER FOUR

PUKAWISS

THE DISOWNED

Winonah gave birth to a second son whose original name is not remembered. From the moment of his second son's birth, Aepungishimook dreamed that this son would be strong and bold like Maudjee-kawiss, a warrior whose mere presence would command peace and respect, and that he would add to the nation's glory and reputation.

Within weeks it was obvious that this boy had a different temperament from that of Maudjee-kawiss. He smiled and cooed much more frequently than any child, certainly much more than his older brother, but this didn't bother his father. Nor did he sleep as much as did other infants and toddlers, being too preoccupied watching and listening to sparrows, squirrels, caterpillars, hawks, moths, dragonflies, and any other creature that came into his view or hearing.

When the boy outgrew toddlerhood, he did not outgrow his fascination with birds, animals, and insects. In fact, Pukawiss's preoccupation increased to the point that it predominated everything, including marksmanship, running, and swimming, that other boys did. All that Pukawiss wanted to do was watch what the birds and animals were doing—watch and laugh, listen and laugh. In this, he was quite unlike any other child.

Much to his father's displeasure and dismay, the boy did not show as much interest in war clubs, lances, wrestling, and war cries as he should have. Furthermore, he was squeamish, turning away from the sight of dead animals and shuddering, much too squeamish for his own good. Ae-pungishimook might not have minded too much if his son had shown half the interest in practical and useful games as he did in trifling pastimes.

Ae-pungishimook tried to wean his son from his amusements—watching, listening, jumping, skipping, and bending his body in hundreds of different shapes. He reminded the boy that whether he liked it or not, he would have to master, as best he could, those skills that would serve him in the future. These fatherly talks and reminders never failed to elicit a promise from Pukawiss to do better and were always followed by a short period of strict observance of the father's wishes. Eventually, Ae-pungishimook got tired of reminding his son to practice and to do something useful instead of wasting his time; he scolded his son and even cuffed him around to knock some sense into him. However, not even punishment could knock sense into the boy and convince him to do his father's bidding and to take the necessary steps to prepare for his future.

In exasperation, Ae-pungishimook turned away from his son and had less and less to do with him until they were estranged. Ae-pungishimook gave all his affection to Maudjee-kawiss.

For having been forsaken, the boy was from that time on known as Pukawiss, meaning cutoff, disowned, unwanted.

As much as any boy, Pukawiss wanted to please his father, but he could not help himself; he could not break his fascination with events in the sky, woods, meadows, and lakes. He could not take his eyes or ears off the ravens, geese, hawks, bears, snakes, or dragonflies. What Pukawiss saw, and others took for granted, was far more fascinating and illuminating than marksmanship and much more rewarding than taking the life of one of these nonhuman creatures.

Wherever Pukawiss went, he saw the drama and miracles of life around him: birth and death; growth and decline; triumphs and setbacks; and acts of love, affection, courage, cowardice, and sacrifice by humankind's cotenants and neighbors on the Earth. In many respects, some birds and animals surpassed human beings in the exercise of certain virtues and morals and values, whereas in other instances, they deported themselves no better than did human beings at their worst. Pukawiss saw human conduct reflected in the comportment of birds, animals, insects, and snakes.

For this reason, Pukawiss began to mime what he saw for the amusement and entertainment of his companions: strutting as cocks strut, sidling nervously up to a meal of carrion as buzzards do, scurrying for cover in fright of a fleeting shadow like nervous squirrels, sniffing a strange creature to determine whether it was friend or foe, strong or weak, dangerous or harmless in the manner of pups and kits. Before long, Pukawiss's talents launched him into a career as a dancer and an entertainer.

As Pukawiss grew up, his interest in dance and drama likewise increased, as did his skill in and reputation for entertainment, so that he was in demand not only in his own villages but in others. Before long, he was on the road more than he was at home meeting his engagements.

Because of his constant travels, Pukawiss didn't have a home; home for him was wherever he happened to be.

As an entertainer, home was not the only attachment that Pukawiss had to forfeit. He was never long enough in one place to form friendships or other close relationships. In going from one Anishinaubae village to another, Pukawiss was always among strangers, himself a stranger, but welcome, an *abeewi-dae*. Without a permanent home, friends, or traditional occupation, Pukawiss was a wanderer with only his clothing and bundle in which he carried all his worldly possessions. As much as he would have liked to linger for a few days in one village, he could not; he had to go on, drawn forward by his people or urged, pressed onward, by some force or instinct within himself that he could not resist.

Pukawiss could have settled down and had a home anywhere if he had only accepted any one of the numerous invitations extended to him to stay. Everyone, but especially young women, begged Pukawiss not to go any farther. Each young woman secretly yearned for Pukawiss as a husband. With his ever-present smile, imagination, and grace, which suggested good nature and a sunny disposition, life with Pukawiss would be a dream fulfilled.

To attract the dancer's attention and affection and perhaps to tempt him to stay, young women, and a few with the help of their mothers, made and presented him with the finest ornaments and garments that they could design: headdresses, vests, loincloths, coats, and moccasins, beaded or embroidered with quills.

Pukawiss wore these ornate costumes, much too fine for everyday wear, during his performances and on such special occasions as festivals, rituals, and ceremonies. In so doing, he set a precedent that became a tradition for dancers and others to be clad in their finest garments during dances and ceremonies.

But these tokens of love, admiration, and affection, fine as they were, were not enough to quicken Pukawiss's pulse and to persuade him to abandon his wanderlust and entertaining to settle down to a life of devoted and contented fatherhood and husbandhood.

Pukawiss invented new performing methods that became traditions. For example, when his younger brother Cheeby-aub-oozoo invented the drum, the flute, and the rattle, Pukawiss invited him to drum while he danced and mimed with a rattle or some other object in his hand. This marked the first use of musical accompaniment in performance that became a tradition.

In the course of his career as a dancer and an actor, Pukawiss choreographed countless dances, as many as there are incidents, conflicts, adventures, tragedies, and comedies. He and the dancers who took up the craft tried to enact human emotions in performances that were therapeutic. One such performance is the Hoop Dance, which characterizes the layered troubles faced by humankind.

In the Hoop Dance, Pukawiss dramatized the trauma that people often go through, their disorientation, and finally their recourse to a counselor for guidance. But instead of giving answers, directions, and encouragement to enable a person to get out of his or her predicament, the dancer who portrays the counselor presents the distressed person with wooden hoops made of willow. The act represents the perception that troubles cannot be transferred to or resolved by another and that the advice dispensed is actually a return of the troubles to the distressed person for sorting out. The hoop is also emblematic of the way things are, in that mischief breeds mischief that eventually returns to haunt and plague the inventor.

Troubles seldom stay single, but multiply. They cannot be given away or put out of sight, but must be borne by the progenitor, as the dancer who portrays Pukawiss demonstrates by picking up the hoops one at a time until he has collected them all and cannot possibly take up one more. And like the distressed person who seeks refuge or solutions outside himself, even in spiritualism and religion, the dancer who portrays Pukawiss forms figures of spiritual patrons and manitous. The manitous are unmoved; they offer no help. Desperate, Pukawiss twists and turns and, commencing with the last turn, presses himself through the hoops until he works his way through all of them, reminiscent of the person who must live and work his own way through his adversities from last to first until he has them all in hand, under control.

It is a spectacular dance that Pukawiss invented. Spectators, even then, were so taken by the costume, imagery, grace, and agility of the dancer that they failed to see the real meaning of the performance and the Anishinaubae understanding of the nature and character of personal difficulties and their resolution.

Pukawiss entertained everyone, but he did not please every person. Young men envied the dancer for his talents, his fine clothing, and his charm and ways with women. They didn't come out and say that they were envious and jealous, nor did they do anything to injure him as jealous individuals are known to do on occasion. They were much too refined for that. Instead, they copied Pukawiss's fine dress and his art. None of them wanted to be outdone by this stranger who, they thought, was no better than they were. They could choreograph dances as well as Pukawiss. Besides, the dancer could not possibly fulfill all invitations to entertain.

Some, like Pukawiss's brother Maudjee-kawiss, thought that he was no more than a slacker who did what he did to avoid work and responsibilities. Others disliked Pukawiss for another reason: They saw in his performances allusions to themselves.

More frequently than not, Pukawiss meant to amuse and entertain, but he also intended to provoke—especially those who took life and themselves too seriously and who could not take a joke. Among these people was his brother Nana'b'oozoo.

It was this predilection for provoking and teasing his younger brother that led to Pukawiss's end.

More than anyone else, probably because he was an older brother and it is an age-old custom for older brothers to pick on younger ones, Pukawiss played practical jokes on Nana'b'oozoo. Nothing serious or malicious, but good-natured jokes that caused no more than inconvenience and provoked laughter and embarrassment in most people. Nana'b'oozoo reacted to these pranks, however, with outrage, childish tantrums, and vows for revenge.

The last straw was the desecration of Nana'b'oozoo's beloved collection of pigeons. Knowing that his brother was uncommonly fond of these white birds, Pukawiss painted the pigeons with pitch while Nana'b'oozoo was away from his camp on business.

Nana'b'oozoo didn't pass this trick off with a shrug or a smile, as some people might have done; no, he took it as an insult that had to be avenged before he could look another person in the eye. He clenched his fists, curled his lips, and looked around with fire in his eyes. Then he dropped what he was doing and what he had intended to do in the coming days to devote his time to setting his hands on his brother.

Pukawiss, knowing that his brother would pursue him, disguised himself as a serpent and crawled into a crevice at the bottom of a mountain. When Nana'b'oozoo came along later, he lost Pukawiss's trail at the base of the mountain. Suspecting that his brother was hiding on the mountain, Nana'b'oozoo called on the manitous Thunder and Lightning to destroy it. The manitous obliged Nana'b'oozoo and unleashed their fire bolts and hammered the mountain until it was reduced to a heap of smoking ash.

Nana'b'oozoo gloated as bolt after bolt of deafening thunder tore into the mountain and pulverized it, shaking the air. But no sooner had these forces spent themselves and moved off then Nana'b'oozoo began to cry, overwhelmed by what he had done. As he dug and sifted the ash for his brother's remains in order to give Pukawiss a proper wake and burial, Nana'b'oozoo cried out against the manitous of storms and destruction for killing his brother and demanded that they restore Pukawiss to life.

While Nana'b'oozoo waited for an answer from the manitous

and for his brother to rise out of the ashes, he heard derisive laugher coming from the woods nearby. His heart quickened, and he felt like crying out. It was unbelievable. Nana'b'oozoo lifted his head, scarcely daring to breathe, and listened to the sound with all the concentration that he could bear. A second peel of laughter. Nana'b'oozoo wanted to believe, but he couldn't bring himself to do so. He was afraid. A third peel of laughter broke out, thin, taunting, very real. Nana'b'oozoo turned and looked into the woods but saw nothing. The laughter came from behind. No matter where he turned to look, the laughter always came from behind him.

In a few moments, Nana'b'oozoo's initial elation and joy turned to resentment, and he sprang to his feet, his mind set on teaching his brother a lesson that Pukawiss would never forget for making a fool of him, leading him into believing that he had died, into making him feel guilty and crying like an old woman, a child . . . for nothing. Nana'b'oozoo ran into the woods following the laughter that mocked him and led him on and on.

Pukawiss wasn't dead; he had not been killed. And from then on, Pukawiss lived out his duty to tantalize and provoke the pretentious.

For his part, Nana'b'oozoo continues to pursue his brother, resting from time to time to look after the affairs and responsibilities that he must tend to, but just as surely as he prorogues his chase, he must resume it. Whenever Nana'b'oozoo interrupts his chase, Pukawiss takes a break from his flight to do his own thing, but he never strays too far from his brother. It is said that a rush of wind bending grass, tearing leaves from trees, driving water spouts to dance over waters, and swirling spumes of snow in the air is caused by Pukawiss and Nana'b'oozoo chasing each other.

Pukawiss is credited not only with the invention of dances and initiating the custom of wearing elegant garments during celebrations but with endowing birds and animals and all creatures with vivid colors and establishing festivals.

Pukawiss lives. His spirit lives on in the bones, blood, genes, and flesh of the Anishinaubaek. It is from Pukawiss that the people have inherited their love for drama, dance, festivals, and elegant attire, and their disposition for practical joking and dramatizing life.

CHAPTER FIVE

CHEEBY-AUB-OOZOO

THE GHOST OF RABBIT

An elder gave the name Waub-oozoo, meaning "white tail," referring to a rabbit, to Winonah's third son, predicting as he bestowed the name that the boy would do great things for the village and people.

Ae-pungishimook, the boy's father, was pleased, thinking that the elder meant that Waub-oozoo would be like Maudjee-kawiss. Winonah's expectations were more modest, limited to the hope that her baby would always at least fare well, whatever he did as he grew up, and that good luck would continue throughout his life. If he became like Maudjee-kawiss, well and good; if not, it didn't matter as long as he wasn't poor and he remained in the village and did not move away as did Maudjee-kawiss and Pukawiss.

As he had done during the infancy of his and Winonah's first two sons, Ae-pungishimook came often to visit to keep an eye on Waub-oozoo's growth and development and to help in the boy's upbringing and training. For him, the first five years passed too slowly; he wanted to take his son hunting and fishing and to teach him the way of the birds and animals, forests and meadows. And Ae-pungishimook was glad that this son was not like Pukawiss, giddy and silly. In one respect, the boy was like Maudjee-kawiss; he was quiet—quieter than any other boy or girl—and, from his reluctance to play, he seemed to dislike merrymaking.

For Winonah her son was far too serious.

But there was one habit that bothered Ae-pungishimook: Waub-oozoo's practice of standing or sitting stock-still for half an hour or so as if he had been struck deaf and dumb and been turned into stone. It was a habit that would later serve the boy well while hunting, but when he was a child, no one understood his behavior.

When asked what he was doing, the boy explained that he was listening. No one could really complain about a habit that was basically good and simple, but it was excessive to the point that Waub-oozoo was warned that a Weendigo would do him in for overindulgence. But these warnings didn't scare the boy for long.

For a while it was sport for the young people to rouse Waub-oozoo from his trances by suddenly shaking him and yelling in his ear, to startle him enough to make him cry out and shake with fright. Their amusement came to an end, though, when the older men and women reminded the youngsters that they could kill Waub-oozoo if they happened to rouse him from a dream. Sleep is half-death; certain dreams occur at a level near death, and a sudden motion or sound could push the dreamer's soul to death.

Other than this habit, Waub-oozoo was like other youngsters his age, without any outstanding traits that would influence his future. From what they saw, Waub-oozoo's parents expected their son to struggle and suffer like everyone else.

If anything was to interfere with his work and detract from his success, it was this habit of stopping whatever he was doing to stand or sit motionless, unconscious of people or events around him, for an entire hour.

When Waub-oozoo recovered from his trance, his companions asked him what he was listening to, and he explained that he had committed himself to the beauty and meaning of the call of some bird, animal, or wind; the crackle in the night sky of the Northern Lights; the boom of ice; or the rumble of the earth. There was nothing as beautiful or full of meaning as these things, and he hungered for his fill of beauty. But more than anything else, Waub-oozoo wanted to know the meaning of echoes and the sounds that gave the birds and animals the gift of speech.

Waub-oozoo's companions thought these explanations of the habit silly and the exercise a waste of time. It was enough to know what these creatures said about the forthcoming weather; . to understand their habits and routines; and to know the coloration, rates of growth, and average size of plants. No one needed to know anything else.

What his companions said may have been true, but it didn't stop Waub-oozoo from continuing to listen to and derive joy and peace from the talk of the animal beings.

With so many distractions, so many other noises and sounds within the village, Waub-oozoo began to go farther and farther into the woods and fields, where boys and girls his age did not normally venture.

Older people sometimes followed him, curious to find out what Waub-oozoo was up to as much as to keep an eye on the boy, so he would come to no harm, but they saw and heard nothing unusual. The boy just stood or sat in one place, and the observers soon grew tired of watching him do nothing and went home.

Waub-oozoo asked the older people, who are supposed to know and to be more tolerant of youth's inquisitiveness than younger people, what made birds happy and to whom they were whistling and warbling when they were not doing so to their mates, little ones, neighbors, or intruders. And he asked why humans and animals do not use their voices as birds do to communicate to others in song. Of course, no one, not even the wisest, could give a satisfactory answer.

Waub-oozoo also wondered whether the birds spoke to the manitous and whether the manitous understood or spoke to birds. The more he heard about the manitous and the more he thought about them, the more Waub-oozoo wanted to know about these beings. It is not likely that he knew that his father was a manitou.

The older people advised Waub-oozoo to leave "them" alone. They said that it isn't good to intrude into the affairs or the world of the manitous.

When Waub-oozoo received little encouragement from others, he turned more and more to his grandmother for explanations. His grandmother listened patiently to all his questions, as attentively as if he were an adult and as if his questions were as weighty as an adult's, answering them as she would an adult's. He asked questions that only crossed the minds of other youngsters and were soon forgotten, questions that baffled adults.

"N'okomiss [Grandmother]! Where did I come from? Where do butterflies come from? Where the rabbit? The beetle? Where does the sun go at night? Where do bluebirds and geese go in winter? Why do leaves drop off some trees, leaving them naked, but others do not? When beavers and groundhogs die, where do they go? Do deer, grouse, and otters cry?"

Waub-oozoo's grandmother was baffled by many of the questions that her grandson put to her. All too frequently she had to admit, "I wish I knew the answers to such hard questions." If his grandmother didn't have answers to his questions, Waub-oozoo didn't mind.

He plied his grandmother with still more questions, questions about the manitous, *Cheebyuk, Auttissookaunuk,* the underworld, the afterlife, the future, the spiritual, and the supernatural. He wanted to know how humankind knew of the existence of these beings, the purpose of their existence, where they dwelt, whether they were friendly or hostile, and what influence they had on humans' fortunes and lives. He wanted to know humankind's relationship to the manitous, Cheebyuk, Auttissookaunuk, and *Matchi-auwishuk* and what their responsibilities were, if any, to these unseen beings.

With regard to the existence of manitous and their kin, Waub-oozoo's grandmother was as certain of their reality and presence as she was of the reality of blood, flesh, and bone beings and of stone and wooden things, although she could provide no tangible evidence in support of her belief. The best she could do was to say, "They are there even though you can't see them. You can sense them. And you can feel them touch your inner being. If you get a feeling that you ought not do something but should put it off, it is the manitous' way of warning you. If you get a feeling that something's going to happen, pay attention; it is the manitous letting your soul know. If you see and hear things in a dream, it is the manitous entering your being and your world through the dream to let you know of certain events that are about to occur. On the other hand, your dream may be scenes in your passage from this reality through the world of dreams, of the spirit, to a different level of existence and being. These are signs."

Waub-oozoo burned inside to know the answers to his questions. He longed to know things that had not yet occurred or were taking place in another part of the world, to leave this world and enter another sphere and then to return, to be transported from one place to another, distant place and then to return, and to send word to another person or persons many days of travel away. To know the secrets of long life; to be able to command life, death, and health; and to understand the nature of the supernatural and the afterlife excited and fascinated Waub-oozoo as nothing else did.

Before he was a man, Winonah's third son began frequenting places that were said to be the dwelling places of the manitous. When he went to these places, his kin and neighbors were afraid for him, and they grew more afraid of him each time he returned unharmed from his ventures. They expected that the young man would sooner or later be done in by the manitous or bring divine vengeance on the village and the people.

It was useless trying to frighten the young man with stories of Weendigoes and Matchi-auwishuk, the Evil Beings; he did not scare as easily as they had hoped.

To win the goodwill of the manitous, Waub-oozoo began to make offerings in apology and conciliation for trespassing on their hallowed, sacred abodes. People who heard Waub-oozoo talk to caves, rocks, groves, canyons, gorges, and recesses believed the young man was deranged, if not "possessed."

Even though Waub-oozoo received no outward sign nor heard an answer to his communications, he continued to go to the sacred places. If he heard or saw nothing during the day, he never failed to dream at night when he slept near the presence of the manitous. And always he awakened in the morning with his mind and spirit at peace.

Finally, after some years of talking to the empty air and listening for some kind of answer, Waub-oozoo had a vision. In the vision, his personal patron manitou showed him a drum, how to construct such an instrument, and what wood and covering were the most fitting and told him that it was to be called *maedawaewae-igun,* the Echo Maker. Waub-oozoo saw men and women cradling small drums and tapping on them while they sang or chanted a psalm in a language that only the very old could understand because it was so unlike the modern language in usage, structure, and cadence. It was the mother of the language now spoken. In the same vision, Waub-oozoo also saw men and women gathered around a large drum, chanting and striking it to make it carry their thoughts, words, and feelings to the manitou dwelling in the skies, in the realm of dreams and visions. He saw as well men and women carve flutes from the bones of hawks and willow wands and blow through them in imitation of hawks. Last, Waub-oozoo saw men and women dance to the beat and throb of the Echo Makers.

On his way home from his vision, Waub-oozoo constructed a small drum according to the directions his personal patron manitou had given him.

But his neighbors and his kin did not accept the drum or the flute, as Waub-oozoo had hoped and anticipated. They were suspicious and afraid of these instruments even if they were gifts of the manitous and therefore sacred in origin and purpose.

To those who had never seen or heard of such practices, drumming and chanting were strange though innocent exercises that Waub-oozoo performed as a ritual before he undertook any trip or major task. They thought it was hocus-pocus to ask for the goodwill and favors of the manitous. But as skeptical as many may have been, they could not deny the results. Waub-oozoo now enjoyed unfailing success in all his ventures, when before he had reaped no better luck than anyone else.

Still his neighbors weren't convinced; at least they refused to say or do anything in public that marked them as having given in to a belief in these rituals.

But gradually people came to him—at first, chiefly the old and the unlucky, who had nothing to lose but much to gain by conducting such rituals and talking to the manitous. Women with sons or daughters long absent came to Waub-oozoo with requests to ask the manitous to tell them if their children were still alive and, if so, where they were. And when Waub-oozoo elicited answers from the manitous that were later borne out, these men and women constructed their own drums to talk to the manitous to gain their goodwill and favors.

There were still skeptics, among whom was a young man who disliked Waub-oozoo. However, this young man went through a period of bad luck in hunting that was so prolonged that he finally swallowed his animosity and went to Waub-oozoo. He asked Waub-oozoo to intercede with the manitous or Kitchi-Manitou and to ask them to explain his bad luck and to suggest a remedy.

For this kind of petition, Waub-oozoo was directed by his patron manitou to erect a cylindrical structure of birch bark whose foundations of staves were driven deep into the ground. He was then bound securely in a blanket and placed within the edifice.

Presently, the audience, which had gathered to witness the communication, heard Waub-oozoo chant in the ancient form of the Anishinaubae language that the present generation could not understand. While the celebrant was chanting, a remarkable thing happened. First, the audience heard celestial voices on high, chanting and talking in an ancient Anishinaubae dialect similar to that spoken by Waub-oozoo, and the edifice in which Waub-oozoo sat began to shake so violently that those gathered there feared it would break asunder. The tremor of the building subsided as the celestial voices faded. When it was all over, Waub-oozoo emerged unbound.

Afterward, Waub-oozoo told the young man in private that his fortunes would improve if he undertook a fast and purification and if he henceforth would exercise greater respect for birds, animals, insects, and fish than he had shown before. The young man did as Waub-oozoo had been told by the manitous, and his fortunes improved.

As far as is known, all Anishinaubae men and women then followed Waub-oozoo's example by making and beating drums; asking the manitous for permission to kill a moose, a deer, a bear, or any other animal on the night before they set out on a hunt; and afterward, whether they were successful or not, paying due respect to the bones and the spirit of their victims and offering condolence to their victims' kin and kind. The ritual before and after a hunt or other venture became the Anishinaubae way of acknowledging that birds, animals, insects, and fish have a right to life and to their own sphere and purpose as bestowed upon them, not by mankind, but by Kitchi-Manitou, the creator of all living beings and things, who had jurisdiction over all life and being. The ritual also acknowledged that humankind's well-being and fate was completely dependent on birds, animals, insects, and fish.

As well, everyone imitated Waub-oozoo's practice of retreating and fasting alone in some secluded place near the presence of the manitous to seek a dream or vision.

Although everyone followed Waub-oozoo's example in communing with the manitous and in questing for dreams and visions, not every person was successful. Not every man or woman who prayed to the manitous for compassion and success was rewarded. If the *anamiewin* (chant accompanied by a drum) did not bring what was hoped for, the failure might be imputed to a number of causes, among them the supplicant's lack of sincerity, the want of real urgency in the family's needs, or less than due respect for the manitous.

In addition to their physical needs, men and women had spiritual needs, for which they had to address manitous who presided over matters of the spirit. These manitous resided not in humankind's world, as did other manitous, but in the skies, in the stars, and beyond. At first, men and women tried to emulate Waub-oozoo in attempting to commune with these distant manitous, but only a few who possessed spiritual medicine could gain the attention and audience of these beings. Only these people were so privileged by virtue of their respect and their character to attract the attention of the manitous and to receive guidance in living a life that was in harmony with the seasons and the Earth; with kin, neighbors, and strangers; and with all other creatures and the manitous.

Waub-oozoo demonstrated that the only form of communication that could elicit an answer from the distant manitous, the only fitting way in which to address the higher beings, was chanting accompanied by a drum. In combining chanting and drumming, Waub-oozoo created music, and in composing lyrics, he created poetry, both spiritual and religious—poetry whose content and purpose were comparable to those of psalms.

Men and women who communed with the manitous were respected and even feared, for no one was quite certain of the extent of their medicine and fellowship with the manitous, and no one wanted to offend them. One never knew. Some of them might even be in league with the Evil One, Matchi-auwish, and his kind.

But the music that Waub-oozoo created also served a secular purpose. When his brother Pukawiss heard the drum and music, he put it to use in his performances.

Waub-oozoo also meant a great deal to his brother Nana'-b'oozoo. As their mother had wished, Waub-oozoo remained in the village of his birth, closer to his younger brother than were Maudjee-kawiss and Pukawiss.

When the day came that Nana'b'oozoo was preparing to get married, Waub-oozoo sent word by drum to Maudjee-kawiss and Pukawiss of the coming event. It was the only occasion, ever, on which all four brothers were together.

It was a marvelous occasion for them all to meet and get to know one another, for the years and distance that separated them made them strangers when they ought not to have been. It was especially joyful for Nana'b'oozoo to meet his brothers, about whom he had heard much, for the first time.

After the wedding, the brothers remained together for some days to get acquainted and to learn what the others were like, how they had fared in life, and what their aspirations and expectations were. They meant to establish a bond between them, a bond of brotherhood that exemplified respect, affection, goodwill, and caring for the others' well-being.

The company was amiable and boded well for the future, until Maudjee-kawiss demanded to know what good was served by dancing, carousing, chanting, and drumming and what good works his younger brothers had performed for their people to compare to his exploits and career in safeguarding the nation. When his brothers defended what they did, Maudjee-kawiss answered that their practices were nothing more than children's amusements, diversions for those with nothing better to do.

While Nana'b'oozoo had nothing to say and Pukawiss didn't allow such remarks to bother him, Waub-oozoo was stung to the quick. He answered back in kind. He told Maudjee-kawiss that his occupation as warrior was sordid and that his idealization of war and killing was grotesque.

As the two brothers' words got sharper and their voices grew louder, Pukawiss and Nana'b'oozoo tried to act as peacemakers to mollify their brothers, but their efforts were useless, and it appeared that the quarrel would end in a brawl.

Waub-oozoo's arguments so befuddled and nettled Maudjee-kawiss, a slower thinker, that the warrior resorted to a personal attack, implying that his younger brother would run and hide at the first sign of danger.

At this aspersion upon his courage, Waub-oozoo lost his composure. He challenged his elder brother to name any warrior and to point to any danger, and he would stand up to them. He said that if Maudjee-kawiss were not his brother, he would not have let him get away with such insults. And Waub-oozoo glared at Maudjee-kawiss.

Maudjee-kawiss sneered and responded, "Strong words. But anyone can utter strong words . . . it's easy. I want to see what you can do. . . . What stuff you're made of. I would like to see what you can do with Beboonikae [Winter Maker]."

Although Maudjee-kawiss had not expected to rouse his brother's anger and was surprised by Waub-oozoo's show of temper and defiance, he was secretly glad. He really wanted to know what his brothers were made of, the character of his family.

"Where," demanded Waub-oozoo, "is this person? What has he done?"

When Maudjee-kawiss told him about Beboonikae, a manitou who dwells in the North and causes winter hardship, Waub-oozoo wasted no time packing his traveling equipment. He was ready to leave at once by canoe, even though the surf and the wind were much too heavy for travel. Despite his brothers' pleas to wait until the wind subsided and the surf calmed down, Waub-oozoo set out immediately. He wasn't afraid of anything or anyone.

The brothers watched Waub-oozoo draw away from shore, with admiration for the way he managed the canoe against the breakers yet with some contempt for his foolhardiness. None of the three took his eyes off the canoe as it mounted the waves and plunged into the troughs until he could see it no more.

As they withdrew their gaze from the horizon, Pukawiss and Nana'b'oozoo looked at their older brother without saying a word. From their looks, Maudjee-kawiss knew that his brothers would blame him if anything were to happen to Waub-oozoo, and knowing their thoughts, explained that he wanted his brother to go later, not at that time. But Maudjee-kawiss also knew that his brothers did not accept his explanation. Even then they were accusing him in their minds of driving Waub-oozoo into a rash act. Maudjee-kawiss stole away.

The next morning, they found the hull and what remained of Waub-oozoo's canoe on the shore not far from the village. The people knew that Waub-oozoo would never be seen alive again.

When told of the discovery, Nana'b'oozoo went down to the shore and wept, calling on the manitous of the Underworld to return Waub-oozoo to the World of the Living, to restore him to his family. The neighbors did what they could to console Nana'b'oozoo and to persuade him to tone down his grief, but for all the good their efforts did, they might as well have tried to stop the wind from blowing.

On the second day, the figure of Waub-oozoo emerged from the lake.

Nana'b'oozoo shouted, laughed, and cried; he wanted to run out to meet Waub-oozoo and to help him ashore.

"Hurry! I thought you were dead. I thought I'd never see you again," Nana'b'oozoo called out, and he began to wade out. But before he took too many steps, Pukawiss caught hold of him and held him back. In one instant, Nana'b'oozoo was sure that this figure was that of his brother, and in the next, he couldn't believe what he saw. Those who were with Nana'b'oozoo cried with joy but at the same time were overcome with dread, for the figure was only a phantom.

The others who were present raised their voices to drown out Nana'b'oozoo. They asked Waub-oozoo where he had been.

Waub-oozoo answered that he'd been to the Land of the Dead and that he had come back, had been drawn back, as it were, by Nana'b'oozoo's tears and grief.

The elders bade Waub-oozoo to return to the Land of the Dead where he now belonged. He was now Cheeby-aub-oozoo, a ghost who did not belong in the world of men and women, of blood and flesh and bone.

Cheeby-aub-oozoo shook his head as he answered that while men and women might want him to remain in the afterlife, he belonged in both the present and the past, in the Land of the Living Flesh and in the Land of the Souls, and that he could move between the two spheres at will. Cheeby-aub-oozoo, a soul of the dead, let his living kin and neighbors know that he need but touch a person or enter a home to take someone with him to the Land of the Dead.

The bystanders shrank back. They entreated Cheeby-aub-oozoo: "Don't touch us! Don't come into our homes. Not now! Not yet! Wait! Go back where you belong."

Cheeby-aub-oozoo turned and went back to sea, subsiding step by step until he vanished.

In pressing Cheeby-aub-oozoo to bid the other Souls of the Departed not to trouble the living and to keep them bound to their proper dwelling place and sphere, the elders made Cheeby-aub-oozoo *ogimauh,* or leader of the Underworld.

Cheeby-aub-oozoo was the first Anishinaubae to communicate with the manitous. Following his example, men and women began to go to secluded places, made holy by the presence of manitous, to quest for dreams and visions. There the people addressed the manitous, and if the manitous were persuaded, they came to the petitioners in dreams to grant favors that were requested. The practice spread. Before setting out on an expedition or preparing medicines, men and women entreated the manitous in chants, to the accompaniment of drums, for their goodwill and success.

Cheeby-aub-oozoo can be credited with bequeathing music, dream quests, and chanting petitions akin to biblical psalms, and for making a regard for the supernatural a part of every life.

CHAPTER SIX

NANA'B'OOZOO

"Tau-hau!" meaning "How extraordinary. . . . What kind of being have you brought into the world?" Winonah's mother was supposed to have exclaimed when she heard her daughter's newborn son talk moments after his birth. Within days of giving birth, Winonah died, and her mother, old N'okomiss, had to care for the baby.

Except for his ability to talk from birth, the little boy, known as Nana'b'oozoo from his first words, "I am Nana'b'oozoo," appeared to be like any other child. Compared to his brother Maudjee-kawiss, who was afraid of nothing, Nana'b'oozoo was timid. Everything frightened him: fleeting shadows, thunder, sudden movements, spiders, snakes, owls. Only with his grandmother's explanations did Nana'b'oozoo eventually overcome his fears. Nor did he have Pukawiss's good nature or his inventiveness or gift for dramatizing what he perceived. No, he was different in disposition, one moment blithe and sunny, the next gloomy and malevolent. And he was as unlike Waub-oozoo as he was different from his other brothers. He was not as attentive to the winds and thunder and waves, nor did he have the same interest in or respect for ceremonies and rituals, dream quests, and purification rites or regard for bears, hawks, sturgeons, and the manitous themselves. In outlook and in conduct, doing what he ought not to have done and neglecting to do what he ought to have done, Nana'b'oozoo behaved more like a human being than a manitou.

As an orphan, Nana'b'oozoo had only his grandmother to care for him and give him the guidance he needed. Daebaudji-moot, the storyteller and his grandmother's friend, taught the boy such practical skills as Nana'b'oozoo needed to know to perform as a hunter, fisherman, and trapper when he grew up.

The boy's father must have been as disappointed with him as he was with Pukawiss and Cheeby-aub-oozoo. If Ae-pungishi-mook had come to see his newborn son, and it must be presumed that he did, there is no mention of the visit anywhere in the Anishinaubae stories, nor is there mention of Ae-pungishi-mook paying his son a visit in his formative years.

At first, Nana'b'oozoo was unaware that he was without a father or a mother. It wasn't until later, when other youngsters his age asked him about his parents, that Nana'b'oozoo awakened to his parentless state and yearned to know about his parents. But as often as he asked his grandmother to tell him about his father and mother and to explain why he didn't have parents as did other children, just as often did his grandmother put him off with "they're gone," which Nana'b'oozoo took to mean that "they are dead." He accepted his grandmother's explanation well enough, but he wanted to know more about his parents, how they had come to their ends and other details that he could not yet articulate. Each time he asked about his parents, his grandmother postponed answering him with the explanation, "Later! Not right now. Wait till you're older."

Months before Nana'b'oozoo was old enough to undertake his vision quest, his grandmother drew his attention to this event, one of the most important events that would take place in his young life. If Nana'b'oozoo was well prepared, the manitous would come to him in a dream, and he would be inducted into the world of adults.

Nana'b'oozoo, as did every youngster, had heard of dream and vision quests as he was growing up and had frequently gone on make-believe quests and fasts in play, but the real quest was much too remote to take seriously. However, when his grand-mother mentioned the quest and that the time was fast approaching for him to undertake it, Nana'b'oozoo grew excited by the idea that before long he would commune with the mani-tous and take his place among adults.

Having no real sense of time, and impatient to boot, Nana'b'oozoo thought that "soon" meant tomorrow. On rising the next day, he was ready to set out.

His grandmother had to disappoint him by refusing to give him leave to set out that very morning as he wished. In fact, she was bemused by Nana'b'oozoo's impetuosity. "Nana'b'oozoo! Nana'b'oozoo!" she cried. "So impatient! You can never wait! You want to do things right away. But some things can't be rushed. You must wait, prepare. Think about life, the manitous, and what kind of person you want to be. You need to be strong . . . unafraid."

"But I am strong and unafraid," Nana'b'oozoo insisted.

"I know!" his grandmother agreed. "But not just yet. Wait a while longer."

For the next few weeks, Nana'b'oozoo asked his grand-mother as soon as he woke up every morning if it was today, if it was time for the quest. And as often as he asked, his grand-mother answered, "No! Not yet! I'll tell you when." His excite-ment and anticipation waned, and he began to believe that his grandmother had not meant what she said, and he resented her for fooling him. Nana'b'oozoo did not like being deceived.

It was high summer and already twilight when Nana'b'oozoo arrived home hungry after playing with his friends in the main village.

"Ahow! The time has come for you to go on your rehearsal for the quest," his grandmother stated.

Her announcement was so unexpected that Nana'b'oozoo forgot about his hunger and stood for a few moments speechless as though thunderstruck. He glanced anxiously in the direction of the growing shadows in the nearby woods and heard the last call of the evening thrush. And as he darted glances toward the woods, Nana'b'oozoo thought that he saw movements in them. He at once envisioned Weendigoes, Pauguk, and Giant Bears, all evil manitous, stealing about waiting for victims.

"Now?" he stuttered after some moments. Up to this time he had expected to rehearse by day.

"Yes! Now!" his grandmother repeated.

"Couldn't it wait till tomorrow?"

"Yes, it can wait, but if you are too afraid to go now, you won't be any less afraid tomorrow."

"I'm not afraid!" Nana'b'oozoo insisted.

"Well, what are you waiting for?" was all his grandmother said.

"N-n-nothing!" Nana'b'oozoo stammered. "Its s-so sudden. I—I wasn't ready."

"All you need is your blanket," his grandmother added.

Without an excuse to offer, Nana'b'oozoo gathered his blanket, taking as much time as possible. Meanwhile it was getting darker. He cast several backward glances as he entered the woods in the hope that his grandmother might call him back, but she didn't even look up from the basket that she was weaving. Nana'b'oozoo made his way forward warily, keeping one eye peeled to the front and one eye peeled backward in the direction of the camp. He was ready to tear back at the first sign of a monster.

With one eye riveted to the rear and the forest growing darker, Nana'b'oozoo had to feel his way forward with his feet, holding one arm in front of him to ward off limbs and branches, but despite the care he took, he stumbled over roots or pitched forward whenever he stepped into a depression. As often as Nana'b'oozoo tripped, he barked and scraped his shins and elbows, broke and snapped brittle twigs, and sprung branches that whipped back and forth and lashed back at him. To Nana'b'oozoo, each crack, each whip, was like thunder.

A hundred paces or so into the woods, Nana'b'oozoo risked calling back, "Is this far enough?"

"What's the matter with you?" his grandmother answered.

"If I looked up, I'd probably see you. You're not yet far enough. . . . Go on! Why, I can hear your every step."

If Nana'b'oozoo's heart beat fast in fear before, it now beat faster. He didn't want to go on but he did—one step at a time, expecting to be set upon with every step, at any moment. He went another hundred paces before he called back, "Am I far enough?"

"No! You're nowhere near far enough yet. Keep walking until I tell you to stop. I can tell how far you are."

Nana'b'oozoo stumbled forward another two hundred paces. "Aaaawoooooh!" a wolf howled, some distance away. Nana'b'oozoo froze; he shook and could hardly breathe. It took some minutes before Nana'b'oozoo could settle down and think. He couldn't go any farther or he would lose sight of the campfire. Already, he was too far from camp for his safety. But how was he to keep his grandmother from finding out that he was afraid, that he was within sight of the campfire and that if it were daylight, he would be in plain view? How was he to deceive the old woman who seemed to sense everything? For some moments, Nana'b'oozoo considered keeping quiet so as not to give his position away, until she called, "Nana'b'oozoo! Where are you?"

He had no choice but to answer; still, he hesitated. She called again in a tone that sounded thin and distant. It was then that Nana'b'oozoo got an idea. Turning his head away from the camp and cupping his hands around his mouth, he called, "Is this far enough?" in as thin a voice as he could manage, to give the impression that he was calling from a distance. He had to call several times, each time louder than the last, before his grandmother replied, "Ahow, that's far enough."

Nana'b'oozoo stood rooted where he was, ready to bolt. Visions and dreams were far from his thoughts on this night. Instead, enemies, evil beings, danger, death, and torture crowded everything else out of his mind, causing him to jump, sweat, and cower each time he heard a noise, whether it was the squeak of trees rubbing together or the rustling of leaves on the ground as a mouse scurried along to attend to its business.

And though he cast anxious glances into the dark whenever he heard a sudden and ominous sound or call, Nana'b'oozoo kept his eyes on his grandmother and on the fading fire. As he watched, he made up his mind to leave his post and return to the safety of the camp or near the camp as soon as the old woman went inside.

But as impatient as Nana'b'oozoo was to return to the lodge, his grandmother was in no such hurry to go in. To Nana'b'oozoo she was slow, insufferably slow.

At long last, Nana'b'oozoo lost sight of his grandmother; all he could see was the faint yellow glow of the campfire.

Nana'b'oozoo stole back toward the wigwam, stopping at the edge of the woods.

Even before he settled down to rest, Nana'b'oozoo heard voices. He strained his ears. Almost at once Nana'b'oozoo recognized the male voice as that belonging to Daebaudjimoot, his grandmother's friend and his tutor. Nana'b'oozoo's anger and resentment mounted as he listened to his grandmother and the old man talk and laugh.

Immediately, he drew a connection between his being sent off and old Daebaudjimoot's presence alone with the old woman. It was now clear to Nana'b'oozoo why his grandmother was so anxious to have him elsewhere, even a place that was dangerous. He couldn't understand why his grandmother had not sent him to a neighbor's lodge, where he could have spent the night in safety. It would have been so much simpler.

If Nana'b'oozoo had a stave, he would have planted it in the fireplace until the sharpened end was reddish white with heat. Then he would have run it through the old man. But no staves were at hand that were small enough for Nana'b'oozoo to manage.

Without the means to revenge himself on his grandmother's guest and indirectly upon her, Nana'b'oozoo kept watch the night through, fighting sleep and hunger and brooding about his grandmother's treachery in sending him into the very den of Weendigoes and other evil beings, so she could indulge in her own amusements.

At dawn, tired and hungry, Nana'b'oozoo stole away from his lookout and returned to the place where he was supposed to have spent the night in solitude soliciting a dream or vision. He waited until the sun was high in the sky and he could no longer bear his hunger before he returned to the lodge.

As Nana'b'oozoo stepped into the clearing around the home lodge, his first words were, "I'm starving! What's there to eat?"

This preoccupation with food was nothing new to Nana'b'oozoo. With him, food was first as well as last, as his grandmother well knew.

As she filled her grandson's bowl, old N'okomiss asked, "Well! Did you dream?"

It was as if the old woman had broken a dam.

Words poured from Nana'b'oozoo's lips; he even stuttered as he spoke of eagles, bears, wolves, hawks, watersnakes, and other beings that boded much good for the future as they appeared to him in succession in the one night-long dream or in a series of dreams, he knew not which. Nana'b'oozoo claimed to have seen a vision that was far richer and deeper in meaning and that had greater promise than had any other person, as far as his grandmother knew, in his first venture into the world of manitous and spirits. And this was but a rehearsal, since children were encouraged by adults to play at vision and dream quests, practicing performances in preparation for the real thing. But with Nana'b'oozoo, this was, as was true of many other things, not unusual. There was no need for other vision quests.

After his meal, Nana'b'oozoo slid down next to the log that he had been sitting on. Within moments his eyes closed, his head nodded, and he slumped sideways to the ground.

The old woman covered her grandson with a blanket. But the boy's sleep was neither deep nor peaceful. For as long as he slept, well into late afternoon, Nana'b'oozoo twisted, whimpered, and woke up in fits and starts with sweat streaking down his face. On awakening and sitting bolt upright, he would look wildly around and demand, bewildered, "Is it gone, Grandmother?" Every time he woke up in panic, his grandmother took him in her arms, stroked his forehead, and assured him that it was indeed gone and that he need no longer fret.

By the next day, the entire village knew of Nana'b'oozoo's remarkable fortune in receiving a vision during his first attempt, which was more a rehearsal than the real quest, but no one could tell about the manitous. Nana'b'oozoo's friends, who were the first to learn of his good fortune, were envious as well as admiring. Their parents and the entire village declared the event unusual but not out of the ordinary for an unusual youngster such as Nana'b'oozoo.

Nana'b'oozoo's grandmother was saddened and alarmed by her grandson's exaggerated accounts and his irreverent broadcast of sacred and spiritual matters. Over the next few years, she often brought up the issue of vision quests, as discretely as she could, to get Nana'b'oozoo to stop deluding himself and others, to take the vision quest seriously, and to undertake it earnestly, but each time she mentioned the sacred exercise, Nana'b'oozoo reminded her testily that he had already had a vision and that he had thereby fulfilled his obligations. There was no need to go on another quest if he chose not to.

Finally, afraid that he might strike her in anger, the old woman mentioned it no more. She could only hope that the manitous would overlook her grandson's impiety and would not be too severe with the impetuous youth if they meant to exact revenge.

As he grew up, Nana'b'oozoo frequently had to be reminded of things, as if he couldn't retain anything in his mind. But there was one thing he never forgot: his grandmother's promise that she would someday tell him about the fate of his parents. And as he got older, Nana'b'oozoo became more insistent about learning about his parents. His grandmother found it ever more difficult to put Nana'b'oozoo off, and he would no longer accept her reasons for keeping the information about his parents from him. As the son, he had a right to know.

The old woman put off telling her grandson what she knew of his parents as long as she could, but she could not defer it indefinitely. Finally, when Nana'b'oozoo was twenty, she told him what his mother was like and how she had died not long after his birth. She also told him about his brothers, whom he didn't know and who had long gone from home. Last, she told him about his father, a manitou, who was believed to live somewhere out in the west.

All of what his grandmother told him was new and disturbing, and it excited and prompted Nana'b'oozoo to ask question after question about his brothers. But Nana'b'oozoo's mood changed from excitement to somberness during the discussion as he thought about his father, who had not cared enough to come to him even once during his childhood.

The neglect of his father disturbed Nana'b'oozoo more than the fact that he had never known his mother's love. As he thought about the loss of his mother, he began to suspect that his father might have caused her death. Before long, he began to cry and left the lodge.

Half blinded by tears and grief, Nana'b'oozoo walked with no particular place in mind; he walked until his moccasin soles were worn and his feet were blistered. When he finally stopped walking, he sat down. Nana'b'oozoo was despondent at the thought that his father was a manitou, dwelling somewhere in the west, utterly indifferent to his son's existence, and that Aepungishimook had used Winonah more as a whore than as a wife.

Because of his father's neglect and maltreatment of Winonah, Nana'b'oozo had been deprived of love and had never learned how to love anyone. Nana'b'oozoo was not an orphan, as he had long believed, but a *waebinigun,* an unwanted castoff.

As Nana'b'oozoo thought about the lot that the fates and the manitous had dealt him, giving him less than what they had granted others, he felt cheated. If he had been given as much as others had received from the manitous, Nana'b'oozoo would have no reason to lament his fate or resent the injustice of life.

If only his mother had lived, Nana'b'oozoo would have had her to turn to when he needed someone during his childhood. If only his father had remained with his mother, life would have been different. He would not be unhappy now, uncertain if he meant anything to anyone.

For several days, Nana'b'oozoo lingered in the deepest gloom, wracked by self-doubt and dejection. For as long as he dwelt on his parentless childhood and what might have been, his mind and his feelings repeatedly settled on his father. There was no doubt that the cause of his misery was his father, as unknown and distant to him as any stranger. His own father had done him a greater injustice than had any person.

That his father should still be alive, unpunished for what he had done and not done, infuriated Nana'b'oozoo. It wasn't right that anyone, whether a person or a manitou, should have perpetrated such an injustice without paying some penalty. In Nana'b'oozoo's opinion, evildoers ought to be made to undo the harms and injuries that they had done and to make amends. Since no one had taken up his mother's or his own cause, the onus devolved on him, as the son of Winonah, to undertake to settle the score for her sake. It was only fitting that he, Nana'b'oozoo, do so to show his love and respect for his mother.

The more Nana'b'oozoo dwelt on justice and injustice, his mother, and his father's neglect, the more bitter be became. He made up his mind to avenge his mother by making his father suffer; he would make his father rue the days that he lived. If he could, he would make Ae-pungishimook cry and then beg for mercy. As Nana'b'oozoo's rage mounted, he forgot that the object of his resentment was a manitou.

With his mind made up to hunt down his father and punish him, Nana'b'oozoo returned home. He told his grandmother what he intended to do and that he would not rest until he had avenged his mother.

Nana'b'oozoo's grandmother was aghast. After the old woman had overcome her initial shock, she didn't think that her grandson could be serious; the idea of a man, a mere youth, daring to challenge the manitou was just too absurd. But her disbelief served only to provoke Nana'b'oozoo into directing some of his venom at her.

It wasn't until Nana'b'oozoo commissioned the arrow maker to make the finest arrows and the finest bow and took to carrying a war club at all times, striking stumps and trees in practice, that his grandmother was convinced that her grandson was serious. This behavior was entirely out of character for him.

His kin and neighbors were both bemused and startled by Nana'b'oozoo's strange conduct and his explanations for practicing war cries and striking posts. They didn't take Nana'b'oozoo seriously, and their disbelief served only to infuriate the young man even further.

About the only people to take him at his word were his grandmother and old Daebaudjimoot, both of whom tried to talk Nana'b'oozoo out of his rash crusade, pointing out the difficulties and dangers to be faced. The first challenge, to find his father without knowing where the manitou was, would be nearly impossible. And if, by some wild chance, he was to find or encounter his father, he would meet an end as horrible as one could imagine. A manitou could destroy him with one blow, blast him into nothingness with a bolt of lightning, or by a mere wish turn him into an insect to be tormented to the end of his days by birds and other creatures. Worse still was the fate he would suffer after death: to spend eternity in the void as an outcast, condemned never to join his ancestors in the Land of Souls.

But nothing that his grandmother or Daebaudjimoot or anyone else, the elders or his friends, said made the least impression on Nana'b'oozoo. For another person to tell him what to do, Nana'b'oozoo thought, was a slight, tantamount to questioning and doubting his intelligence and judgment. It was not they who were aggrieved; it was he. And it was always easy for those who were not personally affected, who had never known what it was like to be abandoned, to counsel forbearance. No! No one was going to talk or scare him out of his mission to avenge his mother.

Eventually they all gave up trying to dissuade Nana'b'oozoo from following through with his course. Since they couldn't change his mind, they urged him to undertake a purification ceremony in the sweat lodge and to seek the patronage of the manitous through dreams, as the least he could do for his sake and theirs. Nana'b'oozoo, like anyone else, needed the goodwill of the manitous to guide him safely in the coming months through whatever dangers might arise along the way.

Skeptical of the efficacy of spiritual exercises, Nana'b'oozoo reluctantly agreed to go through the purification rites and to go on a retreat to solicit a dream, more to please and patronize his grandmother than for any other reason.

Alone in a dreamer's place deep in the forest, Nana'b'oozoo made up his mind to fast for the four days as prescribed and to keep his mind on the manitou and nothing else; he prayed and chanted for a dream. For two whole days Nana'b'oozoo tasted no food while his thoughts were fixed on thunderbirds, manitous, and sacred objects. And during those two days, though deer and moose, rabbits and partridges passed and even paused well within range, Nana'b'oozoo paid little attention. But despite his single-minded fixation on sacred, spiritual objects, Nana'b'oozoo neither saw nor heard anything resembling the supernatural during his sleep or waking hours.

On the third morning, Nana'b'oozoo awoke weak and aching with hunger. He tried to forget his discomforts, especially his craving for food, by dwelling on holy and spiritual things, such as thunderbirds and departed ancestors. But Nana'b'oozoo couldn't hold his attention on the spiritual and mystical for long. Up to this time, he had never felt the pain of starvation, and now that it afflicted him, the sensation was disquieting. It felt as if there were a tiny creature within his innards struggling, gnawing to get out. As far as he was concerned, it was the worst form of torture that a person could be made to suffer.

Hunger was too much for Nana'b'oozoo, and with the immediate presence of food and meat in abundance, the torture was increased a hundredfold. There would be no difficulty killing one of the deer that was grazing nearby. With one arrow, Nana'b'oozoo felled the nearest buck.

For the next two days, Nana'b'oozoo did little else but eat

and sleep. And he dreamed as he had never dreamed before, of vultures, crows, ravens, mice, dragonflies, bats, snakes, and worms.

On his return home, Nana'b'oozoo recounted all the extraordinary dreams that he'd had, in which eagles soared and called, bears walked by his side as companions, and cougars brought him food. Such dreams boded well for him in his upcoming venture. Such were the dreams to which all dream seekers aspired, but, alas, only such individuals as Nana'b'oozoo could have had every dream filled with propitious figures and symbols. Mortals had to go often and for years before they had a dream or vision. To Nana'b'oozoo, it was common.

On the night before he set out, Nana'b'oozoo performed the war ceremony in the presence of the entire village. He had never gone on a raid, and his performance lacked the realism that warriors lent to such events. He could not refer to past experiences and triumphs to demonstrate what he could do. His war dance was a charade.

In the morning, with a quiver fitted with special arrows made by the arrow maker and a bow, and with his pack filled with provisions and medicine, Nana'b'oozoo bade farewell to his grandmother.

With his quick pace, Nana'b'oozoo was soon out of earshot of the shouts and clamor of the village and of the barking of dogs. But as he walked farther from the village, misgivings set in. At first, these misgivings were small and insignificant, not worthy of much attention, but they mounted in size and in number with every step and were transformed into real fear. As his fear increased, Nana'b'oozoo slowed down until he came to a complete stop.

For the first time since he had made up his mind to hunt down his father and to punish him, Nana'b'oozoo began to consider the implications and the consequences of his intended act. His father, whether human or supernatural, must be ancient. If his father was mortal and elderly, killing or injuring him would be an act of cowardice. And suppose, as Nana'b'oozoo had been told by his grandmother, that his father was indeed a manitou; then there was not a chance that Nana'b'oozoo could defeat him. On the contrary, it was he who would be done in. His objective was presumptuous, blasphemous, sacrilegious. If the manitou found out, it was Nana'b'oozoo who would be hunted down and destroyed.

As he thought about the possible consequences, Nana'b'oozoo was almost paralyzed by a sense of foreboding. He didn't know what the manitous could or could not do. He couldn't think straight. He had heard that they knew or could know the thoughts of human beings, learning of them from the winds that bore the words and thoughts of men and women into the skies and beyond into forever. On the other hand, Nana'b'oozoo had heard that the manitous could know nothing of a person's thoughts anymore than a man or woman could know what was in the minds of the manitous . . . unless someone, perhaps an enemy, relayed messages to the manitous.

If the manitous could know hidden things, they would not long be in the dark about Nana'b'oozoo's venture after his braggadocio, his performance of the war dance ceremony, and his warlike preparations. And as the object of Nana'b'oozoo's crusade, they would surely be angry. Under these circumstances, it would be better for him to make offerings to the manitous in atonement for his profanity and to return home, except that he could not well do so after having made such a display of his cause and courage. Nana'b'oozoo could not now return home and announce that his decision to take up against the manitous was rash and unwise. It was too late. Both his kin and his neighbors would laugh at him behind his back and think he was a blowhard. Nana'b'oozoo knew that people were expected to do what they publicly announced or be subject to derision. He could not bear to be laughed at or to be regarded as a coward.

Before he did anything else and before the manitous struck him dead, Nana'b'oozoo made offerings to appease them in the hope that they would withhold their wrathful vengeance. As to how he could save face, Nana'b'oozoo had no idea. But if a person, regardless of mental ability, dwells long enough on some predicament, he or she will chance on some solution, as Nana'b'oozoo did in this instance.

The solution was simple: Provided the manitous didn't destroy him, Nana'b'oozoo would have to absent himself from the village for an extended period to make it appear that he was on a prolonged expedition. During his absence, he would visit distant lands, meet different peoples, and even discover where the butterflies and the bluebirds went to escape the winters; he would follow the sun to the rim of the earth and see for himself where it fell or discover why it went out every night. There was no shortage of ventures that Nana'b'oozoo could pursue in the coming months to while away his time instead of scouring the land for a manitou whose whereabouts were anyone's guess. One might as well try to find a ghost or a spirit.

More than anything else, Nana'b'oozoo longed to know where the sun spent the night in hiding or whether it had been captured and imprisoned. With this thought in mind, he resumed his journey.

In one story, before he had gone too far on his journey, Nana'b'oozoo came upon an old man living alone deep in the forest. After some preliminary observations, the old man remarked that what had drawn Nana'b'oozoo so far from home must be of overwhelming importance. Nana'b'oozoo explained that it was indeed important, and he told the old man the entire story of his family situation and that he had originally set out intending to punish his father. The old man asked Nana'b'oozoo what he would have done to his father had he found him. Nana'b'oozoo explained that he would have forced his father to beg for mercy and cry like a beaten dog. The old man then revealed that he was Ae-pungishimook.

In another story, Nana'b'oozoo trekked all the way across the plains. Near the great mountains, he was unnerved by misgivings to the point of praying. A flicker appeared to him in a dream telling him of his father's fatal weakness and how to take advantage of it, for even the manitous had weaknesses.

At the base of the mountains, Nana'b'oozoo stumbled upon the camp of an old man, who spoke the same language as he did. The old man was curious to know why Nana'b'oozoo was so far from his home. Nana'b'oozoo readily obliged by explaining his abandonment by his father and his avowed mission to whip the old man.

When Nana'b'oozoo finished his explanation, the old man identified himself as Ae-pungishimook and, in proof of his identity, told Nana'b'oozoo things that only someone close to the family would know. At the end of his explanation, the old man assured Nana'b'oozoo that he was ready to be whipped any time his son was set to try. He wanted to see how his son had turned out and if he was as bold as his words were brave.

Nana'b'oozoo coughed and sputtered before laughing nervously. He stammered as he looked for words to say that his threats were spoken in jest, and he laughed some more. And as he tried to talk his way out of his embarrassment, he eventually stumbled upon a reason for not going through with his boast. He did not strike old people, and he would not lay a hand upon the old man despite what the old man had done to him.

Ae-pungishimook commended Nana'b'oozoo for his principles. But if Nana'b'oozoo was unwilling to raise a hand to strike an old man, but would stand up to and trade blows with someone of his own generation, then Ae-pungishimook would gladly oblige. At that moment the old man was transformed into a youth, taller, bigger, and more muscular than Nana'b'oozoo.

"Now!" the young man thundered. "Am I young enough?"

For a few moments Nana'b'oozoo was too thunderstruck, too dumbfounded, to speak. He looked at the giant warrior standing before him and felt like bolting, but his knees were too weak even to move. Nana'b'oozoo had backed himself into a corner from which there was no escape; he had to fight his way out.

Feebly, Nana'b'oozoo looked about and asked, secretly afraid, in as even a tone as he could manage, whether they would battle at close or distant quarter, with what weapons they would fight, and whether they would fight to the bitter end. His opponent casually replied that he would let Nana'b'oozoo decide the manner, means, and terms of the battle.

With so many weapons to choose from, it was difficult at first to decide which one would give him some chance against the giant. After some deliberation over the relative merits of the various weapons, Nana'b'oozoo granted his father the use of a bow and arrow while he would use fist-size stones. Ae-pungishimook agreed.

Nana'b'oozoo then paced off the distance and drew the battle lines more than 120 paces apart, a distance well beyond the range of arrows but well within the reach of pitched stones. With the battle lines drawn, he collected flint rocks until he had assembled a large stockpile as his arsenal. Meanwhile his father quietly watched Nana'b'oozoo's preparations. When Nana'b'oozoo guessed that he had enough missiles, he hailed his father with "Ahow [All's ready]."

Without waiting for his father to get set, Nana'b'oozoo launched a fusillade of rocks in the direction of his opponent as hard and as fast as he could pick them up. Despite the accuracy of his throws, the stones veered to one side just in front of Ae-pungishimook, as if an invisible shield was standing upright in front of him.

Meanwhile, Ae-pungishimook looked on for some time before drawing his weapon and aiming it at Nana'b'oozoo. The arrow whined as it streaked toward its target, leaving behind a blue-white trail of smoke. The flaming arrow kicked up gravel as it bore into the ground at Nana'b'oozoo's feet. Nana'b'oozoo leaped. Before he landed on his feet, another arrow streaked toward him, sizzling as it tore into the ground, where it disappeared. Other arrows came at him steadily, one after another.

Soon Nana'b'oozoo was leaping up and down and from side to side to avoid the spitting, deadly arrows. He looked as if he was performing a macabre dance on hot stones, leaping like a dervish. In his frantic efforts to save his life, Nana'b'oozoo forgot about casting stones. Even if he had remembered, he could have done nothing about it. He couldn't take his eyes off the whizzing arrows, not for a moment.

In a short while, Nana'b'oozoo lost the spring in his legs; he didn't leap quite so high or so quickly. Beads of sweat sprang on his forehead and then ran down his nose and into his eyes. His legs grew heavier, and he could do no more than bob up and down, as infants bounce without their feet leaving the ground. Still the arrows came like bolts of lightning. Bolt after bolt hissed and spat at this feet and then sizzled by his ears.

Now Nana'b'oozoo cried and prayed. He slumped to the ground in front of his arsenal. As he lay prostrate upon the ground, Nana'b'oozoo instinctively covered his head with his arms, as if bare arms could ward off the arrows. He closed his eyes. Every part of him stiffened in anticipation of an arrow driving into his back, goring and burning and drilling ever deeper.

The hiss and spit of arrows broke off, but Nana'b'oozoo was not aware of the end of the fusillade, so rapt was he in awaiting the end. He didn't even hear the footsteps.

"Eeeeeeeyoooooh!" Nana'b'oozoo let out a scream of pain when he felt something press on his shoulder.

"Oh, get up," a voice said. "You look silly lying there like a she dog."

Nana'b'oozoo felt no searing, burning pain of fire in his shoulder. He put his hand to his shoulder tentatively but kept his eyes closed. At last, feeling no pain or blood, he opened his eyes and looked up into the face of his father. He tried to rise to his feet as bidden, but he was too weak to do so. He had to wait for a while until his strength returned.

Back at the old man's camp, Ae-pungishimook unwrapped an object from a buckskin casing such as Nana'b'oozoo had never seen before. The old man explained that the object was a pipe, *pawaugun,* that came from the manitous and as such was a hallowed object. Among the manitous it was smoked to foster goodwill, peace, and brotherhood. The old man explained that he meant to give it to Nana'b'oozoo as a symbol of their reconciliation, if Nana'b'oozoo so wished, so Nana'b'oozoo could promote its use among the Anishinaubae people. The pipe was to be smoked in ceremonies before meetings to compose passions, to be carried as a sign of peace, and to seal pacts of peace after war. Then Ae-pungishimook invited his son to smoke the pipe as a gesture and token of their conciliation.

Nana'b'oozoo accepted the offer and smoked the pipe. He also accepted the pipe as a parting present from his father, on his behalf as well as that of all the people, promising to encourage its use.

No one in the village of Nana'b'oozoo's birth ever expected him to return from his foolhardy mission and to escape the wrath of Ae-pungishimook for his blasphemy and impudence. Therefore, when Nana'b'oozoo walked into the village years later, people screamed and ran as if they had seen a ghost. It took some effort, but Nana'b'oozoo and the elders finally convinced the villagers that it was indeed Nana'-b'oozoo, not his ghost, who had come back. From the moment that the people of the village were convinced that it was Nana'b'oozoo in the flesh, they all believed that he either was a manitou that was endowed with powerful medicine to protect him or that he had to have a special relationship with supernatural beings to have received a sacred gift from the manitous. From then on, Nana'b'oozoo was regarded with a mixture of awe and fear, and stories about his mission into the very dwelling place of the manitous and his epic battle and triumph spread fast and wide, without anyone ever asking him to tell what really happened.

Rumors grew as they spread. Soon, without his knowledge, Nana'b'oozoo was known as a champion. Moreover, he was a champion who lived in their midst, unlike his brother Maudjee-kawiss, who was supposed to be their defender, but was too far away to help when he was needed.

Not too long after Nana'b'oozoo came back from his odyssey, a courier from a distant village on the north shore of Lake Superior arrived in Nana'b'oozoo's village looking for the champion. He had been sent by his chief and his people to ask Nana'-b'oozoo to take up their cause against a certain war chief who had been terrorizing their village for some years.

The courier described the raids that his kin and neighbors had suffered. The ruthless, bloodthirsty war chief came into the village from time to time, no one knew when, and made off with whomever he chose, men or women, the old or newborn, victims who were never seen again. Or he stalked the outskirts of the village, falling upon anyone, it didn't matter whom, who happened to venture alone beyond the confines of the village. After killing his victims, the cutthroat mutilated their bodies and scattered their bones, so the dead never received a proper burial, and their souls-spirits could never enter the Land of Souls to rejoin their ancestors. The warriors of the village were powerless against this war chief, who was much too big and much too strong for any number of warriors sent against him, as had been attempted in the past.

Tears coursed down Nana'b'oozoo's cheeks as he listened to the courier's description of the cries and screams of babies, men and women, and old people. It was as if he himself had been aggrieved and sensed personal loss.

He eventually stanched his tears, and his mood changed from grief to rage. Nana'b'oozoo was nervous as he began to denounce the warrior as a coward and a sadist who was better off dead; as one who should be killed in the same way as he had killed his victims, the war chief deserved to die slowly, to be tortured and then hacked from limb to limb, forced to beg for mercy, for a quick death. As Nana'b'oozoo described what ought to be done, his voice grew louder and more violent, frightening his audience into thinking that he might strike one of them. Nana'b'oozoo ended his diatribe by performing the war dance ceremony to prefigure what he meant to do to the warrior and as a sign of his acceptance of the invitation of his kin of the north shore to take up their cause and to put an end to the war chief.

The moment that he finished his war dance, Nana'b'oozoo was ready to set out without consulting the elders or the soothsayers, who were about to remind him that it was customary for warriors to perform other rituals before they mounted a raid. But Nana'b'oozoo didn't give them a chance.

When he and the courier arrived at the village of the north shore people, Nana'b'oozoo was insistent upon setting out against the enemy at once, declining food and rest, saying that there would be ample time for food and sleep after the enemy was vanquished. Feasting, dancing, and celebrating following the defeat of the enemy would be more gratifying. In the meantime, Nana'b'oozoo would begin to carry out the purpose for which he had been invited.

Nana'b'oozoo was impatient to get under way and asked where the enemy dwelt and what his strengths and weaknesses were. His hosts pointed to an island offshore that was visible but some distance away. They described the island as a stronghold that was unassailable by their warriors. Watchdogs patrolled the beaches day and night, and no one could approach the island without being seen or heard by these dogs, who barked and howled at the first sign of a trespasser. Even if a large force of warriors were to land on the island, as a company had once done, they would still have to face Waub-meegwun himself, a warrior whom no individual or group had ever bested. This is what Nana'b'oozoo had to face.

While his hosts were informing him of the position and strength of the enemy, Nana'b'oozoo studied the distance and features of the island through squinted eyes, as if he was estimating how long it would take to cross the strait and how best to gain the shore. But as his hosts talked and suggested what chances there were against such a formidable enemy, Nana'b'oozoo began to anticipate, not so much how to breach the island, but how to find a way of backing out of the venture. He began to shake and to fidget with his war club, twisting it this way and that so it appeared from the whiteness of his knuckles and the tautness of his neck muscles that he was thirsting for blood. As he stared at the island and the swell of the lake, Nana'b'oozoo foresaw his doom, from which there was no way out.

His hosts brought him a canoe and asked him if he needed a band of warriors to accompany him. Nana'b'oozoo declined the offer. Boys and girls and old men and old women looked on Nana'b'oozoo with admiration and with worry for his safety.

Nana'b'oozoo gazed at the island for a long time without saying a word, until someone suggested that it would be better if he waited until nightfall to leave, when he would have more of a chance of getting on land. That person further suggested that a canoe-load of warriors should accompany Nana'b'oozoo to the island, to act as decoys and enable him to go ashore.

Nana'b'oozoo agreed to this idea, postponing his assault until nightfall. But all afternoon he trembled and tried to contrive some scheme whereby he could bow out of the venture. Failing to come up with a satisfactory excuse to go home without fulfilling his promise, Nana'b'oozoo turned his attention to the manner and the means of battling a warrior one and a half times the size of an ordinary man and with one and a half times the strength, not to speak of his years of experience in battle. He would have to resort to cunning and hope that he had enough to triumph over the fierce warrior.

It was well after dark, midnight or so, when Nana'b'oozoo set out in a canoe. He was preceded by warriors on board another canoe whose purpose was to attract the attention of the watchdogs and Waub-meegwun on one side of the island, to allow Nana'b'oozoo to land undetected on the other.

Everything went according to plan. The decoy canoe aroused the watchdogs, who set off a furious uproar that echoed across the water.

On the other side of the island, just as Nana'b'oozoo stepped ashore, there was a roar, "Who are you? What do you want? What do you mean by coming to my island in the middle of the night like a thief?"

Nana'b'oozoo's hair stood on end. His heart almost stopped. His legs wobbled and nearly gave way. Nana'b'oozoo dropped his canoe and ran, without thinking, holding the back of his head in anticipation of a blow of a war club on his skull.

If Nana'b'oozoo had one gift, it was speed. He didn't know of it until now. He was fleeter than any being upon the bosom of Mother Earth, particularly when he was frightened. And in this instant, Nana'b'oozoo took to his heels, faster than a falcon, as fast as the wind. He ran following the shoreline. Behind him the pebbles that he kicked sounded to him like footsteps as they fell. To Nana'b'oozoo, the enemy was at his very heels. He couldn't see behind him, and he didn't dare look. Nor could he see well enough in front of him to see overhanging branches, hillocks, depressions, fallen logs, and loose rocks. As often as he ran into a branch, slipped, stumbled, and tumbled head over heels, Nana'b'oozoo screamed, thinking that the enemy had struck him and was about to club him to death. But he quickly got back on his feet and was off again, screaming and yelping, so that with his speed, his shouts, coming from various points in his course around the island, sounded like they were produced by a score of warriors.

Even though Waub-meegwun had seen only Nana'b'oozoo, he was convinced from the numerous shouts that there were many invaders on shore. For his own safety, he retreated to his lodge, which was situated in the middle of the island, to await the assault near his weapons.

Nana'b'oozoo kept running around the island in the belief that he was being pursued. When Waub-meegwun ran into his camp, he grabbed his largest war club and stood in the middle of the clearing, rotating clockwise to face the direction from which the shouts came. With so many enemies closing in on him, Waub-meegwun didn't dare relax his vigilance. Round and round he turned, twisting and spinning about, until dizzy, he staggered, listed, and then fell in a faint that was transformed into a deep sleep.

At dawn, with his pace diminished by fatigue, Nana'b'oozoo glanced behind him and saw no one; he had outdistanced his pursuers. He stopped to catch his breath as well as to listen, but there was no sign or sound of a pursuer. It could easily mean that his pursuer or pursuers were hiding to ambush him. They could be behind or in front. To avoid running into an ambush along the shore, Nana'b'oozoo slipped into the woods and walked inland up the slope and into the enemy's camp, where he found Waub-meegwun fast asleep.

Nana'b'oozoo took the enemy's war club, and with all the force he could muster, clubbed Waub-meegwun's skull to a bloody pulp until he was certain beyond all doubt that Waub-meegwun would never draw another breath or harm another being.

Taking the enemy's headdress and weapons as plunder and as a sign of his victory, Nana'b'oozoo returned to the mainland in the morning, uttering triumphant war cries along the way.

A feast and a celebration were immediately begun to commemorate the end of the terror and the beginning of a new era. There was no more Waub-meegwun to fear. The people could go about their affairs without looking over their shoulders or stopping to listen to strange and unfamiliar footsteps in the forest. They could go to sleep at night, reasonably sure that none of them would be assassinated during the night and that they would see the morrow.

Some of the villagers wanted to invite Nana'b'oozoo to remain in their midst as their *ogimauh* [chief], but some of the elders advised against such a move. As much as they were indebted to Nana'b'oozoo and admired him, they were secretly afraid of him. Either he was a manitou or had so much of the goodwill and patronage of the manitous that he could accomplish anything, even slay a monster as he had just done, when no other warrior had been able to do so. With a manitou in their midst, the elders argued, they would constantly have to be watchful lest they do or say something to displease him. Besides, manitous had their own dwelling places and, as far as was known, did not cohabit with human beings. One never knew about the manitous. The villagers could easily offend other manitous if they were to invite Nana'b'oozoo to dwell among them. Anyway, if they ever needed his help again, for any reason, they could always invite him, as they had done on this occasion. Moreover, they argued, other people needed Nana'b'oozoo.

Hence, when Nana'b'oozoo prepared to leave, the north shore people did not press him to stay, but bade him farewell and let him know that he was always welcome in their village. They invited him to come back often and join in their festivals.

The people of that village did not forget Nana'b'oozoo and what he had done. They talked about him among themselves and told strangers who they met in their travels and visitors who came to their village about him.

Word spread like a forest fire that there was a champion, a manitou; a half manitou, half human; or a manitou in the guise of a man or woman. Yes, Nana'b'oozoo was a champion for everyone. Nana'b'oozoo cared. He was a manitou, a human, who could not bear to see anyone unhappy. Nana'b'oozoo cried to see others cry, was unhappy to see others unhappy, mourned when he saw others mourn, and laughed when he saw others laugh. He was a champion who understood. He wouldn't turn anyone down.

Nana'b'oozoo was especially fond of children. He would do anything for them—restore smiles and laughter to their faces when they were unhappy and tearful.

In those days children had no toys except sticks and stones, bark, and ants and beetles. The infants and toddlers in Nana'b'oozoo's village were suddenly stricken by a severe case of melancholy that was so deep that they ceased to laugh and even to smile. Instead, these children had a forlorn look and were constantly on the verge of tears. Their parents and the older children tried all sorts of amusements and schemes to get the little ones to cheer up, but nothing worked. A permanent sadness had settled in, spreading even to the adults, who were worried about them.

Along with sadness, the children lapsed into a listlessness, without the life, energy, or interest to run or reach out to extend themselves. They began to weaken.

At first the adults suspected that an enemy had put a curse on them and their children and tried every remedy then known to remove the curse—but nothing worked.

As a last resort, the people in this village sent for Nana'b'oozoo, more out of desperation and for the sake of appearance than from a real belief that this "champion" could do anything.

Nana'b'oozoo was no more successful than anybody else. Actually, he frightened the children even more, so they cried and screamed without let up until the people had to ask him to leave the children alone.

To have failed, and worse, to have been asked to go away, wounded Nana'b'oozoo's pride.

Unable to forget the children and their condition, Nana'b'oozoo made up his mind to speak directly to Kitchi-Manitou. For this purpose, he went in search of the highest mountain in the land, from whose summit he hailed and cried out to the Creator.

Kitchi-Manitou answered with a riddle, but Nana'b'oozoo could not decipher it. "Even stones have wings," Kitchi-Manitou said.

Later, exasperated by his inability to solve the riddle, Nana'b'oozoo took a handful of colored pebbles and pitched them over his shoulder in frustration. In midair the pebbles turned into butterflies of every color, shape, and size behind Nana'b'oozoo, who didn't notice the miracles. The transformation of stones into beautiful butterflies is not fiction; it occurs in the natural physical world when butterflies emerge from their little casements.

Nana'b'oozoo was still nowhere near solving the riddle or finding something that would uplift the spirits of children, when he decided to go home, empty-handed. Behind him followed the butterflies.

Children's eyes that had been dull and dim lit up, little arms that had been limp came to life, legs that had been wasted broke into a run, and faces that had been woebegone broke into smiles as the little boys and girls ran after these soft, small creatures that fluttered in the wind.

Since the day that Nana'b'oozoo returned from the west followed by these fragile creatures, butterflies have been the symbols of children's play and happiness. Our people called them *maemaegawauhnssiwuk*, little feathers, kin to the little people in the forest, the maemaegawaehnssiwuk, who appear only to children and sometimes play with them and care for them in the forest if they are lost.

Children then, as now, resisted eating vegetables and fruits, objecting that cabbages and such were a disagreeable green and unappetizing. To persuade children to eat vegetables and fruit, Nana'b'oozoo stumbled on the idea of dying them hundreds of different shades to confer beauty and flavor on them. But before he was half done with this enormous task, an enemy came along during the night and stained everything with a film of fine cold, white dust. Nana'b'oozoo was forced to start over, not once, but many times, before he learned who his enemy was. From the first Nana'b'oozoo had suspected that it was his brother Pukawiss, but it wasn't until he heard derisive laughter, muted and disguised though it was, that he was sure. Finally, unable or unwilling to put up with the despoliation of his work by frost or snow, even if it was done in jest, Nana'b'oozoo caught a cicada and put it to work painting the fruit and vegetables, so he could devote his time and energy to pursuing the enemy.

The cicada took up the assignment readily, but because Nana'b'oozoo's instructions were rather vague, he painted everything, including the grass and leaves. Nana'b'oozoo was so preoccupied with overtaking his mischievous brother Pukawiss, that he quite forgot the cicada. To this day the cicada can be heard on hot days, sometimes as early as mid-July, starting the duties that Nana'b'oozoo assigned him—painting the land to usher in the autumn.

Nana'b'oozoo's concern for his friends and real compassion for others were traits that endeared him to his kin, his neighbors, and other Anishinaubaek. He often voluntarily did a service or undertook a cause for others, and he was regarded as unselfish and kind. He put an end to the harassment of two blind men by an inconsiderate young lout and exemplified that it was unfair for the whole to take advantage of the disabled. He gave spikes to the porcupines so they could protect themselves. He performed hundreds of small services for everything around him, caring for his fellow human beings, elderly or infant, blind, disabled, or poor, and for bears, wolves, eagles, snakes, and beetles and trees, flowers, and blades of grass. To Nana'b'oozoo, care was not merely a sentiment or a word, but a deed to be carried out whenever someone needed it. No one had a better heart than he did.

There were occasions when Nana'b'oozoo applied harsh measures to those who did not demonstrate kindness and concern, especially when he was the object of an offense. In the case of an old woman who refused to give Nana'b'oozoo a crust of bread to allay his hunger, he changed her into a woodpecker and condemned her to subsist on insects and to bore trees for a single drop of bitter sap to quench her thirst. The punishment was harsh and unusual, but in his judgment and in that of his people, there was nothing worse than selfishness.

Nana'b'oozoo meant well, but he did not always carry out what he intended to do. He was encumbered with all human shortcomings: sloth, gluttony, envy, lust, pride, anger, and impulsiveness, among others. Nana'b'oozoo suffered from bouts of laziness, putting off hard and unpleasant work and spending days devising plans and techniques to make hunting and fishing less laborious, frustrating, and time consuming and more efficient and productive for his people. He wasn't happy with the existing spear, club, and bow and arrow. His countrymen's hunting and fishing techniques had not changed in generations because the people were too hidebound and attached to old traditions and methods to try new ways. Something new was needed to make life and work easier.

The first chance that came to him, Nana'b'oozoo broke with the practice of harvesting no more than an individual or family needed; such practice, he thought, was wasteful of time, energy, and talent. He labored mightily from morning till dusk for several days, delivering cargo after cargo of whitefish to his grandmother to clean, filet, smoke, and dry while he rested and looked forward to days of leisure and travel, such as men and women of foresight and industry earn and deserve. But Nana'b'oozoo's leisure and expectations of ease lasted only until the next morning when his grandmother discovered that their entire stock of dried whitefish had vanished.

If Nana'b'oozoo had known who had victimized him and his grandmother, he would have slit that person's throat and cracked his or her skull. After he got over his anger and cooled down, Nana'b'oozoo set to work to replenish the depleted stock.

When the food racks were bending once again under the weight of newly caught fish, Nana'b'oozoo kept vigil and spent a frantic night beating off poachers and freeloaders. Nana'b'oozoo ran here and there to repel the marauders, but when he was in one place beating in the dark with a club and uttering threats, other thieves were helping themselves elsewhere to Nana'b'oozoo's viands.

If Nana'b'oozoo and his grandmother thought that they could rest when day broke, they were mistaken. As soon as it was light, crows, ravens, magpies, jays, eagles, hawks, and mice began raiding Nana'b'oozoo's stores. He and his grandmother ran to and fro beating at the birds with branches while yelling and screeching to drive the birds off until they were both weary and out of breath. There were just too many birds. Nana'b'oozoo collapsed where he was, and his grandmother went to bed, leaving the birds to plunder the stores.

Birds and animals, though plentiful, were not easy to come by, and Nana'b'oozoo needed to devise another method. Men and women often had to go out in freezing rain, biting cold, or driving snow and wait in a place for hours to get one shot with a bow. Nana'b'oozoo knew there had to be an easier way to hunt geese and ducks than the traditional way. Rather than go to their haunts, nesting places, and feeding places, Nana'b'oozoo thought that it would be better to lure the birds to one's place for an ambush. To invite the birds to him, Nana'b'oozoo learned their language. After he gained command of the languages of geese and ducks, along with several of the dialects, Nana'b'oozoo invited the waterbirds to a festival, intending to massacre them, but the birds discovered the plot just before their host could murder them.

Despite his elaborate hunting schemes, Nana'b'oozoo often had to go without a meal and would even be forced to beg strangers and kin for a morsel of food.

Nana'b'oozoo wouldn't listen to advice, nor would he defer to another person with more experience and perhaps more knowledge than he. Even when he sought advice and knew that the counsel was sound, his impulsiveness would negate the advice. Like many people, he was easily beguiled by appearances.

Despite his unwillingness to listen to others, Nana'b'oozoo did seek guidance on one occasion. Dissatisfied with the results of many of his expeditions, he asked his friend Wolf, considered to be one of the foremost hunters in that part of the world, to tutor him in the art of hunting so he could improve his skills. But it was soon clear to Wolf, after a few simple questions, that Nana'b'oozoo did not have the slightest idea of what traits and personal qualities were necessary to be a good hunter. When asked his opinion, Nana'b'oozoo said that speed, grace, style, sight, and strength were the essential characteristics of a good hunter. Wolf had to correct him. Wolf said, "See that one?" referring to the smallest, scruffiest wolf. "He bids his time; he'll stay with his quarry until the very end—he'll not take his eyes off his target. He'll make do with what little he can eat during the hunt, and draw on what's at hand for his needs and know his quarry's strengths and weaknesses and habits. In other words, patience, endurance, fortitude, resolution, resourcefulness, and knowledge are what is necessary." Nor did Nana'b'oozoo exercise any better judgment in discerning the use of certain objects; in fact, he found these objects useless encumbrances.

For example, Nana'b'oozoo neglected to bring a wrapper with him that would have served as a blanket and kept him warm at night. Thus, despite his distaste for the smell and squalid state of his companions' tails that the young wolves spread over him to keep him warm, Nana'b'oozoo gritted his teeth and breathed in wolf stench all night.

For the most part, Nana'b'oozoo was grave and serious, but there were times when he gave frivolous answers to serious questions. Seldom were these answers taken so seriously as to cause hardship or accident. But there were times when others took them at face value and acted on them. In the case of Myeengun (Wolf), who asked Nana'b'oozoo how to cross a lake during the spring thaw, Nana'b'oozoo gave a flippant reply, recommending that the best way to get across safely was to cast a sapling on the ice that would turn into a bridge.

Now whether Nana'b'oozoo gave such a direction out of exasperation at the stupidity of the request or whether he meant the trusting Wolf to act on it in revenge for the number of times Wolf had insulted him while he was studying the art of hunting and surviving in the snowbound country, none can say. Perhaps he meant no more than to see how gullible Wolf was and to watch him fall into the cold water near shore and then scramble out shivering.

Wolf broke a sapling, as directed, and cast it in front of him on the lake, believing what his friend Nana'b'oozoo had told him. But instead of foundering in the shallows and scrambling ashore, dripping wet and howling with rage, Wolf was sucked under the ice by the current, drowned, and borne into the Underworld.

To exact revenge on the Mishi-bizheu, the Great Lynx who dwelt at the bottom of the sea, for having lured and dragged Myeengun to his death, Nana'b'oozoo ventured into the depths of the sea. But he found neither the Great Lynx nor his friend.

Nana'b'oozoo was inconsolable for months. Someday, he vowed, he would hunt down Mishi-bizheu and destroy the monster in revenge for his friend's death.

Nana'b'oozoo envied young men his age, wishing that he could go out with girls as they did. He wondered what it was like to be alone with a girl somewhere at night, and he wondered why girls did not seek him out as they did other boys. Nana'b'oozoo didn't know that the girls and their parents were afraid of him because he was part manitou. He believed that the girls didn't like him.

Though the girls were cool to Nana'b'oozoo, he liked them and was fond of one in particular. He didn't know that the girl was his sister, until his grandmother told him. By then it was too late because Nana'b'oozoo was hopelessly in love. He loved this girl desperately, passionately, but he had to fall out of love; he had to forget her. But before Nana'b'oozoo would give her up, he wanted to find out if she had any feelings for him, for she appeared to be indifferent to him, which made him disconsolate.

Before Nana'b'oozoo let go this illicit love he put the girl to a test, feigning death to induce her tears to see if she cared for him. If she cried, Nana'b'oozoo would be content that she at least cared for him. But Nana'b'oozoo's plan didn't work out the way he hoped it would. Before the wake was conducted, his sister learned of Nana'b'oozoo's chicanery. Instead of crying, she and her sister laughed.

Nana'b'oozoo not only wanted to know what it was like to be a man with a woman, but he was equally curious to know what it was like to be a woman with a man. Perhaps he wanted to learn how to conduct a romance by being the object of a man's embraces and kisses.

Nana'b'oozoo disguised himself as a woman by wearing women's garments and attaching rabbit's fur between his legs. In the dark in another village, he lured a young man to bed. The young gallant, panting with wanton lust, reached down the lady's mound of seduction, and in his anxiety and inexperience pulled off the false organ in the early stages of foreplay. Before the aroused young man could recover from his surprise and do him in, Nana'b'oozoo made off, just barely escaping the clutches of the embarrassed and cheated paramour. If it had not been for his fleetness of foot, Nana'b'oozoo would have been dismembered.

He asked why girls went into retreat on the occasion of their first "change of flow," what they did, and why men were not permitted in or near the "first change of blood flow" lodge. No one could give Nana'b'oozoo an answer that made sense to him and that he could accept; the answers he was given, such as "men aren't allowed," "it's none of your business," and "leave the women alone; it's their affair," only roused his curiosity further. He suspected that the women might be inducting the girls into the mysteries of witchcraft and medicine during those times. Nana'b'oozoo burned to know what the women were trying to keep to themselves and away from men. He asked young and old men alike to tell him what they knew of women's customs, but none of them knew anymore than he did. What was disturbing, as well as inexplicable, was that the men seemed indifferent to what the women did during their rituals. In Nana'b'oozoo's opinion, it was not right for part of the community to perform rituals in secret and only for themselves.

If the menfolk preferred to remain ignorant and to allow their womenfolk freedom to do certain things in their own way, without the help and knowledge of the men, then it was their loss. But Nana'b'oozoo wasn't going to be kept in the dark; he wasn't going to abide by custom simply because others had done it in a particular way and as a matter of practice for generations.

But anxious as he was to witness the girl-becomes-a-woman ritual, Nana'b'oozoo had to wait for a while before he could actually spy on a young girl and her attendants. On the first night of the ritual, Nana'b'oozoo stole to within seeing and hearing distance of the women's lodge, hiding under a blanket of ferns and cedar boughs. In the morning several dogs belonging to the women attending the young girls discovered the mound of cedar boughs and began to bark furiously. The women, alarmed by the barking, picked up sticks and ran toward the place where the dogs were congregated, creating an uproar. Before the women arrived at the mound of cedar boughs, Nana'b'oozoo got up and ran off amid the imprecations of the women and the baying of the dogs, which, besides howling, nipped at his heels.

To the women, although Nana'b'oozoo was part manitou, he

was most unmanitou in his secular and lurid curiosity about women and their bodily functions. It may have been from this incident that people, especially women, began to regard Nana'b'oozoo with less awe and reverence than in the past, referring to him as *aupitchih igoh nauh w'gageebaudizih,* saying that "he is foolish beyond words, imagination" and is not to be trusted.

The men teased him and found his venture amusing. Nana'-b'oozoo was not all manitou, and although he seemed to be more man than manitou, they thought he must have been more manitou than man to have had the audacity to try to enter the world of womanhood. When the men asked him what he saw and heard that they had not seen or heard, what would better their lives, Nana'b'oozoo laughed to think that he had been discovered by dogs.

Still single, he lived with his grandmother, coming and going whenever he felt like it, leaving the old woman to manage for herself during his absences.

But as time passed, it became more difficult than before to leave the old woman alone; she was becoming too frail to look after herself. Before he left on some trip, Nana'b'oozoo had to entrust her to the care of neighbors and kin, and if he could find no one to look after his grandmother in his absence, he had to take her with him.

Up to this time, Nana'b'oozoo had been accustomed to leaving on the spur of the moment. Now, when he decided to set out and had to take his grandmother along, he had to wait and wait, pacing and chewing his nails in impatience while she dawdled and stood uncertain in some spot as if she could not decide what to do next or as if she had forgotten something, unconcerned about time or her grandson's anxiety to leave for his appointments. She moved like a turtle or a snail, without a sense of time or urgency. Not only did Nana'b'oozoo have to wait for her when he was prepared to leave, but he had to wait on and serve her when they arrived at their destination, pitching their camp, making the fire, cooking her meals, and washing her clothing while she sat and mended a torn garment or simply sat staring into space seeing visions of life as it had been years before. Not only did Nana'b'oozoo have to wait on his grandmother while she rested, but he had to carry her up and down slopes and over portages when she got too tired. She held him back; he could no longer go as far as he would have liked to go in one day or at his pace. Nana'b'oozoo was no longer in full control of his life.

And he resented the demands and the impositions that his grandmother made on him and his time. She had become a burden, a millstone, that he couldn't get rid of but had to carry about with him wherever he went for as long as she lived. And she was a burden that would get heavier and more cumbersome with time.

At first, Nana'b'oozoo said nothing when his grandmother tarried, could not remember where she had put something, or rested too frequently to catch her breath and her strength. But as time passed and the old lady's steps grew shorter, Nana'-b'oozoo spoke brusquely as he bade her hurry and move along. He even scolded her as if she were a disobedient child, going so far as to call her names. But none of these measures made the slightest impression on the old lady; she didn't walk one step faster because her grandson told her to move along, nor did she complain when Nana'b'oozoo called her "a deadhead."

Eventually Nana'b'oozoo's patience gave out. He had enough and decided to get rid of her. According to one story, Nana'b'oozoo cast his grandmother overboard as they were crossing a lake, in which she drowned. It was said that an island formed in that part of the lake where she sank out of sight as a monument to Nana'b'oozoo's heartlessness and ingratitude.

Had Nana'b'oozoo actually done this, however, there would have been no more Nana'b'oozoo-grandmother stories. But there is another account. In this other story, Nana'b'oozoo simply abandoned his grandmother, telling her that he was going to leave her alone for an afternoon while he paddled up lake to study the route and the availability of deer and food.

Nana'b'oozoo should have been relieved to leave his grand-mother behind because she had held him up so frequently and for such lengths of time and forced him to perform extra, unnecessary labor, but he wasn't. He was disturbed to the point of looking back, half expecting to see his grandmother and half expecting to see someone who might have observed what he had done, and he couldn't keep his mind on where he was going or what he intended to do. His mind kept returning to the image of the old woman like a magnet. Different images of her appeared to him; one moment, as she stirred the soup that she was making, and the next, as she braided her hair—over a hun-dred reflections of her, as many postures as she had taken over the years as she went about her work. Nana'b'oozoo tried to put these images out of his mind by fixing his thoughts or recalling other events that he'd experienced in his short life, but these memories were soon superseded by images of his grandmother. Still he paddled farther and farther on.

No matter how far he went, Nana'b'oozoo could not shake the thoughts of his grandmother. Everything he saw, heard, or smelled reminded him of old N'okomiss: waterlilies, cedars, mist, waves, the call of robins, the flight of hawks, all of which delighted the old lady, his mother's mother, and reminded him of her.

On the third day, these images of his grandmother changed from ones of his grandmother as she had been in the past to the present, pathetic images of old N'okomiss—frail, gaunt, crawl-ing to the edge of the lake to get a drink of water, and eating grass and moss to nourish herself just to sustain her life a few days longer. Last, he saw her emaciated, unmoving image upon the ground, surrounded by crows, ravens, buzzards, and other birds of death that fed on the flesh of the dead. And Nana'b'oozoo would be to blame.

Consumed by guilt, Nana'b'oozoo turned his canoe around and paddled back on the double without stopping to eat. A day and a half later, he was back where he'd left his grandmother, relieved to see that she was still alive and well under the care of some people who had come upon her by chance in their travels. When his grandmother asked about his prolonged absence, Nana'b'oozoo explained that he'd lost his way.

Sometime after his return home, Nana'b'oozoo courted the arrow maker's daughter. Some people felt sorry for the young woman and secretly urged her not to go through with the marriage to Nana'b'oozoo, even though he was a manitou and capable of supernatural deeds. Life was hard enough with an ordinary man, they said. However, the arrow maker had agreed to give his daughter to Nana'b'oozoo.

Word spread that Nana'b'oozoo was going to get married to the poor arrow maker's daughter. Nana'b'oozoo asked a "divine" to perform the shaking-tent ceremony and to drum a message to his father and his brothers inviting them to attend his marriage and the feast and celebration afterward.

Nana'b'oozoo didn't expect his brothers to come, since he did not know their whereabouts or how to get in touch with them. So when they came, there was a double cause for celebrating. Even Pukawiss came dressed in his finest garments. This occasion was the first time that Nana'b'oozoo met his oldest brother, Maudjee-kawiss, and the first time that the four brothers came together; it also was the last time. In the meeting, Nana'b'oozoo's wife was almost forgotten.

This meeting of the four brothers ended in tragedy when Cheeby-aub-oozoo, stung by Maudjee-kawiss's taunts that he and Nana'b'oozoo lacked courage, set out across a lake during a storm to show his daring. Before he got far out on the lake, Cheeby-aub-oozoo's canoe capsized and he drowned.

Nana'b'oozoo was, of course, downcast by the people's decision to forbid Cheeby-aub-oozoo from entering the homes of the living or touching any living being. He accepted their decree and learned to live without ever having his brother as a guest in his home or touching him, for he, too, was bound by the edict.

After the wedding, Nana'b'oozoo never saw Maudjee-kawiss again. Pukawiss was now the only brother to call on him.

For the most part, the two brothers got along well enough. Nana'b'oozoo was fond of Pukawiss and might have gotten along even better with him except for his brother's inability to resist playing practical jokes on others, but especially on Nana'-b'oozoo, who couldn't take a joke. Nana'b'oozoo had a quick temper, and Pukawiss was fond of provoking him into a rage. It was then that Nana'b'oozoo prayed for his brother's death, and his prayers were answered.

With Cheeby-aub-oozoo and Pukawiss gone, Nana'b'oozoo had only his grandmother and his wife.

For the arrow maker's daughter, life was not the state of companionship and well-stocked stores that she imagined from the courtship, when Nana'b'oozoo was with her constantly and kept the arrow maker's food racks bent, sagging with meat and fish. Like her father and mother, the daughter was beguiled by Nana'b'oozoo's attentions and his wizardry with the bow and arrow, club, spear, snares, traps, and deadfalls.

Before long, she was spending long periods alone as Nana'-b'oozoo undertook some cause on someone's behalf and having to scrounge and beg or borrow food from neighbors.

If Nana'b'oozoo and his wife often went without, it wasn't because deer and geese and fish were scarce or that he had lost his touch, as much as it was his unwillingness to listen to others, to learn from his experiences, or to abide by time-honored customs and the practice "of leaving something for others and for tomorrow."

In one of the spells of bad luck that he experienced, and from which his wife suffered during the early days of their marriage, Nana'b'oozoo watched Heron, a fisherman, go to the lake several times each day for several days and catch fish without fail. Nana'b'oozoo envied the apparent ease with which Heron caught fish. He therefore asked Heron to show him the art of fishing and the secret of his success.

Heron obliged, reminding Nana'b'oozoo to take no more than what he and his family needed, so there would be fish the next time Nana'b'oozoo needed it. Nana'b'oozoo assured

Heron that he would respect the laws and practices governing the taking of fish and promised to exercise proper respect for the fish.

With Heron's method, Nana'b'oozoo caught a fish at once. He could not believe the results. Not sure that the ease with which he caught a fish could be attributed to method or to luck, Nana'b'oozoo put Heron's method to a second test to make sure. He caught a second fish with like ease. Still not convinced, Nana'b'oozoo tried the technique many times until there was no doubt in his mind that getting fish was a matter of skill, not chance. By the time he was absolutely certain, Nana'b'oozoo had a large pile of fish behind him. It was all so simple and easy. He didn't stop, but kept drawing fish after fish from the lake without regard for Heron's reminder to take no more than was necessary to feed him and his family for the next day. As Nana'b'oozoo added to his harvest of fish and forgot Heron's advice, he foresaw a winter of ease and comfort with no shortage of food.

At the end of the day, Nana'b'oozoo had an immense stockpile of fish by the shore. Taking two large whitefish with him for supper, he went home and told his wife about his good fortune and how they would always have more than enough to eat from then on by following the method that Heron had shown him.

In the morning, Nana'b'oozoo and his wife returned to the lake to retrieve the fish that he had left there. When they arrived, there was no trace of fish in the place where he had left a small hill of whitefish. Nothing was there except a small mound of icicles. Nana'b'oozoo couldn't understand what had happened; he could only insist that he had indeed speared more than two hundred whitefish and that he had left them where the icicles now stood.

"Fool!" Nana'b'oozoo's wife shrilled, and she unleashed a hail of invective at her husband. The words poured out of her mouth in no particular order, cold and cutting, like sleet. "Greedy! Weendigo! Selfish! Mindless! Idiot!" She snarled and spat. "Fish! Enough fish to last all winter! Promises! And more promises. That's all we ever get to eat and wear. Fish! Food. Never have to worry. More than enough. How do we know? Maybe it's just a lie to make us feel good, a pipe dream.

"And if it's true! If it's true that Heron showed you how to catch fish and to save something, you wouldn't listen. You knew better, didn't you? You had to get greedy, be like a Weendigo. Think only of your belly, your hunger now, for you there's only today.

"Because you lie, you cannot . . . will not listen . . . you're greedy. You don't know when to stop, you don't care for customs and have no common sense. Now we don't have anything to eat for tomorrow. The children will have nothing to eat except roots and moss if we're lucky and you can find some! What kind of father have they got? . . . Why did my father give me to you? You're supposed to be a manitou, humph! If they only knew."

Nana'b'oozoo's wife was right, of course, not only about her husband but what fare their children were going to eat. They ate moss, bark, and dried berries for some days as she had predicted. That experience ought to have made some impression on Nana'b'oozoo and brought about a change in his behavior and attitude, but alas it did not. After a short period of reformation, Nana'b'oozoo fell back into his old habits that resulted in hardship for his wife and family. Following each lapse, Nana'b'oozoo was contrite and made up his mind to improve for his family's sake, and he meant it. But despite his good intentions, he soon reverted slowly to his old ways without noticing that he was falling from his good habits. Stand up, fall, regain balance, and stumble again; such was the pattern of Nana'b'oozoo's life.

During the hard times, when his children (the number of whom he sired is not known) were forced to eat moss and had to wear ragged garments, Nana'b'oozoo acted as if he were a hunter whose food racks were fully stocked, leaving his wife and family at a moment's notice and staying away from them for protracted periods. It was as if they didn't exist.

In fact, it seemed as if Nana'b'oozoo cared more for others than he did for his family. Even after he was married, people came to him frequently, expecting him to leave his family and to suspend whatever he happened to be doing at that moment to champion their cause. And Nana'b'oozoo did; he was always ready.

The Anishinaubaek of Nipissing had long been beleaguered and harassed by local Weendigoes. As soon as they heard about the new champion of the nation, they sent a courier to Nana'b'oozoo to invite him to their part of the country to drive their oppressors out and put them to flight or club them to a pulp.

As the courier described the atrocities committed by the Weendigoes, Nana'b'oozoo couldn't hold back his tears or contain his outrage. He whimpered and gasped to catch his breath during the recitation, unable to bear the thought of struggling, screaming old women trying to fight off the Weendigoes or of shrieking children being torn asunder by the monsters. Everyone else, his wife, his children, his grandmother, his friends, was cast into the background and forgotten. Long before the entire story was told, Nana'b'oozoo was on his feet, brandishing a tomahawk and shrieking war cries. Nana'b'oozoo was ready.

Days later Nana'b'oozoo was at the foot of the Mattawa hills, the dwelling place of the Weendigoes, where he had been led as he had requested.

When the Nipissing Anishinaubaek saw Nana'b'oozoo, they were dismayed, for they had been expecting a champion, a large and brawny man. Instead, they looked on this man of average height and slightness of build, who presented himself as a champion, a man who was supposed to inspire hope and confidence in his friends and dread and respect in the enemy. They felt sorry for this man, for he could not begin to hold his own against the Weendigoes; he didn't stand a chance. Yet they admired his spirit.

On the shores of Lake Nipissing the Anishinaubaek waited.

At the foothills of the Mattawa highlands, Nana'b'oozoo bellowed a taunting challenge. "Ahow! You child killers! You abusers of old men and old women. Come on down and lick my moccasins, or . . . shall I have to come up for you? . . ."

Before Nana'b'oozoo could add another word, about forty Weendigoes, according to witnesses, came thundering down the hillside, screaming and brandishing war clubs. They shrieked, "Murder! Blood! Meat! First one gets all of him! Quit complaining. At least it's a meal!"

Even one Weendigo was more than enough for one man, no less forty. Nana'b'oozoo took one look, heard the ear-piercing war cries, and dropped his war club. Then he turned and bolted.

The Anishinaubaek spectators watched their hero run, as they expected he would, their slight hopes dashed. They were downcast, as downcast as could be.

As fast as Nana'b'oozoo was, he could not outrun the enemy, who closed in on him. Nana'b'oozoo didn't have to glance backward to know that the Weendigoes were drawing steadily nearer. He could hear their pounding steps and their shrieks. Nana'b'oozoo pushed his legs to the limits of their speed, but he couldn't pull away from the Weendigoes. There was nothing he could do except cry and pray; teardrops and sweat washed over him. Bleary-eyed, the champion ran blindly—straight into Lake Nipissing.

As Nana'b'oozoo ran headlong into the water, a miracle took place. Flat stones rose to the surface in front of him the way he was to go. Without breaking stride, Nana'b'oozoo leaped from one stone to the next. But the Weendigoes followed right behind, matching Nana'b'oozoo step for step, vaulting forward on the same stepping-stones.

When Nana'b'oozoo and the Weendigoes were well out into the lake, another miracle took place. The stones behind Nana'b'oozoo sank, pitching the Weendigoes into the water. The Weendigoes thrashed the water while trying to stay afloat. They screamed in terror as they sank out of sight, one by one, never to be seen again. Only bubbles broke the surface where they vanished.

Nana'b'oozoo ran on, unaware of the miraculous tragedy behind him. He cried and he prayed to the manitous of the Weendigoes to spare him for his family's sake, promising never again to take the name of the Weendigoes in vain.

On the opposite shore, Nana'b'oozoo staggered and then collapsed steps from the water's edge. He covered his head and closed his eyes in tense expectation. But for all his waiting, no blows came and no hands tore at him. He listened but heard no footsteps or outcries, nothing except the break of waves and the screech of seagulls. Nana'b'oozoo opened one eye, then two; he saw no one. Utterly spent and relieved, he was unable to move. There he lay and fell into a deep sleep.

Meanwhile, on the opposite shore, the Anishinaubaek who had seen everything from the beginning and witnessed the drowning of the Weendigoes were inspired by the turn of events. They cheered when the Weendigoes were engulfed, observing in admiration that "only Nana'b'oozoo could think of such a stratagem. Only Nana'b'oozoo could do such a thing!"

When Nana'b'oozoo failed to return to the village of the Nipissing Anishinaubaek, their chief sent out a search party to find him and bring him back. The party found Nana'b'oozoo asleep and brought him back to the village to celebrate a festival in his honor. Never had a nation such a champion as Nana'b'oozoo. No man, woman, or manitou was deserving of more honor.

From what they saw, the Anishinaubaek of Nipissing and elsewhere believed that Nana'b'oozoo was a hero, a manitou, a guardian of the weak, caring, daring, and cunning. They didn't see the terror or the tears in his eyes or hear his prayers. They were too distant, too absorbed in their own cares, to see beyond the surface to the fundamental reality of what Nana'b'oozoo did.

If the spectators had known Nana'b'oozoo as his grandmother and his wife knew him, they would not have been fooled. They would have known that Nana'b'oozoo, in this instance as in every other one, was not faking, but being true and faithful to himself. His tears and prayers, as well as his actions, were genuine. In going to Nipissing to render aid, Nana'b'oozoo meant well. In returning home to his family and his village intending to look after his wife, grandmother, and children, he meant well, as did most men and women.

Yet, despite his good intentions, Nana'b'oozoo often fell short of carrying out his objectives. Something always interposed itself between his intent and his fulfillment of it and resulted in mishap or indiscretion. Whenever Nana'b'oozoo failed to fulfill his intentions, such failure was invariably caused by his human shortcomings: fear, curiosity, forgetfulness, envy, lust, and intemperance. If he sometimes succeeded in accomplishing anything, such success was earned quite by accident.

In his village, his kin and neighbors were bemused by Nana'b'oozoo's blunders and follies, unable to understand how a manitou, as many still believed him to be, could lack such common sense or be so blind as to fail to foresee the consequences of his schemes. They attempted to predict what Nana'-b'oozoo would do next.

Eventually, the Anishinaubaek applied the name "Nana'b'-oozoo" to anyone who committed blunders as a result of acting on impulse and instinct, rather than on reason and common sense. Nana'b'oozoo came to exemplify the foolishness that men and women are capable of. "Ha! Nana'b'oozoo!" means "fool" or "folly."

Whether "Nana'b'oozoo! Ha! Nana'b'oozoo!" was said with a smile or with a note of scorn, it was meant to keep men, women, and children in line and to prompt them to exercise common sense and reason. Everyone is susceptible to foolishness. In most instances, the utterance of "Nana'b'oozoo" was sufficient to bring about reform, because men and women normally do not like to be regarded as incapable of exercising good judgment. Pride and a sense of worth and dignity would not allow most men and women to be scorned for long.

As Nana'b'oozoo got older, he committed fewer and fewer misdeeds and bumbled less often. And if he hurt someone, he was invariably sorry. He learned, but slowly, as do most men and women.

In the end, years later, Nana'b'oozoo left his home, his family, and his village, accompanied only by his grandmother aboard his canoe. No one was on shore to bid him farewell. Some say that he left his village and the people in disappointment, heartbroken by their rejection of him and by their turning away from him to accept the pale-faced latecomer and his new ways. They say that he also left word that he would return some day when his people were ready to welcome him into their lives once again.

That Nana'b'oozoo left with his grandmother was fitting, for at the end he had cast off the ways of youth and espoused the values, aspirations, and understandings that his grandmother had tried to instill in him in his youth. Finally, he deserved to take a place at the side of the elders.

Since forsaking the land of his ancestors, his brothers and sisters, the Anishinaubaek, Nana'b'oozoo has not been seen or heard from. No new stories about him have been made up for generations, and the old ones have been all but forgotten. Because of the present generation's indifference to its language, traditions, and heritage, the spirit of Nana'b'oozoo is unlikely to return to inspire storytellers to add to the national Anishinaubae legacy, enriching the meaning and the value of the bequest as it is meant to be enriched. And there are few who mourn the loss to the Anishinaubae nation.

CHAPTER SEVEN

THE MANITOUS OF THE FORESTS AND MEADOWS

Four young men, not yet in their twenties, had been friends since childhood. When they were children, they would often sit on the shore in the evening, watching the sun set and speculating on what lay beyond the horizon, certain that the land on the other side was much fairer than their own encampment. As they grew older, they still met frequently in the evenings, but the topics of their conversations had shifted from speculations on the fairness of the land to the west and life's prospects to their present lot and outlook.

The discussions that these young men had about their conditions and a better life was not just idle talk. Theirs was a bedraggled little band, constantly on the move in pursuit of animals who also were constantly on the move, in retreat before the onslaught of hunters. If the band's lot became desperate in winter, it was not because moose, deer, elk, and other animals were scarce, but rather because the herds had no fixed habitat. Seldom did the band remain in one place for long before the men and women had to dismantle their lodges, pack their possessions, and resume their trek in search of the territory where animals dwelt permanently and in large numbers. If the band was to come upon such a land, they would erect their lodges and found a village that would be home. But the fulfillment of that hope and dream was always one night off and just beyond the horizon.

In the meantime they would all have to suffer hardship, forced to eat bark and moss from time to time and listen to the cries of hungry children and to leave behind the bodies of their kin and neighbors who had succumbed to sickness. There were times when blood would be spilled, both theirs and that of other bands, for the same bounty.

The years of moving without ever coming on "the land of plenty" took a toll on their spirits. All the hunters and their families grew discouraged, humiliated, and dejected by their failures; distrustful of their holy men and women and even doubtful of the manitous; more and more anxious over the well-being and future of their children; fretful of the winter; and fearful of the Weendigoes who stalked the hungry camps, lying in wait for an incautious hunter. In their gloom and depression they quarreled with one another. They were not a happy lot, but they pressed on, solely to survive.

The four young friends at last agreed that if every family had enough food, clothing, health, and strength to survive the winter, everyone would be content and enjoy peace of mind and spirit. This was all that men and women sought in life.

If *only* there was enough food in winter, if *only* the animals had a fixed habitat, if *only* there was a way of storing food, life would be rewarding. If only, if only . . .

The idea that such a place must exist or be in the hands of the manitous preoccupied the four friends. They made up their minds to find this place.

When they confided their convictions and their plans to the wise men and women, they didn't receive as much encouragement as they had hoped or as much opposition as they had expected. The holy men and women weren't helpful in giving them direction and guidance. About the only worthwhile information they were given was that only a manitou could bring about the changes they craved and that such a manitou dwelt somewhere in the west.

The four young friends left with good wishes for a successful mission, along with the doubts and sarcasm of skeptics.

For some months the four traveled on foot before they came to a great river about which they had heard much. To get across the river, they had to construct a raft.

A day's travel beyond this, the greatest of rivers, they came upon a hovel recessed in a grove of trees. From within came moans, barely audible. Drawn by these faint and pitiful groans, the young men entered the hovel and found an old woman, all skin and bones, who, from her pallor and glazed eyes, looked as if she had not much longer to live.

The old woman was beyond help. There were only two things the young men could do: keep her as comfortable as possible and watch over her until the end came and they could bury her. Since the old woman's lodge was cold and she shivered and convulsed with chills, two of the young men cut wood and made a fire while the other two went hunting for food for their meal.

When the lodge warmed up from the fire, the old woman ceased shivering and fell into a deep sleep. In the morning she awakened hungry. After the young men gave her some broth, the old woman immediately fell asleep once more.

The young men waited, one always in the lodge next to the old woman's pallet, the others nearby outside, watching, waiting for the end to come. But it did not come as they expected it would. Each time the old woman woke up, she said she was hungry, and the young men fed her; then she would fall asleep again. So certain had the young men been that the old woman was doomed that her recovery was akin to a miracle.

It was gratifying to the young men to provide some service during the old woman's recovery, but what they should do with her when she had fully regained her health bedeviled them. They guessed her age to be about ninety. They could not very well leave her alone.

As yet they dared not ask her personal questions for fear of offending her, and they weren't certain that they had done the right thing by caring for her.

But it was the old woman, as curious about them as they were about her, who asked the first personal question the moment she was well enough to sit up on her pallet. She wanted to know what had brought them so far from home.

At first they refused to tell her where they were bound, thinking that she would laugh at them as a few others had done, but in the end they overcame their reservations and told her what they were doing in her part of the world.

To their relief, the old woman didn't laugh at them. Instead, she asked, "And for yourselves, what do you want?"

They answered that they wanted no more than what they wanted for their kin and neighbors. They would be more than content if sustenance were more readily available in winter than at present. What they wanted more than anything else was enough food and remedies to keep them from starving, to restore them to health when they were sick, and to prolong their lives. And what they wanted as much as anything else was to see their brothers and sisters, kin and neighbors, live in friendship instead of the spitefulness and petty jealousy that prevailed in their communities. If such a life was possible, what more could men and women wish for?

The old woman told the young men that she could grant them what they wished.

This was what they had come to hear, but when they heard it, they didn't believe it. They asked her who she was; they needed to have some proof that she could do the extraordinary.

The old woman told them that she was Muzzu-Kummik-Quae, Mother Earth, and to show that she could do what only a manitou could do, she asked for a branch and caused it to bloom with apples.

The young men were convinced.

Before they left, Muzzu-Kummik-Quae gave each of the young men a little medicine bundle with instructions that under no circumstances were they to open the bundles until they returned to their village. If they opened the bundles sooner, the talisman would be undone. At home each young man was to make a beverage with the medicine from his bundle and then drink it.

On the way back the four young men were tempted many times to open their bundles. The farther they drew away from the old woman, the more skeptical they became, questioning how such small bundles could possibly benefit their people's ills and needs. They even began to harbor suspicions that Mother Earth might be gulling them. But, in the end, the four friends kept their bundles unopened out of fear of what might happen.

Amid welcomes, the young men were also greeted with good-natured kidding and irony at home. "Well did you bring home a better life?" the people asked, which was well meant, but nevertheless nettled them.

In secret, along with a great deal of skepticism, the four friends each prepared a beverage from the contents of the medicine bundles. Nothing happened, as they had feared.

The four friends did not long survive their disillusionment and sense of betrayal. Within days of one another, they died from broken hearts.

But a remarkable thing happened. Out of the grave of the first young man grew a tree whose seeds begot countless offspring that became thick green forests. In these forests, deer, moose, caribou, elk, rabbits, and partridges took refuge and made their homes, and the men and women set their lodges and shelters. The hunters and their families no longer had to trudge through snow, day after endless day, in quest of food. And they found that the leaves, cones, resins, boughs, roots, and bark of the evergreen trees were medicinal and healthful.

The second youth's grave yielded a plant that grew into a tall tree whose bark was white and soft yet strong. This tree produced other tall white trees that the Anishinaubae people called *weegwauss* (birch), whose outer bark is white and luminous, fragile, and delicate. From the delicate bark of these trees, the people constructed their *wigwamun* (lodges), canoes, utensils, and containers, and their holy men and women inscribed their chants, psalms, prayers, and ideas on sacred scrolls. Even woodpeckers and their kin drew their drink from the sap of the birch.

Atop the third youth's burial mound there appeared slate-colored stones of different sizes, quite unlike any seen up to that time in that part of the country. And unlike any other stones, they multiplied until they covered the ground.

For a long time, the people would have nothing to do with the stones because of a presentiment born out of the unnatural origin of the rocks. This foreboding turned into fear when some people discovered that when the stones were struck together, they produced sparks. These stones had within them a property that was manitoulike. It took time, but eventually the descendants of this youth overcame their fear and learned that the sparks fed best upon birch bark, tinder, and resin and gave birth to fire that was of both immense benefit and destruction.

Once they possessed this flint, the people no longer needed to carry coals with them wherever they went. From then on, they carried two wedges of flint, a handful of tinder, and layers of birch bark. Life and work became a little easier.

The fourth grave also yielded a new and different plant that flourished like the other plants. But unlike most other plants that served some useful purpose for humans and animals, this new plant didn't appear to have any use to any living thing.

For years people neglected the plant, until someone finally stuffed its leaves in a pipe for something to smoke. These leaves certainly produced a more fragrant aroma than did ordinary leaves and grasses, and they burned more slowly. There was something about this plant, neither medicine nor food, that made it more fitting than any other substance to be used as incense to be offered in thanksgiving to Kitchi-Manitou, in propitiation to the manitous who presided over victims slain for their flesh, and in gratitude and respect to Muzzu-Kummik-Quae. The Anishinaubae peoples called it *saemauh* (tobacco). From a neglected plant, saemauh became sacred, hallowed by its use in the Pipe of Peace Smoking Ceremony.

With tobacco, people sought the goodwill of the manitous. But with so much ill will, suspicion, and disagreement within the village, there was as much need to obtain the goodwill of kin and neighbors.

Since tobacco was meant for the manitous, and was therefore sacred, the Anishinaubae people, like other North American Indians, gave it as a gift whenever they needed a favor from their kin and neighbors. The donor could give nothing of greater benefit or worth than that which would bring the recipient the goodwill of the manitous.

The Spirit of Maundau-meen (Maize)

In the story about the coming of corn to the Anishinaubae people and country, corn is personified as a stranger who arrived in a village looking for one person, a man or a woman, who could prove that the Anishinaubaek were worthy of the name they had chosen for themselves: "The good men and good people." In representing corn as a stranger, the Anishinaubae storytellers were historically and factually correct. Corn came from afar, from a land that the Anishinaubae people had never heard of, Mexico, advancing as an adventurer and a migrant from one garden to another against formidable odds: hostile climates, unfriendly soil, short seasons, and people who preferred chasing animals and spearing fish to farming. But the stranger prospered.

As corn went onward, it dared hunters and fishermen to master it, promising them life if they could cultivate it. As often as hunters and fishermen and their wives accepted the challenge and squared off with this challenger, they domesticated it. In caring for and giving respect to the stranger, they gained for themselves a life better than they had hitherto known.

The Anishinaubae peoples were reluctant to accept the challenge. They had many reservations about doing battle with a stranger, but like their kin and neighbors to the south, they overcame their doubts and the stranger as well, tended his grave, and derived benefits that they had not dreamed of. They prospered.

In commemoration of the coming of the stranger, his origin, and the remarkable fertility and multiplicity of dishes that the plant he left behind produced, the Anishinaubae people called the new plant Maundau-meen, the seed of wonder, or the wonderful food.

But after some years of plenty, the corn harvest began to fail, and other harvests faltered as well. There was not enough meat and fish to sustain the Anishinaubae people through the winters, and they were forced to eat bark, moss, lichen, and frozen berries. The good life had ended, and the people were forced to return to their traditional hunting and fishing ways.

No one could understand the crop's failure any more than anyone knew what to do to restore the harvests to their former quantities.

Finally, the people asked their spiritual leaders to speak to the manitous on their behalf, to request the restoration of the harvest of corn and other fruit of the earth, and for direction in what measures they ought to take to help revive the harvest.

During his dream quest, the figure of a manitou, who revealed itself as the Spirit of Corn, Maundau-meen, appeared to a sage. Maundau-meen told the sage that because men and women were ill-using corn by feeding it to dogs, wasting it by eating only a portion and casting away the uneaten portion, and leaving it to rot in the fields, it was aggrieved. And unless the Anishinaubae peoples changed and cared for and exercised a regard for corn as it deserved, corn would die out and vanish from their lives, leaving them as badly off as they had been before.

Forewarned, the Anishinaubae peoples asked pardon of the manitou of corn and promised to care for corn as one would a friend. Once again, corn grew in abundance.

The Spirit of Gawaunduk

Until her mother remarked with a mischievous smile that the young man who had become a frequent visitor to their home in recent weeks was a good boy and would some day make a fine husband for some lucky girl, Gawaunduk (the Guardianess) had not given the boy, South Wind, any more thought than she had given any other boy.

"Him!" she had said with some surprise and with a bit of disdain, not realizing that her mother's observation was meant for her benefit.

"Yes, *him!*" her mother emphasized. "He's a nice boy, a good worker. He's like his dad, always busy. That's why they've always got something to eat and good clothes." After a short pause, she added, "You know, he's not coming around here just to see your dad or me."

Up to this time Gawaunduk had not attached any particular significance to South Wind's visits and as far as she was concerned he was just another boy in the village—a good friend and neighbor, kind, considerate, shy, but boring. The notion that he could be a husband who could make some girl happy, even her, set her back up. She could not imagine, as her mother had intimated, being married to a man she didn't love. The idea repelled her.

As she thought about her future—marriage, a husband, and children—for the first time, she understood that all she wanted was to love a husband and be loved by him, to care and be cared for, and to have children with him. It was not unreasonable or vain or anything like that; it was no more than what other young women longed for and anticipated. If she was espoused to a man she loved and who loved her in return and together they provided the wherewithal to fulfill their needs, she would have everything she wanted. Her dreams would be fulfilled, and she would be as happy as any woman who has had all her hopes come true.

It was a modest enough goal, but one that few woman were

lucky enough to attain, since arranged marriages were the rule. To Gawaunduk, such a marriage must be akin to slavery, captivity by an enemy from which there was no escape.

Upset by her mother's insinuation that South Wind would be an ideal husband, Gawaunduk asked her grandmother about arranged marriages, so she could express her opposition to the practice and perhaps win the old woman's support.

But her grandmother was not as much help as Gawaunduk had hoped. Instead of condemning the custom, the old woman seemed to condone it. She suggested that it was a practice that did not always lead to unhappy results, just as love as a prelude to marriage is no guarantee of lasting bliss.

To illustrate her point, the grandmother told Gawaunduk an ancient story about two young women who asked each other as they were fantasizing, "If stars were men and could descend upon a summons, which one would you choose?" The first chose the reddest star in the firmament, and the second chose the whitest. After each had made her choice, the two young women, in turn, described what qualities they expected in their dream men, their star men. Afterward each fell asleep with the image of her dream man firmly implanted in her mind and in her dreams.

Each awakened the next morning with a man lying by her side.

The girl who had picked the brightest red star in the sky found a handsome young man lying next to her, her dream fulfilled. She married the young man, but within a short time regretted that she had ever dreamed or laid eyes on him. Other women longed for him; he was vain beyond belief, thinking only of himself; and his temper made her life a living hell.

The other girl also awakened with a man lying next to her, but he was an old man. She was appalled that she had shared the night, the bed, and her flesh with an old man many times her age and, what was worse, that she was married to him. Afterward she resigned herself to her situation and accepted what the manitous and the fates had bestowed on her. But during her lifetime with the old man, she never had to go without, nor did she ever hear an angry word from him.

At last when her husband was very old and feeble and unable to look after himself, the woman looked after him and would not leave his side. On his deathbed, a miraculous thing happened. The old man was transformed into a youth—bold, strong, kind, and endowed with all the qualities she had admired. Only at the very end did the woman have her wish fulfilled.

A silly story is not what Gawaunduk wanted to hear, especially an improbable story of a young woman being better off with an old man rather than with a younger one. She wanted to dream, and she wanted her dream to come true.

Before her dream was broken, and to forestall her parents from making arrangements without her consent by committing her to South Wind, Gawaunduk took it upon herself to discourage the young man from continuing to court her, telling him that he was wasting his time. She would never care for him. She tried not to hurt his feelings, but she didn't know how to avoid offending him. But she, too, was hurt by telling South Wind to stay away.

Not only was Gawaunduk hurt by the experience, but she was frightened as well, frightened by South Wind's remark, "You'll be sorry." She didn't know if his remark was a threat, but she took it as such.

To her relief, South Wind came less often.

One evening some time later, Gawaunduk and some companions came together to pass the evening in talk and laughter. To liven up their spirits and the gathering, one of the girls proposed playing *waugizih* (an ancient marriage raffle or draw), in pantomime of the real game.

Even if it was just a charade, Gawaunduk didn't want to play; she was afraid that the charade might foreshadow what would actually come to pass. Her companions laughed at her silly, superstitious fears and forced her to take part.

At stake in this game was the oldest, ugliest man that the girls could imagine in the community. According to the rules (improvised because no ears of corn were available, as was customary), the girl drawing the plum stone as the "trump" would win the prize. On the first round Gawaunduk drew the trump, to the squeals and giggles of her companions. She was horrified and oppressed by a foreboding that she tried to laugh off but could not.

Afterward she tried to convince herself that waugizih was only a game, played thousands of times without the events that it depicted ever becoming reality.

She now thought about the old man, the "prize," something that she had never done before. Until now she had regarded him simply as a nice old man, sprier than most old men of comparable age, reported to be around seventy; wrinkled like the bark of ironwood. She knew little about him except what her parents, neighbors, and others said. He had been widowed for some years and had not gotten over the loss of his wife. In his youth and until his wife's death, he had been *ogimauh* of his band for many years. Few men or women had done as much for the people as he had done.

People deferred to him, spoke to him in terms of respect, saying that he was a good, kind man, still able to look after himself, and that he thought of others, making sure that no one went without.

As she thought about the old man and, indirectly, all the elderly, she realized that they belonged to another generation, to another time, not to the world of the young. It was unthinkable that a young girl would be married to such a one.

But this was self-induced anxiety. She put the old man out of her mind with thoughts of a young man of her own generation who had not yet come into her life.

In the autumn during the corn harvest, waugizih was arranged by the village elders for the benefit of young women who were unmarried and not yet promised to young men. At stake was the old man who had been the "prize" in the game that Gawaunduk and her friends had played earlier. Many of her companions who had taken part in the pantomime were participants in this lottery, for that is what it was. It was also undertaken for the benefit of the old man. It was the tribe's way of doing something in return for all the old man had done for the tribe and the people. At the same time, it was the fulfillment of a duty that the community and nation had undertaken on behalf of all its members.

For those who were forced to take part by virtue of their unmarried status, there was no escape. Everyone had to go through with the ordeal or be forever outcast. Gawaunduk could no more obtain exemption than could anyone else.

Except for a few, such as Gawaunduk, many girls did not seem to object to the practice and appeared even to welcome it. And the parents of the girls who were taking part condoned the practice.

For the villagers who were present as spectators, the event was as exciting as gambling, and there was much betting on the outcome of waugizih.

An old woman set a pile of corn in front of each participant. At the word *ahow* (start), the girls who were indifferent to the results wasted no time in peeling off the husks of the corn, while the girls who dreaded the outcome had to be prompted and threatened by the cries of the spectators and the other contestants, some of whom may indeed have been disappointed by the girls' failure to draw the crooked, discolored ear of corn.

Gawaunduk had just removed the last layer of green casing when she gasped and then slumped sideways to the ground. She had drawn the ear with the warped, discolored kernel. She belonged to the old man and he to her.

After all the corn was husked, the villagers returned to their homes and to their lives and routines that had not changed for the Anishinaubaek in generations.

But for Gawaunduk there was no return to anything familiar, certain, or comforting. Her world was in shambles, devastated by a single upheaval. Her dreams, hopes, and visions were shattered, never to be fulfilled.

If Gawaunduk could not return home, she blamed her parents for her fate as much as she blamed the elders and the entire village for allowing such a practice. Once she realized that she, at fifteen, could not run away, for she had nowhere to run, her dreams were ended. She could never again hope to fulfill any dream, ever.

She hated the old man, hated him more than anyone in the world. She wanted to die.

But Gawaunduk was not only a romantic, an idealist, she was also a realistic, proud, and defiant young woman who didn't know this about herself until, after languishing for several days and even thinking about doing away with herself, she ventured outdoors.

At the lake where she had gone to fetch water, Gawaunduk met a girl, the village sharp-tongued wit, who never allowed any situation or event to pass without comment that was meant to give embarrassment and laughter. And she didn't let this occasion slip by her. She said something akin to some people having all the luck in the world, which Gawaunduk caught only a part of because she was trying to ignore the girl. With the village wit was South Wind. He didn't say anything; he didn't have to say anything to remind her that his threat that someday she would be sorry had come true.

Gawaunduk was the object of laughter and pity. She was mortified, but weak and shrinking she was not. Despite her humiliation and the urge to run and hide somewhere, she walked on, her head held high; she would not allow them or anyone else to beat her spirit down.

A year and a half later, Gawaunduk gave birth to a baby girl. With the birth of the baby, Gawaunduk's private "hell" was no longer quite so insufferable. She now at least had someone to love, and she no longer felt the same revulsion for the old man. Yet she still wished that everything had been otherwise. If only she had listened to her mother.

Gawaunduk was not fully resigned to her fate, and though she allowed the old man to touch her body and to father their child, she had no use for him. He would never fulfill her dreams as a younger man might have done. Since their marriage, the old man had not raised his voice or shown any sign of impatience, and he provided for all their needs as well as did any man in the community. Nevertheless, she resented the old man, who was much to blame for having snatched her dreams from her grasp.

By the time Gawaunduk had a third child, she was considered fortunate by her neighbors. The love that she felt for her children and the affection they gave her more than compensated for all the anguish that she had suffered. She felt differently about life and the manitous, looking on all favors and hardships with resignation, rather than with acceptance. Her feelings toward the old man had softened. Instead of seeing him as an abomination, unfit as a consort, Gawaunduk now looked on him as a decent but humdrum sort. But she did not love him, and she did not know or care if he loved her. If something was to happen to him, it would be a pity but she would not cry.

There were women who said they would have exchanged places with her, but Gawaunduk didn't take them seriously, believing them to be patronizing her. Even the sharp-tongued village wit who had married South Wind would have traded places with Gawaunduk to escape his beatings and neglect.

When Gawaunduk heard these stories, she was grateful, but she still believed that she would have been happier and that her life would have been far more fulfilling had she married someone closer to her age.

Gawaunduk and the old man had two more children before she was thirty. He now was eighty-five.

A couple of years later the old man fell ill, not critically, but seriously enough to confine him to bed.

Gawaunduk was frantic, as anxious for his recovery as she was when her children were sick, and she remained by her husband's side, watching over him and tending to his health with medicines prescribed by the medicine people. While he slept, she kept vigil; as he labored for breath and sweated, she prayed to the manitous while imagining the worst.

She was now afraid that at his great age she would lose him. She wanted him to live forever. And she wanted her own life to be one with his.

When the old man recovered, there was no happier woman in the village or one more thankful than was Gawaunduk. She didn't say *K'zaug-in!* (I love you), nor did she think in terms of love, but she wished what lovers wish for their loved ones: life, health and happiness, and the fulfillment of their dreams.

One night, when her husband was in his hundredth year, he told Gawaunduk as they lay next to each other on their pallet, "I am tired; I've never been so tired. . . . If only I were not so old . . . for your sake . . . I would not be so tired." It was the closest that he ever came to saying "I love you." Before morning his soul-spirit left him.

On the final day of the four-day vigil, when the bereaved were free to leave, Gawaunduk's daughters, sons, and grandchildren were ready to go home. They offered their arms to escort their mother home, but she refused, and nothing they said or did could persuade her to accompany them. At last they left their mother by the graveside, where she continued to keep her own vigil, rocking to and fro upon her knees and keening.

At home the family decided that they would take turns watching their mother and keeping her company until she was ready to come home. They brought her food and water, but she refused their pleas to eat, drink, or to come home.

As the days passed and their mother took no nourishment, the family's alarm grew, and not knowing what to do, they asked the elders to intercede on their behalf. But the elders also failed.

On the tenth day of Gawaunduk's fast and mourning, she broke her silence, saying to her eldest daughter who was at her side, "Your father is waiting for me. I want to go to him. I belong there with him." That was all she said. That night Gawaunduk died.

The family buried their mother next to their father.

That spring, a small plant grew out of the burial mound, and in the years that followed, the plant grew into a tall tree.

Years later, when the daughters, sons, and grandchildren gathered at the graveside of their parents on the Feast of the Dead, they felt a light mist fall on them. The eldest daughter was moved to explain, "It is Mother shedding tears of love for Father."

And so it is, still. On certain days, spruce trees, infused with the spirit of Gawaunduk (the Guardianess), shed a light mist of tears of love.

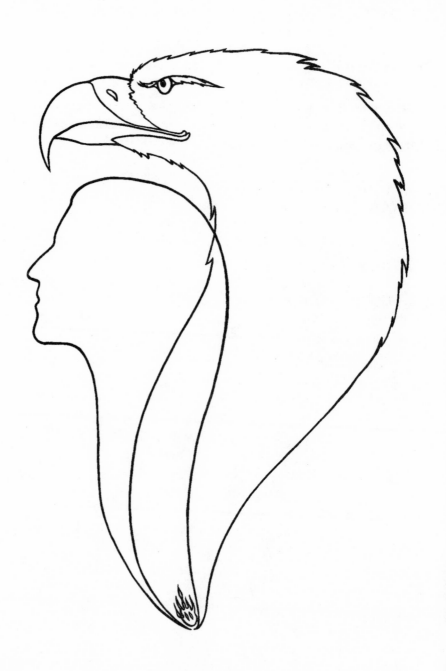

CHAPTER EIGHT

PERSONAL MANITOUS

Right from the beginning, before the Anishinaubaek came into being, animals, birds, fish, and insects were in existence. At the time that our ancestors were conceived by manitous in the sky and the world was covered by flood, humankind's predecessors were struggling to stay afloat to keep from drowning.

Yet, despite their plight, the animals took notice that Sky Woman's time was at hand to give birth to a new being, but she had no place to deliver it. Out of compassion for the manitou and her offspring, the floundering animals persuaded one of their number, the Giant Turtle, to ride on the surface of the flood and to offer his back as a place where the manitou might rest and even give birth.

The Giant Turtle rose to the surface, and the animals invited Sky Woman to come down.

Upon settling on the Giant Turtle's back, Sky Woman asked for and received a moiety of soil retrieved by one of the least of animals, the muskrat, from the bottom of the sea. With this small amount of soil, she created an island that became her world and that of her children and their descendants.

From the beginning, animals, birds, fish, and insects have served not only humankind but the manitous, spirits, and deities that abide in the supernatural, to enable them to fulfill their earthly purposes.

When Nana'b'oozoo, the prototype of all Anishinaubaek and of all human beings, was castaway on the sea in yet another flood, he, too, called for the delivery of a moiety of soil, and it was an animal who delivered the soil that enabled him to re-create and restore the world.

In human experience, as exemplified by Nana'b'oozoo in the flood, it was not this prototype human being with all the advantages and attributes of humanity who retrieved the soil, but a little muskrat without a single outstanding quality to compare with those of his kind and kin.

Nothing is more graphic than the image of Nana'b'oozoo, half manitou, half human who symbolizes all humankind, clinging to a makeshift raft and begging the animals to fetch a pawful of soil as a last, desperate measure to stave off death. Without the animals, he would die; with them, he lived. He ate; survived; created an island, his world; and, in the end, restored the Earth. The story exemplifies humankind's relationship to the animals, a dependence that is absolute.

Although the animals are neighbors and cotenants with men and women on the Earth, they are much more than mere nearby dwellers. They are indispensable to humans, not only as sacrificial victims, whose flesh, blood, bones, fur, and tissue sustain men and women in their struggle for life, but as exemplars whose habits, character, and works provide insights and knowledge that humans would not otherwise have.

Long ago, when our ancestors had only the bow and arrow, club, spear, snare, and deadfall as weapons with which to slay an animal, they had a higher regard for their cotenants and neighbors than many do today. They knew that they owed their lives, much more than they could ever imagine, to the creatures that dwelt in the sky, forest, meadows, seas, and underground.

From infancy, children were taught that the sudden calls or unexpected shadows of animals or birds meant no harm, that these calls were talk in the animals' and birds' own languages, and that all creatures had their own purposes and affairs to conduct. Men and women had less reason to fear bears and such than they did their fellow humans. Children were advised to give animals and birds their distance and not to provoke them.

If children would attend to and understand the languages of humankind's neighbors, they would profit. The chatter of animals and the cries of birds were the key to understanding what was taking place in the woods beyond one's vision, as well as to gaining foreknowledge of the weather in the near future and the climate in the coming seasons. What the animals did and said were nothing less than public proclamations of the presence of enemies, danger, or death. Once children understood the languages and the habits of birds, animals, and small creatures, they would know things that they would not normally get to know as human beings.

How did the eagle, the bear, the wolf, the turtle, and the butterfly know what they know? Did they learn by listening to the words of others, as humans learn? Men and women have other humans, animals, and an inner sense to tell them what they want and need to know, but who tells the loon, the skunk, or the gnat when to take cover and when to emerge; when winter is coming and they must go, and when it is safe for them to return; where to go and what direction to take; what to eat and what not? Instinct? Sense? The manitous?

Only a higher being, a manitou, could tell them what they need to know and give them foreknowledge of events and changes and the wisdom to take measures for their well-being and safety.

Experience and observation lent strength to the conviction that there was something, someone, presiding over the affairs of the animals and safeguarding them. How else could one explain and understand success and failure? Every person has the same skills in marksmanship; similar training; and equal knowledge of the weather, the seasons, and the dwelling places and habits of the quarry, yet some hunters return home from almost every expedition with cargoes of meat, whereas others return home empty-handed, failures more often than not.

In the belief that manitous directed the fate and safeguarded the well-being of birds, animals, small creatures, and fish, men and women began the practice of entreating the manitous, asking for leave to take the lives of animal and soliciting the sanction of the higher, supernatural beings. In their supplications, the hunters adverted to need.

PRAYER TO A DEER SLAIN BY A HUNTER

I had need,
I have dispossessed you of beauty, grace, and life.
I have sundered your spirit from its worldly frame.
No more will you run in freedom
Because of my need.

I had need.
You have in life served your kind in goodness.
By your life, I will serve my brothers.
Without you I hunger and grow weak.
Without you I am helpless, nothing.

I had need.
Give me your flesh for strength.
Give me your casement for protection.
Give me your bones for my labors,
And I shall not want.

Afterward, a hunter offered tobacco in thanksgiving to the manitou of the victim and, more remotely, to Kitchi-Manitou, the Master of Life, for sanctioning the taking of life and for fulfilling the hunter's family's needs. For the victim to come within range of an arrow or to stumble into a deadfall or a trap was seen as nothing less than the tacit approval of the manitou for the hunter to take the life of the quarry. It was only fitting that the hunter express his apologies to his victim and his thanksgiving to the manitou for allowing the killing.

In many respects, the manitous and Kitchi-Manitou were more generous with birds and animals than with men and women, bestowing on them faculties, aptitudes, and qualities that they did not bestow on humans: speed, flight, sight, smell, strength, patience, and length of life.

Men and women coveted these attributes and the advantages they conferred. If they themselves were not meant to be so gifted, then might they not at least hope to derive advantages and benefits from those so endowed with the goodwill of the manitous?

Human beings had special regard for certain qualities and virtues of the animal world. To possess and exercise comparable qualities and virtues would exalt and dignify the human spirit and soul, and men and women aspired to deeds that would make them proud. Few men or women, for example, will dare what every sparrow will do: to stand up to an assailant many times stronger and bigger . . . and drive him off for the sake of her young, exercising two virtues in the one act. Few men or women have the self-control and patience of the heron, the persistence of the wolf, the foresight of the eagle, or the resourcefulness or industry of the beaver.

Men and women especially valued attributes that would enable them to achieve their dreams and visions more readily, to carry out their duties and responsibilities more easily, and to safeguard their lives and health in times of great need. They wished that they had been as endowed and favored by Kitchi-Manitou as were the eagles, sparrows, bears, deer, turtles, butterflies, and sturgeon.

To obtain the benefits of the attributes that they did not possess, the Anishinaubae peoples dedicated their families to birds, animals, small creatures, and fish in the hope that these beings, by the exercise of their attributes and faculties, would obtain for men and women the favors that were needed.

The animals that were chosen as patrons also served as emblems that identified and distinguished families who were dedicated to the same ideals and were entrusted with certain duties. The Anishinaubae peoples called their patrons "totems," a term derived from *dodaem,* meaning action and duty serving as inspiration. Men and women who belonged to the same totem regarded themselves as brothers and sisters of the same family.

But a family's dedication and commitment to a particular totem did not bar the family members from seeking the patronage of the manitous of other creatures of the animal world as their personal manitous. Men and women sought patrons to conduct them through crises, to protect them from sorcery, and to overcome difficulties that they would not be able to surmount alone. The image of the creature, its spirit, became their personal manitou.

Men and women did not always have to dream to conjure a manitou. Sometimes a manitou came unasked, knowing better than men and women what was needed.

Whereas only a limited number of birds, animals, small creatures, and water beings served as totems, any nonhuman being could become a personal patron, manitou, of any man or women.

Thunderbirds

Of all the manitous who presided over the destinies and affairs of humankind, none was more revered for its potency and preeminence than was the thunderbird. Many manitous were once men and women, but the thunderbirds had always been manitous, from the beginning of time, dwelling in the mountains and serving Mother Earth behind clouds that they themselves generated.

The manitous and totems of Mother Earth, the thunderbirds were created by Kitchi-Manitou to tend to Mother Earth's health and well-being, to give her drink when she is thirsty, to cleanse her form and her garments when she needs refreshment, to keep her fertile and fruitful, and to stoke fires to regenerate the forests. From early spring to late fall, the thunderbirds were vigilant in tending to Mother Earth, and in winter, they rested.

The Anishinaubae people believed that the thunderbirds looked like and were kin to eagles, and that eagles might be thunderbirds in disguise, passing from the heights and ascending into the sky until they are seen no more. Thunderbirds were beings of mystery and power and good. Yet they were to be feared.

Days before the thunderbirds began their preparations to cleanse Mother Earth, the owls and other night birds warned one another that the thunderbirds were stirring and that they were about to open the floodgates and let loose fire bolts, and they urged one another to take shelter.

And as the thunderbirds stoked the fires in their forges, great dark clouds billowed, and small birds and animals took shelter just before the floodgates were opened and the flaming arrows were unleashed. The thunderbirds were indifferent to animals or humans.

Most men and women had nothing but the highest respect for thunderbirds, but there were a few who longed to go to the thunderbirds' sanctuaries, to set eyes on these manitous, and trusted that the thunderbirds would not be too offended by their trespassing. Perhaps some believed that they could enter the manitou's domain, as they could infiltrate an enemy's camp, and leave unnoticed.

Those who dared intrude on the sanctuary of the thunderbirds never came back to their families and homes. They were destroyed.

Though men and women could not enter the world of thunderbirds, these manitous occasionally came down from their sanctuary disguised as human beings.

A man once fell in love with a woman, not knowing that she was actually a thunderbird, and asked her to be his wife. Without telling him who she really was, the woman warned him that as much as she loved him, she would have to go back to her people whenever she was summoned. The man readily agreed that she could visit her family any time.

Other men noticed their neighbor's wife and thought the young man was lucky, but there was one young man in particular who lusted for the young woman.

He watched for some weeks, keeping an eye on the husband's habits and routines—when he left in the morning, when he returned in the evening, and in what direction he went.

One morning, he saw the husband board his canoe and paddle across the lake. He waited. As soon as the husband disappeared among some islands, the libertine went to the lodge as a visitor under the pretext of calling on the unsuspecting young woman and her husband.

He tried small and sweet talk at first. When these drew laughter from the young woman, he was encouraged. At last he stated what he had come for. In shock, the young woman reminded the intruder that she was married, but the rake wouldn't accept her excuse. He grabbed her and tried to wrestle her to the ground, but she fought back, raking his arms and face with her nails. She was stronger than he had thought. In desperation he drew his knife and slashed at her. He lashed out again and again, blindly. He forced her back. Before long she gasped and reeled away from the libertine's attack. She slumped to the ground, gashed and bleeding. The assassin drew back and fled.

When the young husband returned home, he found the yard in shambles, some shreds of his wife's garments . . . and the grass stained with blood.

Distraught, he immediately followed the trail of blood, expecting the worst. The next day the young man came to the bottom of a mountain whose crown was reputed to be the dwelling place of thunderbirds. The trail led directly up the mountainside. The young man didn't care what happened as long as he could find his wife.

At the crest, he came upon a flock of enraged thunderbirds. Had it not been for the wounded thunderbird who revealed herself as the woman whom he had married, the thunderbirds might have killed the young man at once. But they still raged at human beings and intended to unleash the hardest winds, the heaviest rains, and the hottest hail of fire and brimstone. The young woman pleaded with her kin to spare her husband and his kindred.

The thunderbirds were at first unwilling, but they soon gave in to their daughter's request. However, they could not allow the man, having set eyes upon thunderbirds and their world, to return to the world of humans. He would have to remain in the realm of thunderbirds. This arrangement could not have pleased the young man more.

But suitable as this arrangement was with his wishes, the young man found his situation a virtual prison, his life a bore, and the outlook bleak. He couldn't go anywhere or do anything, and he was unable to eat what the thunderbirds ate. Unless the thunderbirds brought him fare that he was accustomed to eat, the young man would starve and die there.

For their daughter's sake, the parent thunderbirds took pity on the young man and changed him into a thunderbird.

Eagles

The eagle is a kin of the thunderbird, and the Anishinabaek strongly assumed that the eagle was indeed a thunderbird, from its flight and mysterious presence. Lucky were the men and women who had eagles as personal manitous. One such man was Ozauw-amik (Brown Beaver). In two bounds one afternoon, he landed at his father-in-law's side. He was excited, but before he could tell his father-in-law the good news that he had seen a herd of deer, Old Raven snapped at him to watch what he was doing.

Not knowing what he had done to incite the old man's wrath, Brown Beaver asked what he had done. Old Raven pointed to the ground, and his voice was like ice. Never had Brown Beaver heard Old Raven speak in such a tone or seen such bitterness in his eyes.

When Brown Beaver looked down at the place where his father-in-law pointed, he saw at once what he had done. He had violated a hunter's code and brought bad luck to a fellow hunter by passing over another man's arrows while they were being consecrated.

The young man immediately apologized, asking his father-in-law how he might set things right. But Old Raven would accept none of the apologies; he neither spoke to the young man nor looked at him for the rest of the evening.

When Old Raven, normally a sure hunter, didn't kill anything the next day or in the succeeding weeks, he had no doubt that he had been jinxed, and the more he thought about his change of luck, the more he was convinced that his son-in-law had done it on purpose. But why?

To think that his own son-in-law would invoke the black magic of the Underworld against him chilled the old man.

To protect himself and to regain his touch and the goodwill of the manitous, Old Raven went to a sorcerer to remove the curse and to regain his luck.

After his visit to the sorcerer, Old Raven felt safer and confident that his luck would return. He concealed his feelings toward his son-in-law with his ever-present smile and ready laughter, so Brown Beaver knew nothing of Old Raven's suspicions and distrust.

But Old Raven's luck didn't change and, as his luck remained bad, his resentment turned into bitterness, for his pride as a hunter was wounded. Whereas he was once one of the more successful hunters, Old Raven was now among the more ineffectual. And he blamed Brown Beaver for his failures. Still, he smiled and laughed as readily as ever, so Brown Beaver suspected nothing of the old man's growing animosity.

Brown Beaver would have known nothing of Old Raven's distrust and enmity if his wife had not overheard by chance her father and a sorcerer discuss the best way to get rid of someone so his or her death would appear to be an accident. The young woman knew that her father and the sorcerer were talking about Brown Beaver.

The young woman told her husband what she'd overheard. She was afraid and begged her husband to take her and their children to another place where they would be safe from her father. Brown Beaver would have liked to oblige her, but he explained that there was no escape from black magic. Their only protection was to consult a seer and to obtain an immunizing prescription that would protect them.

Besides giving him a talisman that would neutralize black magic, the seer told Brown Beaver to seek a manitou patron. No less than an eagle appeared to Brown Beaver in dream.

From the time of his wife's warning, Brown Beaver kept a wary eye on his father-in-law. Yet he saw nothing untoward in Old Raven's behavior or demeanor.

In the latter part of spring, Old Raven invited his son-in-law to accompany him to help gather seagull eggs on an island some distance from the mainland. Brown Beaver was only too willing.

On the way over to the island, they arranged that, because of his youth, Brown Beaver would gather the eggs while Old Raven would wait on shore and keep an eye on their canoe. No sooner did Brown Beaver disappear amid the undergrowth than the old man pushed his canoe off shore and called on manitous to command the seagulls to attack and kill his son-in-law. Then Old Raven paddled away.

At that moment, the seagulls, who up to then had done no more than squawk while retreating before Brown Bear, now turned on him, coming at him from every direction. They tore at his flesh as hawks tear at carrion.

Brown Beaver was frantic. He lashed out at the birds. He yelled and bellowed. But within seconds of the attack, before the seagulls could inflict wounds, a mighty crash of thunder shook the island, and blinding flashes of lightning raked the skies. The seagulls retreated. Brown Beaver tried to look about him. It was almost as dark as night. The air was heavy and silent. In the distance came a rumble as of far-off thunder. A few drops of rain fell, thick and heavy, but that was all. Brown Beaver now forgot about the seagulls, for it was the rumble that unsettled him.

The rumble grew louder. As it grew, it no longer resembled distant thunder, but was like a rush of water, a mighty waterfall. No, it was a landslide, with rocks, huge and small, colliding and cracking. Then came a whine, piercing as if thousands of hawks shrilled at once. This storm of storms was bearing down on Brown Beaver.

In the dark, Brown Beaver could barely see. He wanted to crawl under something, but there was no place to hide. There were only a few stunted trees on this desolate little island. He crawled to one of these emaciated cedars.

At the first blast of wind, Brown Beaver flung his arms around this tree and hung on. The next moment he felt the tree tremble and totter, and then both he and it were airborne. His heart pounded. He dared not open his eyes. He dared not let go. Then, when he expected to be pitched and dashed to earth at any moment, he and the tree were in the water.

Brown Beaver opened his eyes. He was not far from shore, which he recognized as his home, and the sky was clearing up. It took a few moments for the young man to guess that a tornado had picked him up, carried him through the air, and set him down in the water without so much as leaving a scratch on him anywhere. To his surprise, his pouch was still at his side, its strap over his shoulder. He felt inside; the seagull eggs were unbroken.

Once on shore he saw the swath of destruction, the broken, uprooted trees that the tornado had unleashed. Behind him was the lake, calm and glistening in the sunlight.

Suddenly Brown Beaver was overcome by a weakness so overpowering that he had to sit down, and he began to tremble as he reflected on how close he had come to being crushed to death. He offered thoughts of thanksgiving and wondered whether his family was alive and well and whether his father-in-law had survived.

When Brown Beaver recovered his strength and composure, he hurried home to his village, not too far from where he had been miraculously set down. To his relief, everyone was safe and well. The twister had bypassed the village.

To most who listened to Brown Beaver's story, it was unbelievable that he should still be alive. To others, it was not so surprising; similar acts had been performed before by manitous. In Brown Beaver's mind, there was no doubt that it was his manitou, the eagle, who had taken him from a place of danger to safety.

His wife and children cried in relief and joy that he was alive, but their gratitude and happiness were short lived and diminished by their anxiety over Old Raven's fate.

The next morning Brown Beaver and his wife went to Seagull Island to look for the old man, more as a matter of form than out of any real conviction that Old Raven or anyone else could have survived the storm. To their amazement, they found the old man alive but thoroughly shaken by the storm and his experience. His canoe was nowhere to be found.

But the old man was frightened, and to win his son-in-law's goodwill, he told Brown Beaver again and again how worried he had been and how glad he was that Brown Beaver had survived. But more than anything else, Old Raven wanted to know how Brown Beaver had managed to survive and return home.

Brown Beaver's account of being picked up by the wind, carried through the air, and then deposited in the water near shore without injury so intimidated and impressed Old Raven that he abandoned the idea of doing away with his son-in-law. When Old Raven's bad luck continued, however, he was humiliated beyond endurance. He compared himself to a mendicant, a helpless one unable to provide for his own needs. Old Raven slowly resurrected the idea of doing away with Brown Beaver.

He waited until fall, when the season would provide him with an excuse. He invited his son-in-law to go spearfishing with him some three to four days' travel from their village.

At the fishing place, Old Raven and Brown Beaver constructed a platform that extended over the churning rapids. But before they started to fish, the old man sent his son-in-law on an errand that required the young man to go out of sight into the woods. While Brown Beaver was gone, Old Raven lubricated the end of the logs with a slippery substance made from elm bark. At the same time he prayed to the Sturgeon of Sturgeons to accept his offering of human flesh.

When Brown Beaver came back from his errand, Old Raven suggested that his son-in-law could start anytime he was ready. He said that he would clean and smoke the fish.

No sooner did Brown Beaver set foot on the slick ends of the logs of the platform then he lost his footing and, with his arms flailing and a wild scream, he pitched into the frothing rapids. Brown Beaver flailed and thrashed his arms to save himself from sinking and then drowning. In so doing he caught a projecting log, pulled himself forward, and clung to it, hanging on desperately as the log was carried forward. He hung on until the log ran aground on a sandbar some distance downstream.

On the riverbank Brown Beaver thanked his lucky stars and the eagle for having saved him from drowning. In going over his close call, he blamed himself for not having taken enough care. He should have known better; he should have known the logs would be slippery from the mist.

Being young, Brown Beaver recovered after a short rest and returned upstream along the riverbank. He thought that the old man must be worried and must be looking for him.

But at the fishing place there was no sign of Old Raven or of their canoe. Brown Beaver didn't know what to make of his father-in-law's disappearance. He didn't know quite what to do except call out and explore both banks of the river for signs of the old man's trail. As he called Old Raven's name, it occurred to Brown Beaver that his father-in-law might have fallen into the river and drowned or might be lying somewhere injured, even on the far side, but without a canoe it would be difficult to investigate.

For two days, Brown Beaver scoured the area without a sign of the old man's presence. Finally he gave up. His family must be worried. But what he must say about his father-in-law's disappearance weighed him down, and he was depressed that some people would surely suspect him of having something to do with Old Raven's disappearance.

When he arrived home, it wasn't as bad as he'd expected. People didn't ask, "What did you do with your father-in-law? Where did you leave him?" They didn't shrink from him. Instead they treated him as if he had come back from the dead. Brown Beaver couldn't figure out what the people were talking about until he learned that Old Raven had reported him dead and that his wife and family were now in mourning. It took a while for Brown Beaver to suspect that something was not right.

But it was Old Raven who now bit the bitter arrow; he had to explain his account of his son-in-law's death and reconcile it with Brown Beaver's survival.

Still the old man wasn't done. He would not accept his son-in-law's inexplicable escapes as signs that a powerful manitou was safeguarding the young man any more than he could accept defeat. He tried a third time.

Because of the scarcity of animals in the vicinity of the village, hunters had to go some distance to procure food in the winter. As partners, Old Raven and Brown Beaver had to leave home to go to distant hunting grounds for animals.

Each time the two men went, Brown Beaver's wife packed an extra pair of moccasins in her husband's travel sack. The young man tried to discourage this practice, but his wife persisted, saying, "You never know." As they were bound for their hunting grounds one morning, Brown Beaver noticed a flicker of a shadow as it crossed his face. He looked up and he saw an eagle. He had never seen one in winter, and its presence both mystified and pleased him. It was a noteworthy thing to see an eagle, but Brown Beaver said nothing.

Sometime during the night, Brown Beaver was startled out of his sleep by a violent shaking and hiss, "Your moccasins! They fell into the fire!"

He sat bolt upright and tried to clear his head while his father-in-law continued to jabber about his carelessness and lack of foresight and the fact that Brown Beaver would now have to stay at the campsite.

Brown Beaver's head cleared slowly, but he didn't offer any

comment or explanation. He was at a loss to understand how only his moccasins, which he had hung beside his father-in-law's, had fallen into the fire and why Old Raven had made no attempt to salvage them. Brown Beaver smelled a rat, so he said nothing.

When Old Raven asked him what he was going to do now without moccasins, Brown Beaver declined to say anything more than "I don't know."

Finally, after some thought, Old Raven told Brown Beaver that the only course they had was for Old Raven to return to the village to fetch a pair of moccasins for him. In the meantime Brown Beaver would remain in the camp and wait for Old Raven to come back.

Old Raven cut enough wood to tide his son-in-law over for two days, or at least until he returned with moccasins for Brown Beaver.

Brown Beaver suspected that Old Raven did not intend to come back. It was a good thing that he had the extra pair of moccasins that his wife had packed in his travel sack. The next day Brown Beaver left for home.

The first to notice Brown Beaver as he neared the village were the dogs. When the dogs barked, everyone who was outside looked to see whether a friend or stranger was coming. When the dogs ran to meet him and run by his side, those who were waiting knew that it was one of their own returning home. Within a few moments everyone knew from his gait that it was Brown Beaver.

The adults who were there sent the youngsters to tell Brown Beaver's wife the good news that her husband was coming.

She had been crying, and the youngsters found it difficult to convince her that it was true. Her own children had already run out. They pulled at their mother's sleeve until they overcame her disbelief and resistance, and she got up and followed them out.

By now Brown Beaver was being followed into the village by a crowd of men, women, and children. His wife ran to meet him.

She flung her arms around his neck, half sobbing, half choking, "Father said that a Weendigo had got you . . . not true . . . you're back . . . ," and her words broke off.

"There was no Weendigo," Brown Beaver explained. "Ask him why he came back alone. Ask him why he made up those stories? Ask him what happened? He knows!" And after a moment's pause he told his wife, "The eagle looked after me . . . and the extra pair of moccasins."

In the excitement caused by Brown Beaver's return, Old Raven slipped away into the woods, into the night, never to be seen again.

Brown Beaver's manitou patron, the eagle, had safeguarded him.

CHAPTER NINE

NEBAUNAUBAEWUK AND NEBAUNAUBAEQUAEWUK

MERMEN AND MERMAIDS

Knock! Knock! Knock!

"Peendigaen!" (Come in!)

Knock! Knock! Knock!

"Peendigaen!" A little louder.

Knock! Knock! Knock!

"I wonder why, whoever it may be, doesn't come in." Zhauwunoo (South) remarked, rising from his place. "It must be a stranger. Everybody else comes in when invited and doesn't wait for a second invitation."

"Could be deaf," someone suggested.

Zhauwunoo pushed back the flap that served as a door and went out.

"Son!" he stammered and staggered backward. "A ghost."

"*Dad!* No, it's me! Don't you know me? I'm alive! I'm real. Don't be afraid. I've come back to visit you and Mother and everybody else. I am not from the Land of Souls, Dad! I've come to visit, and I knocked. I just didn't want to walk in and frighten someone to death, Dad!"

"Son! Where did you go? Why didn't you come home? Don't you know that we thought you were dead? And that Mother and everyone was in mourning?" Zhauwunoo stammered. "Why did you stay away? Why did you choose to visit us on the Feast of the Dead? Come in."

After the family overcame their initial fright, there were tearful "welcome back" greetings. The questions were asked over and over. "Where did you go? We've been so worried. Where did you go? Didn't you think of your friend? People around here have blamed him for your disappearance, and he's borne the accusation hard. He won't look at us or speak to us. What happened? Where did you go? Why didn't you come back with your friend?"

"Let me explain," said the son. "I'll tell you what happened."

"When I left to go fishing, I didn't offer tobacco, as you told me to do, because I didn't believe in those practices and . . . I thought they were just superstitious fairy tales.

"While Waubigun (Clay) and I were waiting out the storm in a shelter, we heard someone crying for help, cries that came from the shore. It was the wail of a woman such as I've never heard, almost like a child screaming from a nightmare or from the sting of a bee, crying out for someone, anyone, to save him from death. And the voice called again and again, 'Help! Help me!'

"I got up, alarmed. And even though my friend attempted to dissuade me with, 'Don't! Leave her! Don't go there! It might not be a woman; it might not be one of us but someone from the Underworld,' I couldn't withhold going to help. I couldn't resist those piteous cries; I couldn't allow that person to continue to suffer or to cry. You see, I thought it might be one of our kin or neighbors. I went down to the shore where the cries came from.

"With the wind driving the rain directly into my face, it was hard to see. Only the voice guided my steps, growing louder the nearer I drew to it. It came from some point just off shore, not too far away. I waded out into the pounding, frothing breakers toward the voice.

"'Here! Over here!' the voice called, thin and pitiful. Hurry! I can't hang on much longer.'

"I tried to hurry, but the thrashing waves and dragging current held me and nearly carried me back. I had to lean and drive forward hard to reach the person before it was too late.

"Then I saw her. She was no more than sixteen, as far as I could tell, her black hair twisted this way and that by the wind and the water. And she was thrashing her arms wildly to keep her head above water.

"'Give me your hand! Your hand!' I yelled into the roar of wind and waves, extending my arm and hand toward her at the same time. She heard me, for she stretched her body and arm as far as she could until she clasped my hand. Her grip was like that of a trap. I drew her toward me, meaning to take her in my arms and carry her ashore. But I couldn't draw her forward, no matter how hard I pulled. Instead, it was she who drew me away from shore and out toward the open sea.

"'No! Don't pull!' I yelled at her. 'Not that way! The other way!'

"But it was useless. She continued to pull me in the opposite direction. Thinking that perhaps she didn't hear me above the roar of the waves, I shouted until I thought my throat would burst. It was as if she didn't hear me.

"As she slowly drew me along, I twisted and jerked my hand, straining to break free of her clasp. But her hand was like iron. My hand was locked in hers. 'Let go! Let go! The other way!' I screamed at her. For all the good my screams did, I may as well have railed at the waves.

"I strained with all my might. I thought that my arm would

be pulled from its socket. I couldn't pull her; she wouldn't listen. She was going to drag me into the deep, to my death. I didn't want to die. I yelled, 'Help! Help! Help!' for my friend, for anyone.

"I thrashed, I twisted—all for nothing. Waves broke over my shoulders and over my head. I held my breath until my lungs burned and could hold out no more. I had to have air. I gasped, gulped, and felt water rush into my nose, and then I lost consciousness.

"How long was I out? I don't know. But when I woke up, I could hear voices and sounds like indistinct hollow echoes that one might hear in a cave or in a canyon bouncing from one wall to another. And I could see, but everything and everyone was enveloped in fog, a sea blue-green fog that felt like water. In this substance, no one, nothing was distinct. All forms were blurred, distorted. The beings near me were talking . . . in our language, though they sounded as if their tongues were tied or their voices were muffled. But I understood.

"'Why did you bring him here? Why didn't you leave him where he belongs? What good is he to you? To us? He's too young. How can he look after you? You'll have to look after him. How are you going to do that?' an older voice, a woman's voice, asked.

"'But I wanted him,' a girl's voice protested. 'He'll get older.'

"I tried to see who was talking, but the light from above was too bright to enable me to see clearly. I had to squint. It was like looking directly into the sun, except that there was no sun. I found that if I turned my head away from the glare and squinted, I could discern shapes and forms. Some I recognized at once as fish, minnows, hundreds of them, which, on seeing me, darted away. The others I had to study more closely to make sure that my eyes were not deceiving me. The dozen or so people who were there looked like men and women, but from the waist down were, in flesh and form, fish: half men, half fish or half women, half fish. I'd heard about such *nebaunaubaewuk* and *nebaunaubaequaewuk,* but I didn't believe in them, thinking that perhaps they were creations of someone's overworked imagination.

"I was in the Underworld. I wasn't dead, otherwise I would be in the passage along the Path of Souls. And this heartened me. But I didn't understand how I could live in an element meant for fish and water beings. I didn't understand how I could sense, see and hear, and be conscious in an element that took these functions from human beings.

"I looked at the Underworld residents, the half human, half fish beings. Their behavior reminded me of my own people in the Upper World when they come to see some spectacle and then go on their way, except that their eyes were round like those of fish and they moved like fish with grace and swiftness. Only five remained constantly nearby, and they seldom took their eyes off me.

"To have them stare at me made me uncomfortable. I thought that maybe I was dreaming. I didn't belong there. But if this was real, how did I get there? How was I to return to my own proper element? I closed my eyes and reconstructed my last movements: my desperate struggle to break free from the young woman, who pulled me down into the water while I held my breath until I thought that my lungs would burst, and then . . . unable to hold out any longer, opening my mouth and nose. Then nothing! I was dead, drowned.

"I should have been somewhere along the Path of Souls, as I had heard that people who die make their way to the Land of Souls along the path, as spirits, shades, and yet there I was, sensible, conscious, mortal. Was this what death was like? Something was wrong. Was I in the wrong world? Was I trespassing. I didn't belong in that world. I must return to my own world, to my own kind—go back to reality.

"I meant to pinch myself for reassurance that this was but a dream. But I couldn't move my arms. I strained, I twisted, I jerked, I arched my back, but I couldn't move. I was bound, as if tied up in a net, every part of me. I got angry. I yelled at the forms nearby, but I only sputtered. I threatened to call upon sorcerers to poison them or to enter their dreams, nay their very beings, and bring about their destruction. I struggled again until I exhausted my strength.

"'Leave me! Let me go!' I shouted. 'Let me go back home! I don't belong here!'

"One of the half women, half fish spoke to me, saying it was useless for me to struggle against the unbreakable bonds. She urged me not to waste my time or strength, but to accept my imprisonment and life in a new and different element and to be patient. I was, as she put it, dead, not in the ordinary sense, but in a condition more akin to sleep, and I would live on in a physical form in the Underworld, seeing, hearing, touching, and tasting as I had when I lived on land. For my own safety, the old woman went on to explain, I would remain bound until I resigned myself to my new life and became like them, changed in form to adapt to my new world. When the transformation was complete, I would be released, free to roam the Underworld and to visit the Upper World. I would become Nebaunaubae, a being of sleep, who dwelt in the water like a merman.

"A dread, a sorrow, suddenly descended on me, threatening to crush my spirit and soul.

"The old woman must have seen my expression of shock, for she continued her explanation in an attempt to console me, but I was too distraught to pay attention or to understand what she meant by the duration of my bondage would be commensurate with the period of mourning observed by my survivors. Nor did I understand or care about her explanation that the grief expressed by the survivors was known to recall people back to life on occasion. They didn't want that to happen, for it would crush their daughter who had kidnapped me from the land of the living flesh, to be her companion and love. I now belonged to her.

"Never would I go back! NEVER! It wasn't a dream! It was true.

"I struggled to break free of my bonds as I had done before. Why I did I know not, for the old mermaid had already told me that the bonds were unbreakable. Perhaps it was because I didn't believe her or did not credit my previous futile attempt, but struggle I did.

"At that moment, I sensed my mother's spirit calling me to return from wherever I happened to be. Joining her calls and adding to the lure of her summons were those of my father, grandparents, brothers and sisters, everyone. Had I been able, I would have returned at once to their side where I belonged. But I knew that I would not ever see them again.

"Memories flooded me, inundating my soul-spirit. Visions came, lingered, and passed on. First and foremost were those of my mother, a vision of her standing or kneeling by my pallet when I was once sick and the recollection of a shadow crossing her brow when I had refused to carry a large bundle of wood for my sister. And I had done nothing to comfort her, no caress, no touch, no word to show that I cared, not since I was a child. Now it was too late. I could never show my family that they meant much more than I could ever say. If only . . .

"If I couldn't fulfill the things that I ought to have done and had wanted to do, I might as well have been in the Land of Souls.

"There had been this young woman. I didn't know if I loved her or not, but I wanted to be near her, to hold her by her waist, to tell her or to show her that I liked her, but I always lost my nerve at the last moment and became tongue-tied. I was too bashful to imitate other young men my age who tossed acorns at a girl or took some article belonging to a young woman to force her to give chase and to wrestle him to recover it. And I wanted to do what other young men had boasted of doing to young women. But I was afraid, afraid that she would laugh at me.

"I don't know if I would have been bolder had I had some badge, but young women preferred young men who had already earned an eagle feather. I did not yet have one.

"To be a leading hunter, fisherman, father, medicine man, chanter, and drummer were all beyond my dreams, beyond fulfillment. I had been only a person with promise, with nothing accomplished. It was as if I had lived for nothing, others having contributed toward my upkeep and well-being. Up to this time, I had not put back into the community as much as I ought to have. I was still the recipient of the community's goodwill.

"I was expected, as was every person, to do something for the people in return for what they had done for me. Whatever I knew, whatever my skills, whatever my beliefs, everything, I owed to my kin, my neighbors, and my Anishinaubae origins. What I was expected to do was not specified. Now I could never do anything in return for the many favors that I'd received. I could never show that my kin and neighbors had not expended their time and energy in vain.

"Other memories came crowding into my mind, demanding attention: memories of my most cherished moments sitting in front of one of the old people listening to stories and accounts that uplifted my spirit and enriched my mind. There was so much to learn, and I had scarcely started. Too often I didn't pay attention, thinking that the old man or the old woman was talking nonsense. I had but a vague notion and an incomplete idea of the accounts of these old people, and incomplete my knowledge would remain. I had always taken the attitude that there was ample time to ask questions and to learn more.

"I became overwhelmed by helplessness and hopelessness, and I gave in to tears.

"'Don't cry!' a female voice bade me, and someone stroked my cheek and temples. 'I will make you happy. I'll make you forget. It was I who brought you here.

"'When I saw you, I wanted you for myself. I could not wait until I was older, as my parents suggested. I thought that by then, someone else might have claimed you, stolen you from me. Rather than lose you, I disobeyed my parents and my kin. I'm sorry that I had to take you in the manner in which I did, but it was the only way I knew how to make you mine.' She went on to apologize for having taken me from my life and youth and freedom and avocation before I had attained full manhood.

"Had I been able, I think I should have done her in or beaten her so badly that she would never walk or see or hear or do anything for herself again. As it was, the only thing I could do was turn my face from her as the only means that I had of expressing my animosity for her and my rejection of her apologies.

"Again I heard my mother's cry; at least I thought I heard her cry. There were no words, but the meaning was in the tone and pitch of her cry. No words were needed to express the keenness of her loss because no words could ever fully express her feelings. It was enough nearly to wrench my spirit from its abode, my body. My spirit struggled to break free of the bonds that held me like tentacles to its physical prison; I fought, groaned, hefted, and did everything else that could be done to snap or loosen the shackles that held me riveted to the ground, until I thought I'd tear my muscles or my bones from their sockets and I had not a single ounce of strength left with which to raise my head. I could not answer or obey my mother's summons.

"I was near to crying in helplessness and rage.

"'Let me go!' I shouted, as if shouting would be more than argument, reason. I shouted that my mother needed and wanted me and that by holding me captive, she was making my mother, as well as my whole family, unhappy. 'Let me go!'

"'I can't,' she said, and nodded at the same time for emphasis.

"'Don't you care? I belong to them, to the Upper World, not to you. I don't belong to you, down here. I shall never belong to you.'

"'I can't let you go! You belong to me!' she responded.

"'Then, if I were to promise you that I will come back to you, if only you allow me to go back for a little while, will you let me go? I must go back and tell my people, my father and mother and my kin that I love them and that I will never cease loving them. I want to do what I should have done. I'll come back. I promise,' I said.

"'I'm sorry, but it can't be done. You are not ready for such a trip. Not just yet. . . . Later . . . when you're remade, recomposed, you may go. . . . I'll let you visit.'

"'But I want to go now! She's calling for me. They all want me back!'

"'Have patience my impetuous man. There are certain things that cannot be done at once. You will go by and by—not till then.'

"For all the good that my solicitations had done, I might as well have tried to persuade the wind to change its course or the waves to be still.

"Over the next four days, which I was able to calculate by periods of darkness and lightness, I suffered torment of the worst kind. I heard my mother cry and her soul-spirit call for my return. It was a call of such intensity that it went beyond the mortal, physical world, entering even into the realm of the dream world and the Underworld and echoing along the Path of Souls. From her cries, I deduced that she believed me to be bound for the Land of Souls, and I longed to assure her of my well-being and of my eventual return. During those four awful agonizing days, I could not, did not, sleep; my mother, father, and kin would not let me sleep or rest. Nor would my own distress let me sleep. I also cried in answer to them all.

"At the end of four days their calls all but came to an end, releasing my soul-spirit from the almost overpowering urge to leave my body in obedience to their summons. The last I remember before I subsided into a deep and heavy slumber was that the girl who had stolen me was still there, near my side. I was now indifferent to her.

"When I awoke, not knowing how long I had slept, I was refreshed but still depressed. I tried the bonds without knowing why, except that I may have unconsciously hoped for some miracle that would have loosened or broken the bonds. She was still there.

"Ignoring her, I looked around. Things had not changed. It had not been a bad dream but reality. It was a blue-green world

illuminated by a blue-green light that had somehow been fil-
tered from its source above, bright, dazzling, almost too dazzling
for sight. Not only was it different in hue from the light that I
had been accustomed to, but it seemed to be in constant
motion, a fluid, watery light. I thought I saw motion as it is
sculpted by the wind on sand, in little ridges, waves, ripples, and
whorls. But I could feel it as well, not as forceful as the wind
that sometimes drives living things to cover and shelter, not like
that at all, but more like a breath, a caress that touched my
entire body, even my heart and my soul, as it swirled and flowed,
ebbed and waned, inviting me to go wherever it carried and to
do its every bidding.

"Nearby, the girl kept watch over me. While, at first, I found
it difficult even to bring myself to look at her for having taken
me from where I belonged, I could now look on this young
woman who was still on the edge of girlhood, but my rancor was
no less than before.

"I wondered how such a young person of no more than
eighteen, about my own age, could do to another what she had
done to me: to take me from what I had loved and from where
I belonged. She must have had nothing but her own needs in
mind, thinking only of herself with no regard for the feelings of
others. People like that are hard and cold; as long as their needs
are fulfilled, it doesn't matter if others are hurt. But one
wouldn't know it to look at her smile or to see how well she
cared for her long black hair; one could easily be fooled by her
attentiveness into believing that she cared more for others than
she did for herself.

"Why did she bring me here? Did she expect me to forgive
her and regard her as a friend or as one who deserved trust?

"As long as I was not in the Land of the Souls or, at the
moment, bound for it, I had hope. When the earthly visits she
had referred to had come to pass, I would escape and return to
the land of my kin. But before stealing away, I would have my
revenge, I would make her suffer no less than what she had put
me through. Between the present and the future time, when I

would be deemed 'ready' for such a visit, I would settle on some plan of revenge that would be just.

"While I was preoccupied with thoughts of revenge, I was suddenly smitten by a powerful hunger that made me forget for the moment my resolve to get even. It was only then that I recalled that I had not eaten for some time. But how and what was I going to eat?

"As if sensing my needs and my thoughts, the young mermaid observed, 'You must be hungry; you haven't eaten for over four days.' That she should know my needs as by a premonition annoyed me. I did not want her to know my wants or to try to fulfill them. 'What is that to you?' I snarled at her.

"I derived considerable satisfaction from seeing the hurt in her features that my sharp rebuke had drawn. I knew how to hurt her, and I resolved that I would hurt her often.

"An older woman, who I assumed to be my captor's mother and who had been ever present in the background, chided me for my sharpness and suggested that I had better make peace with my situation by accepting the fact that I now belonged to the young mermaid and that she would decide when I was to be unbound.

"'No! I want nothing from her or from anyone here!' I cried.

"'Then,' she hinted ruefully, 'you'll starve and waste away in our home. . . . You'll never see your parents again.'

"'I don't care,' I responded.

"Even after this exchange, neither woman went away. Both of them remained nearby, whispering, the older woman doing most of the talking as if advising or consoling the younger. While I watched them and their kin and visitors come and go, I had time to reconsider my decision to accept nothing from any of them, but I was too proud to ask, even though hunger was tearing at my stomach, as if someone within me were clawing to dig his way forth. I would wait. I would swallow my pride.

"My hunger came and went, returning with greater intensity each time it renewed itself. I wished that someone would ask if I wanted something to eat. I would even answer . . . the girl.

"'Do you want something now?' the girl asked as if she could read my mind.

"I nodded. They knew my thoughts, my needs. And their presence disturbed and angered me. I nodded anyway. Maybe if I cooperated, I could be restored to my proper element. It was the only thing that mattered.

"Almost at once the young mermaid brought what appeared to be some kind of tray that she set near me. Sitting beside me, she introduced herself as Mino-idjiwun (Fair Current). She said she had brought some small fish for my meal and that, since I was fettered, she would feed me.

"I almost refused to be fed like a helpless infant, asking why I couldn't feed myself. The young girl explained that she would have to feed me until my arms were set free. She held something near my mouth. It was as she had said, fish, uncooked, dead. I had never liked fish, even cooked, smoked, or dried. I was not only humiliated; I was also insulted.

"I cast my head away, screwing up my face to show my distaste as a means of getting her to understand that I did not like fish, no matter how hungry I was.

"Even though I said nothing, the girl understood, for she withdrew, taking away the tray and the putrid fish. She returned a little while later with a tray of water buttercups and plantain.

"I had eaten all kinds of plants, leaves, stems, roots, their fruits, and even bark, but I had never tasted what was now been set before me. Only because I was at the point of collapse, I ate the plants. Bland as they were, they were vastly better than was the rank fish.

"Over the next few days I ate nothing but water lilies, cattails, arrowheads, pickerelweeds, reeds, sweet flag, and other greens that Mino-idjiwun brought, until I grew weary of the unappetizing flavor of this unchanging menu. When I asked if there was anything else to eat, Mino-idjiwun shook her head. As a consequence of her answer, I held out another month against eating anything else except what greens were set before me but finally agreed to try some fish, only because I needed something more substantial than what was akin to wood.

"For my meal Mino-idjiwun brought me what looked like rolled plantain leaves about the size and shape of spruce or pine cones. Each one contained a small fish . . . uncooked. Even though the leaves neutralized the oily, rancid, slippery, slimy taste that I'd always associated with fish, I nearly gagged. Eventually my stomach gave in and kept the offerings for its own good and mine.

"After that meal, I slowly overcame my distaste for fish, until I acquired a taste for trout, whitefish, and their kind; on the other hand, it may have been more a developed tolerance.

"I didn't know it then, but accepting the food of the Beings of Sleep and the yield of the World of Sleep was the first stage in my adaptation to the new sphere in my own physical form.

"The second stage began almost simultaneously when I accepted my dependence on Mino-idjiwun. As she brought and prepared my food and kept watch over me without complaint, my attitude toward her changed and, instead of believing the worst of her, I now saw her as kind, patient, and good natured.

"All of me changed, not at once or in a short time but over some time. The bonds that held my hands, arms, and head were loosened, enabling me to sit up and feed myself. I accepted the idea that I would never return to my family and my former home, and I began to care less and less about not returning as I reconciled myself to the notion that this was my new home and that these were now my kin.

"If I were changed into a half man, half fish, I could no longer go back to my previous form or to my prior existence. I thought of my family and former home less, and when I did think of them, it was not with the same urgency. Now my desire was rather faint, about as sincere and full of feeling as the wish to see an old acquaintance.

"What I found most difficult to accept was the change in my physical being. When I was able to sit up, I saw that the lower part of my body, from the waist down, was at the final stages of transformation from human to fish; the skin was scaly and smooth as that of fish, and my legs were no longer in existence, having been fused into one organ, the tail of a fish. Without legs, how was I to make my way about on land when the time came? I was becoming like my captors in nature and in form, half man, half fish, a merman, a being of sleep.

"I was also growing impatient to leave my place of confinement, as a sick person is anxious to leave his pallet when his health improves. I wanted to move about and was tired of being kept in one place for so long.

"When I asked if I could be set free, promising that I would not try to escape, Mino-idjiwun readily agreed, as if she had anticipated my request. With her 'yes' she added that she would accompany me, if I wished, to show me how to navigate with my new limb and how to read and ride the current.

"I told her that I would try my maiden voyage on my own. 'Yes,' she said, 'you may now come and go.' But after I floundered, turned upside down, nearly broke my back, and nose-dived into seaweed, I accepted Mino-idjiwun's offer and took her proffered hand. With her guidance and support, as a parent walks beside a child taking his or her first steps and extends a hand to the child for support, so did Mino-idjiwun swim beside me in my voyages, setting me upright when I capsized and swam belly-up or steering me away from entanglements and teaching me the fine art of balance and sense of distance to avoid collisions with other travelers.

"When I could manage to stay upright and navigate passably well, Mino-idjiwun took me on a trip. One aim of the trip was to show me what I had not yet seen: the Underworld, my home. She also had another reason for taking me there.

"To one used to forests and meadows, hills and valleys, rivers and lakes, bright day and black night, it was hard to imagine a world without many of these forms and whose color was a uniform blue-green, never too hot or too cold. There were canyons rather than valleys, scarps rather than hills, some gravel and sand, but mostly the Underworld was made up of rock and boulders and some refuse from the Upper World—stumps, logs, and trees. There were some plants, such as water lilies, which grew near shores and were more like swamps, as well as underwater grasses and mosses. The largest plant I found in the main part of the Underworld was the underweed, which was knee high. Such was the seascape between the point where we started and a secluded spot that was our destination, the mating place of the Merman Beings, where she led me.

"There we mated.

"On the return trip Mino-idjiwun led me back by another way. About half way back she stopped and pointed out a graveled slope that ascended into the Upper World. 'This is where I lured you into my life and my world by pretending that I was in distress. If you had not come, I would not have persisted. But when you came down into the water to give help, I knew that you were a kind man worth having, that you would risk your life for a fellow human being. I'm glad I did. I don't feel sorry for having taken you from your family and village.'

"'I wonder how they are,' I mused matter-of-factly. 'I should like to see them,' I said, as the nearness of home evoked memories of my parents, family, and kin.

"'You can if you want,' Mino-idjiwun volunteered.

"I looked at her, wondering what she meant.

"'I guess it's safe enough to tell you now. Like all mermen and mermaids, you can transform yourself into a full human being with the consent of the elders and mine and your will, to make periodic visits to the Upperworld to visit your family. But you cannot stay too long, otherwise you'll die. As half human, half fish, dwelling at the margin of the Upper and Lower worlds, you may pass some time on the banks and beaches and remote points of land at night and on dark stormy days. Because of your eyesight, don't go to the surface on sunlit days. You won't be able to see and, not being able to see, you'll lose your way and your life, as some of our kin have lost their lives. Take care.'

"'One other thing. When you do choose to make a visit to your parents, you must go alone the first time. I cannot go with you because it is not certain that they'll accept me. You must tell them about me. When they say that I will be welcome, I will accompany you. And tell them that soon they will be grandparents.'"

Mermen and mermaids were set in the waters during creation and will be there as long as they and human beings long for illicit ends. As manitous, they can propagate their own kind, but as half human in nature and form, they are themselves susceptible to concupiscences by luring, abducting, and mating with human beings. This is but one way of reproducing their kind.

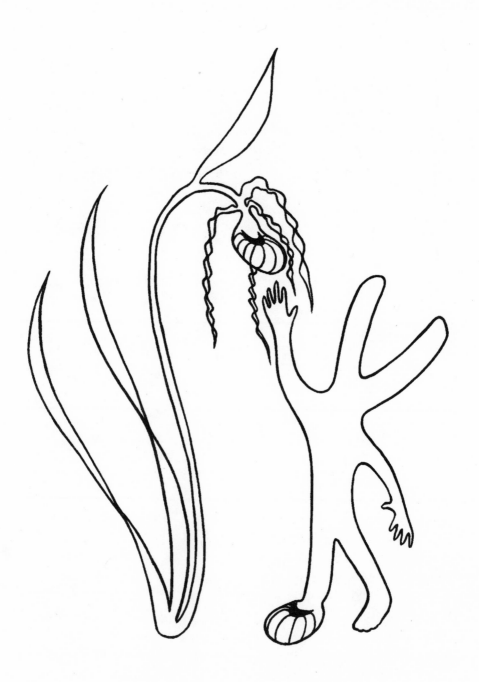

CHAPTER TEN

MANITOUSSIWUK

LITTLE MANITOUS AND SPRITES

As well as giants, or evil manitous, there were several different kinds of little manitous who dwelt in hidden recesses in the forests and meadows, on banks of rivers, and on the shores of lakes. There were the pau-eehnssiwuk, who make their homes near the water's edge to warn and safeguard human beings from the wiles of the nebaunaubae beings (sirens). Then there were the mizauwabeekummoowuk, the copper manitous, who kept to themselves on the mountainsides and descended from time to time to cut some overbearing human or supernatural being down to size. It was unknown whether the little manitous resembled human beings, as did the maemaegawaehnssiwuk and Chekaubaewiss, for no one had seen them. But people knew that these little beings existed, for men and women sensed their presence and could swear that they had been safe-guarded by them from the sirens.

Best known and best loved of the little manitous were the maemaegawaehnssiwuk, little people, beloved for their special care and regard for children. Adults who claim to have seen them described the little people as shaggy, hairy, unkempt miniature grown-ups, but these adults may have mistaken them for the mizauwabeekummoowuk, who live in mountainous regions and escarpments, deriving their name and appearance from the gold, copper, and pyrite embedded in the rock. It may well be that these were maemaegawaehnssiwuk that had disguised themselves to keep their identity secret. This description conflicts with the report of children and grown-ups who had the company and protection of these little manitous, who say that they appeared to them as children, full of play, laughter, and mischief. The maemaegawaehnssiwuk did not appear to all children, only to those who lost their way and needed to be brought home and restored to their families.

Some years ago, in the early 1980s, a four-year-old child disappeared from her yard one afternoon in Whitefish Falls, Ontario. When the mother could not find her child where she had been a few moments before, she was frantic. Her neighbors, hearing her cries, helped her search the yard, the house, the neighborhood, and the nearby woods. They searched all afternoon and well into the evening. Some neighbors who were still looking saw the child emerge from the woods. The distraught but grateful mother asked her little daughter over and over where she had gone but could get no satisfactory explanation except this one: "A little girl came into the yard and asked me to go to the woods with her to play. I went with her, and we played in the woods until she told me that it was time to go home; she brought me to the edge of the woods. When my friend saw some men and women near the woods, she ran away." Nothing the mother said could shake her daughter's story or make her alter it. Every afternoon for some time after the incident, the little girl wanted to go into the woods to play with her little friend. The mother had to keep special watch and restrain her daughter from slipping away.

Again in the early 1980s, a child went missing from his home in Cape Croker in November. After several days of futile search, the men and women gave up hope of ever finding the child alive. They could not see how a child could survive the subzero nights. Yet, despite their misgivings, the searchers found the child covered from neck to foot by a blanket of leaves. The only explanation was that the maemaegawaehnssiwuk looked after the lost child and kept him safe until help came.

The maemaegawaehnssiwuk also look after grieving, despondent children, as exemplified by the story of the Little Boy in the Tree.

Maemaegawaehnse

All at once the waters tumbled, tossed, and rumbled as if huge rocks were cast upon them. Waubizee-quae (Swan Woman) looked up from her work. Her heart nearly stopped. She gasped. She began to shake.

Although terrified and weak, she sprang to her feet, seized her son's hand, and fled, dragging him into the lodge.

"Eeeeeyooooh! You're hurting my hand," Nawautin (Unruffled), a little boy of six, cried out. "What's wrong, mother? Who's that coming across the lake?" the little boy asked, for he, too, had seen the giant. "Why did we run inside?"

Waubizee-quae didn't have time to explain and didn't want to frighten her little son, so she blurted out, "It's grand father!" She didn't want to tell Nawautin that the giant was a Weendigo surging through the shallow lake and roaring, "I know where you are! You can't hide from me!" It was too late to tell her son that Weendigo was a giant cannibal who fed upon human flesh, blood, and bones. She didn't want to frighten her son by telling him that this monster, Weendigo, taller than the height of seven tall men, would eat them alive in the next few moments.

"Come out!" Weendigo roared.

Even though Waubizee-quae was pressing her son to her bosom, he still managed to break free from her arms with a sudden twist that she did not expect and was too weak to prevent. Nawautin bolted outside.

"Come back! Come back!" Waubizee-quae cried out.

But Nawautin was already outside greeting the giant, "Grandfather! Grandfather!"

Weendigo, the giant, stepped ashore, water dripping from his sides. He stopped and looked down at Nawautin. Never had anyone addressed him as "grandfather."

"Where's your mother?" Weendigo demanded in a thunderous voice.

Nawautin pointed to the lodge.

"Where's your father?" Weendigo roared.

"He's away hunting," Nawautin replied without fear.

"Do you have anything to eat?" the giant blared.

Nawautin ran into the lodge to inform his mother that "Grandfather is hungry."

But all Waubizee-quae could offer Weendigo was a hindquarter of a deer, which the monster devoured in an instant. Then he lay down to sleep, snoring loudly. The mother and son went about their work quietly, lest they disturb the giant.

It was already late evening when Pawaugun, Waubizee-quae's husband, returned home. As Pawaugun stepped from his canoe, he threw a deer on shore. At that moment Weendigo awoke. Seeing the deer, he took hold of it, ripped the flesh apart with his hands and jaws, and wolfed it down, while bones crackled and blood dripped down the sides of his mouth. Then he lay down to sleep again.

Later that night Waubizee-quae urged her husband to kill the giant. But Pawaugun said that it would be as useless to try to murder the monster as to run away. The best they could hope was for the monster to go away in his own good time.

But the monster remained there for some time, seizing for himself whatever game Pawaugun brought home from his hunting expeditions. At times, when he was displeased with the quantity of meat that the hunter brought home, Weendigo would roar and threaten to kill him. Only Nawautin, on these occasions, could soothe the monster by saying, "Grandfather, don't be angry."

At last, after what seemed like months, the monster told

Nawautin, "I'm leaving. If it wasn't for you, I would have killed all of you by now. If I stay any longer, I will indeed kill you. I need to eat more than what your father has been bringing me. I must go." And the monster bellowed as he brought his huge club down upon a rock. Fragments flew in all directions, one of which struck Waubizee-quae in the temple, killing her instantly. When Pawaugun got home, he found his son crying at his mother's side. "Mother, wake up! Mother won't wake up!" Pawaugun guessed at once that Weendigo had killed Waubizee-quae.

After preparing his wife's body, Pawaugun buried her next to the great oak that had been her favorite tree. Then he held vigil for four days by the graveside.

Within a few days Pawaugun had to resume hunting to provide for his son and for himself. But because Nawautin was too young and small, the hunter had to leave him at home in the care of an old woman from the village.

When Pawaugun returned from his hunting trip late in the afternoon, his son cried as he gathered him in his arms. "Dad? Can't I go with you? I don't like that woman. I'm lonesome and I have nothing to do. Will you take me with you tomorrow?"

Pawaugun felt sorry for his son, and he explained that he had often to walk miles in the forest before he came upon game; Nawautin would never be able to keep up. It was time, however, for Nawautin to begin practicing his marksmanship with a bow and arrow, and it would give him something to do.

With the bow and arrow that his father had made for him, Nawautin shot at squirrels and chipmunks and sparrows for most of the next morning. For a while it was fun and even exciting for him to stalk the little birds and animals and to aim and fire at them, but after a while, he grew discouraged from missing the little targets that always sprang out of the way at the last moment.

From time to time, too frequently as Nawautin saw it, his guardian, called, "Nawautin! Where are you?"

"Over here!"

"Don't go any farther now, do you hear?"

"No! I won't!"

Nawautin resumed playing, but by now he had grown tired of shooting at targets he could not hit; he found a new sport in firing his arrow into the sky to see how high he could send the arrow and then watch it fall back to earth. The last time that he drew the arrow back to his ear and let fly, he then watched it fall into a clump of bushes near the oak tree. Nawautin unstrung his bow and hung it by the entrance to the lodge, just as his father had told him to do. Then he went in search of his arrow.

It was strange; Nawautin could not find his arrow in the clump of bushes where he had seen it fall.

It was not until his father asked him how his marksmanship had gone that day that Nawautin made mention of his futile attempts and the loss of his arrow. Pawaugun consoled his son by telling him that marksmanship did not come in a day or several days. As for the loss of the arrow, Pawaugun was stern. "Hunters do not lose their equipment; they look after their bows and arrows," he told his son.

Even though Nawautin eventually shot a squirrel the following day and was filled with a momentary sense of triumph, he soon grew tired of the sport. Before he put away his bow and arrow, he fired one last time; he watched his new arrow come down, into the same clump of bushes where his other arrow had fallen the previous day.

To his astonishment, Nawautin saw a little boy standing by the bushes; this little boy caught the arrow just as it fell to the ground and made off with it. This strange little boy ran directly toward the great oak, into which he vanished.

The instant the little boy disappeared into the tree, Nawautin ran, shouting "My arrow! My arrow! Give me back my arrow! Give me back my arrow!" and moments later he was standing next to the oak. Nawautin walked around it deliberately, looking at it from every angle, and sounding it with his knuckle. The tree was solid, yet Nawautin had seen the strange little boy enter it.

As far as Nawautin knew, the little boy was still somewhere in the tree and would answer if Nawautin, with the faith of a six year old, would only speak to him. "Give me back my arrow! Father will be angry with me for losing my arrow. I have nothing else to play with. I need it so I can practice to be a hunter. Why have you taken my arrow?" As Nawautin talked, the image of a boy's face appeared on the trunk of the oak like a reflection in a pool of water. Nawautin continued, but he changed his plea, "Come out. Come out and play. I have no friend, no one to play with. I'm all alone. Won't you come out and play?"

The little boy in the tree replied, "I'll come out if you promise not to tell your father or your guardian. And I'll have to leave as soon as somebody comes. Do you understand?"

Nawautin promised, and the little boy was transformed from an image to reality as he stepped out of the oak. The two boys began to play at once and continued throughout the afternoon until the little boy, whose name was Waemetik (Heart of an Oak), drew up short during their race. He trembled, and his voice was harsh, "Someone's coming. Your father. Don't say anything, and I'll come back tomorrow." Then Waemetik ran to the oak, into which he faded.

Nawautin ran down to the shore to meet his father and to tell him the good news that he had found the arrow he had lost and that he had shot a squirrel, but it had ran away. Pawaugun was pleased; he wiped perspiration and dirt from his son's brow. "What were you doing?" he inquired.

"Nothing. Just playing . . . running," Nawautin panted, still trying to catch his breath.

"It's good to play, son, but you must not play too hard. You must rest from time to time," Pawaugun said.

As soon as his father rounded the point next morning, Nawautin ran to the oak. "He's gone. You can come out now," he called. Waemetik emerged.

All morning the two boys ran races and wrestled, until both were exhausted.

But every now and then Nawautin had to return his guardian's call, "Nawautin! Where are you? Are you all right?"

"Yes! I'm alright."

"Don't go too far away."

These calls from Nawautin's guardian frightened Waemetik. Each time the guardian called, he wanted to leave at once. And Nawautin had to beg his friend to stay and to assure him not to worry about the guardian; she was old and feeble and short of sight.

After a rest or an interruption from the guardian, the two boys returned to play. They went into the forest, where Waemetik taught Nawautin how to stalk and shoot rabbits and partridges. By following his friend's directions, Nawautin killed a rabbit. Waemetik even knew how to strike a fire and prepare and cook rabbit, but he would not eat.

The moment that Nawautin had finished his meat, he pulled his friend to his feet to resume playing. Beside playing hide-and-seek or wrestling, there were many other things to do, such as guessing the names of birds who called and whistled in the forest, gathering plants, climbing trees, and imitating raccoons, all new games that Waemetik invented as soon as Nawautin tired of one. That his friend knew so much more than he and was stronger and quicker did not bother Nawautin at all. He was too young and too happy to take notice of these matters.

But for all the delight that Nawautin derived from the many different games, he liked best to pit his strength against that of Waemetik in wrestling, when they both groaned in effort and triumph as they fell to the ground.

Nawautin had just thrown Waemetik to the ground, when his friend stiffened and his eyes blazed in fright. Waemetik stammered, "Someone's coming! Your father! Don't say anything, do you understand?"

As soon as he got to his feet, Waemetik fled, disappearing into the oak. Nawautin stood there transfixed, wishing that he, too, could enter a tree; then he ran to the shore to await his father.

"Who was here?" Pawaugun asked, even before he stepped from his canoe.

"No one! Why?" Nawautin asked in feigned surprise.

"Because I heard voices long before I came around the point," Pawaugun explained.

"It was me you must have heard. I was shouting and yelling at some crows and ravens who were at the food rack," Nawautin replied, and he wiped his face.

"I'm almost sure that I heard another voice besides yours," Pawaugun insisted. He set about unloading his canoe.

"Father! I killed a rabbit," Nawautin suddenly exclaimed, his voice strong with pride,". . . cleaned it and cooked it, too," he added.

Pawaugun placed his hand on his son's shoulder. He was proud. "I'm glad. You're going to be a good hunter. Before you know it, you'll be going with me. And you made a fire . . . and cooked it, too?" he asked, scarcely believing what he heard.

Nawautin said nothing.

As he was leaving the next morning, Pawaugun told his son that instead of taking the canoe, he was going to walk straight back into the forest behind their lodge.

Anxious for his father to leave, Nawautin watched him disappear beyond the knoll. As quickly as his legs could carry him, Nawautin ran to the oak. "He's gone. You can come out now," he said.

Waemetik's face appeared on the surface of the tree; he seemed reluctant to come out. "Are you sure?" he asked.

"Yes! He's gone. He won't be back for a while. Anyway, you'll know when he is coming."

Slowly Waemetik came out. To start their day, Waemetik taught Nawautin the plum-stone game, each trying to guess how many stones the other had concealed under a wooden bowl. With each wrong guess, they yelled out and burst into laughter.

But they had scarcely begun when Waemetik's countenance changed, "Someone's coming! Your father! I must go!" He dropped the plum stones, rose quickly, turned, and gasped.

There, by the great oak, stood Pawaugun.

Waemetik had nowhere to run, and his voice broke as he

pleaded, "Don't hurt me. Don't hurt me. I don't mean any harm," and his whole being trembled.

Nawautin, afraid to lose his friend and stirred by his friend's terror, ran to his father. "Father! Don't hurt him. He's my friend. Let him stay."

Deliberately Pawaugun assured his son, "I have no reason to hurt your friend. You need not fear so. He can stay if he wants." He could not take his eyes off the strange little boy.

There was something familiar about the little boy that at first eluded Pawaugun. As he continued to study Waemetik, he recognized Waubizee-quae, his wife and the mother of Nawautin, from the boy's features, manners, and voice. Though dead, she came back daily in the form of a little boy to care for their son; she had come back as a maemaegawaehnse.

One morning two years later, Nawautin, as he had done every day, ran to the oak to summon his friend to play, but there was no answer; Waemetik did not appear that day or ever again.

Chekaubaewiss or Chekaubishin (Poked in the Eye)

Waubun-anung (Morning Star) didn't want to tell her brother what he wanted to know about the fate of their parents, at least, not just then. She would have preferred to wait until he was bigger and a little older. She felt sorry for her little brother, not only because he was an orphan, but because he was nine years old yet was no bigger than a four-year-old, and she found it difficult to tell him how giant bears had murdered their parents when he was just a baby and that she had looked after him since. Chekaubaewiss bore the news better than she had expected. The only hint of feeling that Waubun-anung noticed was a hard glint in her brother's eyes and a tightening of his jaw and mouth. Chekaubaewiss boasted to his sister that he would get even with the giant bears for her and their parents' sakes—that he would kill them. To Waubun-anung, this promise to avenge their parents' deaths was nothing more than child's talk, cute but absurd.

But Chekaubaewiss meant what he said. That day, he began to prepare for the time when he would grow up and confront the giant bears by practicing marksmanship in earnest and exercising his arms and legs to make himself strong and swift, tough yet agile. The trouble was that he grew no more, so he remained the size of a four-year-old but without the disabilities or the ungainliness of children that age. He could, when he felt so inclined, move with the speed of lightning, and he was stronger than any four-year-old, stronger than he or anyone else could imagine. Besides these attributes, Chekaubaewiss had the mind and the disposition of an adult.

Before he was ten, Chekaubaewiss was killing more deer, bears, and sturgeon than any of the skilled hunters in the village. Such deeds aroused disbelief and suspicion that the boy was stealing his catch from other hunters' traps. As well as hunting like an adult, this child was smoking and doing other things that grown-ups do, and there were other things that Chekaubaewiss would like to have done but was not allowed to do by the adults. Chekaubaewiss hoped and prayed to grow as other boys his age grew. He waited. He measured himself often, but he remained the same stunted little boy, the object of pity and of ridicule. That he didn't grow as he longed to grow was a bitter, cruel calamity to Chekaubaewiss in his dreams for revenge. And he began to think that he would never gain the revenge that he so coveted.

In the same village there lived a man who, because of his size and height, was called Mishi-naubae (the Huge Being). He was everything that Chekaubaewiss wanted to be but was not. To Chekaubaewiss, the man was a giant, a freak betrayed by nature in the opposite way that he was.

Although Chekaubaewiss felt sorry for Mishi-naubae's condition, he envied him and often wished that he and the giant could trade places. Mishi-naubae was a harmless sort and meant well, but he often offended Chekaubaewiss by patronizing him, kidding him about his size, and suggesting that he ought not to impersonate an adult and that he would be better off sticking to pastimes better suited to his age and size. Chekaubaewiss accepted these remarks with tolerance and grace, but what most upset him were the insinuations that Chekaubaewiss was plundering the traps of other hunters, instead of earning his food honestly as did other men.

Finally, Chekaubaewiss retorted that there was no proof that Mishi-naubae himself killed the animals and the fish that he brought home.

After this rejoinder, Mishi-naubae challenged Chekaubaewiss to a pipe-smoking contest to see if he could smoke like a man. If Chekaubaewiss could smoke his pipe as long as did Mishi-naubae, then he deserved to continue to smoke as an adult; otherwise he should stop smoking until he was old enough and big enough to do what adults did.

Chekaubaewiss accepted the challenge readily, observing that the test was too easy. The two contestants started at sunup with a large audience of spectators in attendance to watch the contest. As good a smoker as he was and with as large as pipe as he possessed, Mishi-naubae was unable to keep his pipe going beyond noon. In one story, Chekaubaewiss drew the last puff from his pipe in the evening; in another story, he smoked for three full days before he burned all the tobacco in his pipe.

The spectators at the contest were amused by the results and had poked fun at Mishi-naubae's inability to defeat a child in a contest. "Imagine," they said, "Imagine, a giant being bested by a manikin."

His pride stung by being defeated by a dwarf and then being laughed at by his neighbors and kin, Mishi-naubae challenged Chekaubaewiss to another contest that was more difficult than the first. The giant had to redeem himself. It seemed unfair to those present, but Mishi-naubae proposed an archery contest, a test of strength and skill to put an arrow into an niche on the face of a cliff set a few hundred paces from the marksman, well beyond the range of the ordinary archer. It seemed that the distance favored Mishi-naubae, but Chekaubaewiss accepted the challenge and the contest. As the spectators saw it, Chekaubaewiss didn't have a chance, and they felt sorry for him. They watched in disbelief and astonishment as Chekaubaewiss, who was accorded the honor of shooting first, not only struck the target twenty times in twenty attempts but drove his arrows, fired from his small bow, into the niche and into the very rock face itself. The watchers were speechless. For Mishi-naubae or anyone else to match Chekaubaewiss would be a miracle. As good as he was, Mishi-naubae could not duplicate the midget's feat. His shots had force enough, but all his arrows struck the face of the rock just wide of the target.

To be bested by a midget was even more galling the second time. Mishi-naubae's neighbors and kin would never let him forget that a midget was more than a match for him. They would wink, smile, smirk, snigger, and even taunt him for his rashness, reminding that he was no longer the first of men and that he was like a crow bested by a sparrow. Mishi-naubae had to do something to restore his honor and reputation and to regain the regard of his neighbors and kin. He proposed a third match in which the quickness of each would be tested. He who caught the greatest number of the twenty plum stones cast into the air by a third party before the plum stones fell to the ground would be the winner. With his long reach and enormous hands, Mishi-naubae caught ten plum stones before the rest fell to the ground. The spectators did not believe that Chekaubaewiss could match this feat. But Chekaubaewiss did the unbelievable: He caught all twenty plum stones. Almost immediately the people in the village began to regard Chekaubaewiss as some sort of superbeing, even a manitou, or at least one who was especially favored by the manitous, enabling him to accomplish what ordinary men and women could not. But to Mishi-naubae, Chekaubaewiss was nothing more than a midget, who most likely used sorcery and magic to humiliate him. The source of his bad medicine must be found and then negated, and then Chekaubaewiss must be destroyed.

Not long after the third contest, Mishi-naubae invited Chekaubaewiss to accompany him on a hunting expedition, so he could get rid of his nemesis. Just what happened between Mishi-naubae and Chekaubaewiss in the forest that day never came to light and was never disclosed by the two rivals. All that is known for certain is that Mishi-naubae attempted to do Chekaubaewiss in and failed and that they must have come to some sort of agreement to let bygones be bygones, for Mishi-naubae never again bothered Chekaubaewiss.

It wasn't until real giants invaded the hunting territories of the Anishinaubaek, plundering the streams and swamps and killing most of the beaver, muskrat, and otters, that Chekaubaewiss remembered these creatures and his promise and thought about venturing into their territory.

Up to this time, Chekaubaewiss had not given much thought to giants and giant bears or what chance he might have against them. He knew nothing about them except that his neighbors and kin were terrified of them. He was uncertain if logs, underbrush, ferns, junipers, or caves would keep him hidden if he was to venture into their territory. Nor did he learn from his neighbors if these giants possessed giant dogs. Not knowing a great deal about these giants, he was uneasy when he set out. He hoped that his speed would be enough of an asset.

Without knowing what the giants could and could not do, Chekaubaewiss went forward slowly, ready to turn tail and to run. Sooner than he expected, he heard a giant long before he saw the monster. Chekaubaewiss hid in some ferns. When he finally clapped his eyes on the giant, who must have been three times the height of Mishi-naubae, he saw the giant leaning forward as he pulled a heavy toboggan in the snow. From where he was, Chekaubaewiss could not discern what was on the toboggan. His heart raced and pounded as he looked for signs of a dog.

But the giant had no dog as far as Chekaubaewiss could see. And from the way the giant kept his head down, leaned forward, and snorted in his efforts as a moose blows, it appeared that he was unaware of Chekaubaewiss's presence.

When the giant had passed and was some distance away, Chekaubaewiss emerged from his cover and followed him.

Since the giant gave no sign of sensing anything other than his work, Chekaubaewiss grew bolder and followed him more closely until he crept forward and leaped atop the cargo of beaver pelts and carcasses. Quickly and quietly, he jettisoned half a dozen pelts and carcasses, which he took home to his sister. While Chekaubaewiss was hijacking the beavers, the giant did not turn around once; he noticed nothing.

As soon as he deposited the beaver meat and pelts with his sister, Chekaubaewiss returned to the woods and the giant's trail.

When he reached the giant's lodge, Chekaubaewiss hid in a hollow log not too far from it, from where he could keep an eye on the giant. He saw a giantess, who he assumed was the giant's wife, emerge from the lodge and look on as her husband unloaded the toboggan. Then the giant transferred the beaver carcasses and pelts from the first pile to another, slowly, one at a time, as if he was counting them. He did this three more times before he straightened up, flung his arms outward as if in exasperation, and raised his voice higher and higher. With a roar, the giant stomped off and returned to the trail, retracing his steps, keeping his eyes fixed on the trail as if he were looking for something he had lost. Chekaubaewiss watched him vanish into the woods.

Chekaubaewiss remained where he was, watching and biding his time. The moment that he saw the giant's wife go into the lodge, he ran forward and made off with three more beaver carcasses, which he spirited home to his sister. Then he returned to his hiding place near the giant's lodge to keep the giants under observation and to see what would happen.

By and by the giant came home. He said something to his wife and shrugged his shoulders, but Chekaubaewiss didn't understand a single word. He gathered that the giant was telling his wife that he could not understand how he came to lose six beaver carcasses. Then he went through the routine of counting them again.

When he was done, the giant started to shout at his wife and to shake his fist at her. The giant's wife was not intimidated; she shouted back at him and shook her own fist in front of her husband's nose. Chekaubaewiss had to stop up his ears so they would not burst from the pitch and volume of the uproar, but it was pure bliss to hear and see this domestic infelicity, and he longed to see a blow struck.

As he watched, Chekaubaewiss went through the motions of striking out at an imaginary opponent with a war club and smiting him. As much as he would have loved to see some blood, Chekaubaewiss was disappointed. The giants did not go beyond the shouting stage, and eventually they stopped yelling and resorted to the age-old domestic custom of silence. Meanwhile, Chekaubaewiss waited outside until the giants went to sleep and he heard them snoring; then he stole into the lodge. In the dim light cast by the glow of the dying embers, Chekaubaewiss found the giant's arrows. He broke off a part of a feather from the end of one of the arrows.

With this down in his hand, Chekaubaewiss stood in the dark, undecided what to do. On impulse he imitated the buzz of a mosquito and then ran the end of the feather lightly over the neck of the giant and then that of the giantess. There were exclamations of "Tau-Hau," followed by the echo of slaps in the dark, delivered blindly, and then cries of indignation, "Tau-Hau! What's the matter with you? Why'd you hit me for?" SLAP! WHAM! BAM! WHOP! SPLAT! "EEEEEEeeeyooooowwau-uuh!"

Chekaubaewiss slipped out of the lodge, the battleground, to avoid being accidentally struck. He didn't need to see the fight that he had instigated. He was quite content to envision the scene.

Although he relished inciting friction and turmoil between the giants, he much preferred to plunder their traps and hijack portions of their cargo, for in doing so, he was repossessing goods that really belonged to the Anishinaubaek and turning the tables on the enemy. As he continued to steal the beaver pelts and carcasses, it was now the giants who began to feel hardship while Chekaubaewiss's kin and neighbors were better off. Eventually, the giants, made desperate by their rapidly dwindling resources and facing starvation, packed up and moved away.

Emboldened by his success, Chekaubaewiss went directly into the giants' country and went about their villages unseen, using his speed and size to remain undetected.

One hot summer day he came upon some giantesses bathing in a shallow stream, naked. Up to this time Chekaubaewiss had not given women any more thought than they had given him.

As he watched the naked Amazons, he began to breath hard, almost panting as if he had been running hard. He felt surges of heat followed by waves of chills that produced a rash of goose bumps on his flesh. He sensed an overpowering urge to seize one of the women, and would have done so if he were bigger. Why he felt this urge Chekaubaewiss could not understand, and what he would have done to an Amazon if he had caught one he didn't know.

While he kept his eyes fixed on the women's dark mosses, Chekaubaewiss felt both a tension and an ache between his legs and a discomfort around his midriff caused by the growing tautness of the thong that bound his loincloth. When he looked down, he noticed a huge swelling in the pouch of his loincloth. To relieve the pressure around his midriff and loins, he undid the thong.

Chekaubaewiss's heart nearly stopped in alarm and fright: His poker was stiff and swollen, many times its normal size. This distension was unnatural and inexplicable, and as far as he could remember, no bees had stung him nor had he dashed his instrument against a rock or some other hard object that would have caused it. Just as remarkable was the absence of pain or mark of a bruise. The inflation was mystifying.

So absorbed was Chekaubaewiss by the anatomical phenomenon taking place between his legs that he quite forgot the women. He gazed at the growth between his legs. If only the rest of him grew in the same proportion, life would be wonderful. While Chekaubaewiss was engrossed in his instrument, he forgot to move to make himself invisible. The women saw him, and one of them seized him.

He squirmed. He wiggled to escape. He screamed. He tried to bite, but his captor held him firm. In fact the woman who held him squeezed even harder to prevent him from getting away, so he screamed again.

The guessing game as to Chekaubaewiss's identity began at once. Concurrent with the guesses as to whether "the little boy" was a maemaegawaehnse or a pau-eehnse or a mizauwabeekum was the Amazons' attention to the little dwarf's projection. The giantesses were unanimous in their appreciation of the size, rigidity, and general appearance of the dwarf's poker. Their only regret was that it had been misplaced and therefore wasted on an elf; it should have been bestowed on one of their men. Chekaubaewiss was flattered. But as the women continued to dwell on his poker, they spoke slightingly of Chekaubaewiss himself. Chekaubaewiss felt so insulted that his poker began to shrink. As it began to shrivel up, the Amazons laughed and struck the instrument with sticks.

Even during their merriment, the women did not suspend their guessing about Chekaubaewiss's identity, but they couldn't agree on it. A few suggested that the dwarf might be the obnoxious Chekaubaewiss, basing their suspicions on the size of his poker, which was more adult in proportion than that of a little manitou, and they convinced their companions that their captive was indeed the one they believed him to be. Once the Amazons were convinced that they had the execrable Chekaubaewiss in their hands, they cut his poker down to more proportionate dimensions and then cast him into a pot of boiling water in which he floated unharmed and unscalded. When the giantesses looked into the pot to see if Chekaubaewiss was boiled and ready for eating, he dashed scalding water into their faces, blinding them. He then fled the scene.

The following winter Chekaubaewiss revisited the country of the giants, entering their land in another part. He challenged the giants to a contest to decide which of them could best withstand the cold during the coldest spell in the winter. The giants agreed.

The wind rose and the snow fell. Soon the wind was whining and shrieking as it drove the snow parallel to the ground. Branches snapped and were torn from trees, the wind and cold bit and cut through buckskin and deep into the bones, flesh, and blood of the giants, but it blunted itself against the thick skin of Chekaubaewiss.

With the destruction of the giants, Chekaubaewiss believed that he had avenged his parents, himself, and his sister. Only later did he learn that the giants he had slain were not the ones who had killed his parents; he should have killed the sacred bears.

Up to this time Chekaubaewiss had challenged and triumphed quite handily over beings of flesh, blood, and bones, but now he found that the beings who had killed his parents were sacred like manitous. It made no difference to him. As far as he was concerned, the giant bears who killed his parents were common butchers that deserved to be hunted down. He felt invincible.

Once more he set out boldly, this time bound for the manitou bears' domain. He entered their territory casually, almost carelessly, certain that he would not be noticed. But the giant bears knew he had come and kept him under observation. When they let Chekaubaewiss know that they were aware of his presence and of his whereabouts at all times and demanded to know why he had come into their sacred grounds, where he shouldn't be, Chekaubaewiss realized that he was dealing with no ordinary beings. He fled with all the speed that he could summon, but he could not outdistance the several manitous that pursued him.

The manitous followed Chekaubaewiss all the way to his village and to his very lodge. For his sacrilege, they turned him and his sister into blocks of stone.

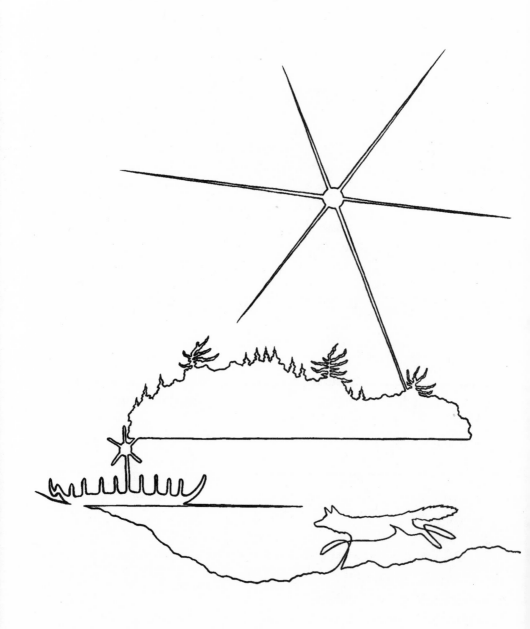

CHAPTER ELEVEN

AUTTISSOOKAUNUK
THE MUSES

Long ago, before there were schools, parents taught their children the practical skills needed for survival. But the burden of passing on most other knowledge, such as customs, insights, understandings, and values, fell for the most part to old women, grandmothers, and the few old men who had survived into old age. Perhaps it is for this reason that N'okomiss, or N'oko for short, is cast as the chief storyteller in many, if not most, of the Anishinaubae stories.

The sole teaching aid of the Anishinaubaek was the story. For every event, belief, animal, or manitou, there was a story. Most of the lessons, or storytellings, were conducted during the winter, from the first snowfall in the autumn to the melting of the last patch of snow in the spring. Storytelling was carried on as much to relieve the tedium of the long, cold winter nights as it was to instruct the young in the traditions and heritage of their ancestors. Only in winter could a storyteller declare "Ahow, N'gah auttissookae," meaning, "Now, if you will attend, I will call upon the Auttissookaunuk (the manitous muses, the North, South, East, West, and others) to inspire me in the creation of a story." With these words, the storyteller was ascribing the authorship of the story that he or she was about to tell to the manitous and, by implication, suggesting that he or she was but a messenger of the manitous, their spokesman or spokeswoman, as it were, in the here and now. It was taken for granted that it was a manitou that had inspired the storyteller.

"Ahow, N'gah auttissookae" was a sacred invocation that was performed only in winter, when the manitous were abroad in the physical world and were proximate to humankind. Once brought into being, the *auttissookaun* became an *awaetchigun*, a story akin to a parable that could be told anytime it needed to be told. Most narrators prefaced their stories with "Ahow, N'gah dibaudjim," meaning "Well, the time has come for me to tell a story . . . to tell what I know of such an event." What followed was more than a story; it was a lesson in the art of storytelling, language, and drama, meant to awaken and enlighten.

Besides these sessions, there were other teaching methods that might be regarded as formal. Certain youths, selected for their strength of character, breadth of mind, and their kinship with the manitous were taken to the *kikinoomaukae-assin* (the teaching rocks), where they were taught the wisdom and the knowledge of the Anishinaubae people by the elders, through stories represented by symbols inscribed on the face of the rock or impressed on birch bark. The purpose of these tutorials was to prepare the candidates to be the future custodians, interpreters, and teachers of the cultural and spiritual heritage of the people. And when their time came and they still led exemplary lives, they would succeed their tutors as "elders," by virtue not of their age, but of their knowledge, wisdom, and integrity.

These were the men and women who sought to understand all aspects of human nature: life, death, the manitous, and the afterlife. These were the dreamers, the visionaries, who called on the Auttissookaunuk for inspiration in the creation of new understandings and interpretations and added to humankind's knowledge and wisdom. These were the men and women whose advice and guidance were sought.

The Auttissookaunuk inspired not only stories but prophecies as well.

The Story: The Man, the Snake, and the Fox

Daebaudjimoot called on the Auttissookaunuk for guidance in telling a story and in making a prophecy. Then he said: "First I'll tell you the story of 'The Man, the Snake, and the Fox.'"

Daebaussigae, a hunter, was a long way from home. He was at the point of turning back when he heard a faint call in the distance. He listened, tilting his head to one side to hear more clearly and to make sure that his imagination was not playing tricks on him. After several moments he was sure that the calls were genuine, but he could not tell whether they were human or otherwise.

Daebaussigae's excitement mounted with each call, as all hunters' senses are sparked by calls and sounds in the forests. Now his senses and his instinct came to life. His spirit, which had been languishing, quickened and his hopes rose. Perhaps he would not go home empty-handed after all.

It was getting late, but that didn't matter. As a payoff for his patience and self-sacrifice, Daebaussigae and his family would feast tomorrow and for many days to come.

Lest another hunter outpace him to the quarry or the animal make off before he got there, Daebaussigae broke off at once, running when the terrain was even and open and walking briskly when the ground was uneven.

Along the way Daebaussigae stopped frequently, just long enough to check his course and to make sure that he was bearing in the right direction. Only when he had reduced the distance to his goal in half did he stop to rest and catch his wind. Almost immediately he was arrested by the unnatural, unusual pitch of the calls. In all his hunting days, Daebaussigae had never heard anything quite like it in the forest or meadow. It certainly was not the call of any animal that he knew; it was too low at times and too shrill at others. It sounded desperate, as if whoever was crying was in pain . . . like a human.

The cries reminded him of the cries he once heard a prisoner utter as he was being tortured. That time Daebaussigae had turned away from the prison and had clapped his hands over his ears to shut out the sight, as well as the shrieks and moans. Still he could not completely shut out the sound. At last, unable to stand the screams any longer, he had run forward and shouted at the torturers, "Enough! End it! You're hurting him!"

Daebaussigae, then ten, had not expected the torturers to pay attention to him, but to his surprise and relief, they let up on the half-dead prisoner.

Few saw Daebaussigae's act as an expression of compassion and secretly commended his deed; rather, many saw it as a display of weakness, a lack of toughness, and called him "woman" behind his back.

But Daebaussigae was like that, compassionate and kind-hearted. Even the spurts of blood; the dying gasps; and the last convulsions of the deer, geese, and beaver that he brought down with his arrows made him ill and wish that he had not killed them.

No longer in any doubt that it was a human being who was suffering, Daebaussigae set off again on the double.

After an hour of hard running and fast walking, Daebaussigae came to the glade in the forest from which the cries were coming. He stopped at the periphery of the woods. The moans were coming from an underbrush on the opposite side where the saplings and vines were bobbing to and from. For a moment Daebaussigae considered going around the glade behind the fringe of trees to avoid being seen. But he rejected the idea.

By now, the moans coming from the underbrush were growing weaker as if the man or woman were losing strength and hope.

There being no sign of anyone else in the vicinity, and therefore no need to skulk in the woods, Daebaussigae went directly across.

Fewer than five paces from the thicket, Daebaussigae came to an abrupt stop; he gasped.

His eyes met the yellow and baleful eyes of a huge serpent lying twisted and bound in a trap made of vines, roots, and thongs; its forked tongue snapped and whipped like little flames. But it was the size of the serpent that daunted Daebaussigae.

From its twisted mass, he could not tell how long it was. The girth alone was awe inspiring. He'd heard of monstrous sea serpents. Here was such a serpent, alive, real.

Daebaussigae was almost frozen to the spot where he now stood, hypnotized by the snake's gaze, by his terror, and by the presence of a mythical serpent. Nevertheless, though weak and trembling, he still had enough presence of mind and strength to back away.

"Needjee! [Friend]" the serpent croaked before Daebaussigae had taken a second step.

When he heard the serpent's voice, Daebaussigae's knees buckled, and he fell in a heap on the ground, senseless. He came to, but collapsed a second time when he heard the serpent speak to him again. Daebaussigae regained consciousness, and the serpent spoke to him for the third time.

"Needjee! I didn't mean to frighten you. I mean no harm. You have no reason to fear me. As you can see, I'm bound and cannot leave this place. Will you set me free?"

Daebaussigae, still trembling, shook his head.

"Needjee! I beg you. Do the favor that I ask. I've been waiting and calling for help for I don't know how many days, hoping that someone would hear my call. I can't last much longer. I will waste away and rot here. Will you not set me free, my friend?"

Again Daebaussigae shook his head.

"Needjee! Don't you know that you have my life and my fate in your hands? You, only you, can set me free and restore me to life and my family. Only you can leave me as I am, bound and helpless and doomed to die. If you leave me as I am, then my death will be your doing. My friend, let me live a little longer!"

By now Daebaussigae had recovered his voice. He said, "No!"

"Needjee! I, too, have a right to live. I have a purpose to serve. Kitchi-Manitou created me to live and to do what I was meant to do. Open your heart a little."

"You might turn on me," Daebaussigae answered.

"Needjee! You are mistaken if you believe that of me. I am

not the mean-spirited being that you take me to be. I will not touch a strand of the hair on your head. Suppose, my friend, that you were in my place: You had no more than a day to live, and you prayed that someone would hear you and a traveler did, indeed, come by and set you free as you implored him to do. Would you not be indebted to him and thankful from the bottom of your heart, and would you not be willing to do as much for the traveler as he did for you? My friend!" The serpent's voice choked. "Don't . . . leave . . . me . . . to die."

Daebaussigae was touched by the serpent's plea. He drew his knife from its sheath and cut away the thongs, the vines, and roots that enmeshed the serpent.

The moment that the last bond was cut, the serpent sprang on Daebaussigae and wound himself around the man. Daebaussigae screamed in fear and in pain. He struggled. He struck out at the serpent with his knife, but his thrusts had no force. The serpent tightened his coils and squeezed. The man and the snake sank to the ground in a deadly struggle.

A fox who happened to be passing in the vicinity was drawn to the scene by the commotion of the struggle. Never having seen such a spectacle, the fox settled down to watch. But within moments, it was clear that the man was finished or would soon be crushed to death.

The fox, curious to learn why the man and the snake were locked in struggle, shouted, "Hey! Why are you fighting?"

Startled, the serpent decreased the tension of his coils. The man gasped out his story. The moment the man was finished, the snake denied Daebaussigae's explanation and gave his own version of the reasons for their fight.

At the end of the serpent's account, the fox declared that he did not understand the serpent's language and asked the serpent to show what he meant.

The serpent released the man and crawled back into the entanglement. From within the tangled web of vine, thong, and roots, the serpent glowered at the fox and demanded to know in a loud voice, "Now! Can you see? Do you understand?"

The fox nodded.

The serpent attempted to crawl back out, but he found that he was once more caught fast in the entanglement. In rage and terror, he screamed at the fox and vowed to get even with him for his treachery.

When Daebaussigae saw the serpent entrapped once more and heard him shrieking in anger and despair, he felt relieved and grateful. He owed his life to the little fox, and he wanted to do something for him. But he also knew that he could never do anything for the fox to compare to what the fox had done for him. Besides, he didn't know what the fox needed and, not knowing what favor he could do for his friend, Daebaussigae pressed the little fox to say what he would like by way of return.

The fox protested. He told Daebaussigae that he did not rescue him to get something in return. He expected nothing. The man's gratitude was enough. But the fox's explanation didn't do any good. Daebaussigae insisted on an answer; he had to have one before he would let the fox go on his way.

Finally, eager to get away from the man and to get on with his own hunting, the little fox explained, "There are times when my family and I must go without meat for a few days when food is scarce, especially in winter."

Before the fox could say another word, the man interrupted him. "There's no need for you to go without any longer. I'll make sure of that. You have my word. Whenever you're down and out because hunting's been bad, just come over to my place. I'll give you whatever you need, or you can just help yourself to my stores."

"You're very kind, very generous," the little fox commended the hunter, deeply affected by the man's goodwill. "I won't forget what you've said."

With an apology for his impatience to be on his way, the fox left.

For the next few years Daebaussigae frequently thought about his encounter with the snake and the fox and often wished that his little friend would come, but as more years passed, he seldom recalled the event.

One day Daebaussigae was in his lodge repairing his snow-shoes, when his youngest child of twelve burst into the lodge stammering, "Dad! There's a fox . . . outside . . . on top of the food racks . . . and he's stealing our meat!"

Deliberately Daebaussigae set his work aside and took down his bow and arrows. Just as deliberately he went outdoors. Sure enough, there was a fox on top of the food racks, tearing at the meat.

Daebaussigae stole to within range before he brought his weapon up. He trained the arrow at the fox's neck and let fly.

The aim was true. The arrow struck and bore through the fox's neck with such force that it sent the fox pitching to the snow-covered ground. There the fox writhed and twisted, gasped and wheezed as blood spurted and spread upon the snow.

For once the hunter didn't feel sorry for his victim because his victim was a thief who deserved what he got. With his knife ready to finish off the thief and to remove the pelt, Daebaussigae walked to where his victim lay gasping and rasping for breath.

As Daebaussigae knelt beside the dying fox and drew back his dagger, the little fox lifted his head with difficulty and gasped, "Don't you remember?" And then he was no more.

The Prophecy

When Daebaudjimoot finished telling the story, he continued.

"Now, I'm going to tell you a very different kind of story. It's not really a story because it has not yet taken place, but it will take place just as the events in the past have occurred." Daebaudjimoot paused to fill his pipe. "And even though what I'm about to tell you has not yet come to pass, it is as true as if it already happened because the Auttissookaunuk told it to me in a dream."

The men, women, and children from the neighboring lodges

who had come, waited for Daebaudjimoot to begin. The adults
had long ceased to believe the tribal storyteller. Still they came,
as they had done for years, to relive the delight and faith of
childhood that moved some of the old to say, "He makes me
feel like a child again sitting at my grandparent's feet." But
unlike the children in the audience who believed Daebaudjimoot, the adults spoke slightingly of the storyteller, but not
without affection. "W'zaumaudjimoh" (he exaggerates) they
said of him. But there was not a man, woman, or child in the
village who was not enriched in some way, either in mind or in
spirit, once he or she heard Daebaudjimoot.

"Tonight I'm going to tell you about white people." There
was a moment of silence, astounded silence, and then an out-
burst of laughter as the audience perceived the incongruity of
the notion. An albino caribou or an albino beaver, yes! But
albino people? Who ever heard of white people? Even Daebaudjimoot had to laugh. The laughter gradually subsided.

"Are they like the maemaegawaehnssiwuk [little people, like
leprechauns, elves]?" a man asked, inciting another wave of
laughter.

"Are they like the Weendigoes?" an old woman inquired,
igniting more guffaws. The old laughed at such notions; the
young laughed to hear the adults giggle, roar, and twist their
mouths and cheeks into a hundred shapes. At the same time the
young wondered what beings, in addition to the Weendigoes,
maemaegawaehnssiwuk, pau-eehnssiwuk, mizauwabeekummoowuk, and Pauguk, lurked in the forests and roamed about at
night.

"What do these white people look like?" another old lady
asked when she dried her eyes.

"The men and women that I speak of are all white—face,
bodies, arms, hands, and legs—pale as the rabbits of winter.
And they are hairy . . . hair growing on their arms, legs, chests,
backs, and armpits . . . and some men grow hair upon their
faces around their mouths, drooping down from their chins, like
moose beards." Daebaudjimoot had to interrupt his narrative

again for the nervous twitters and embarrassed cackles that set off another uproar. The children chuckled and chortled as they imagined their playmates, maybe brothers and sisters, goateed like moose. Daebaudjimoot continued, "Different, too, is the color of their hair; some yellow as goldenrod, a few red as cranberries, and others black as our hair. In old age the white people's hair turns white; on some men the hair falls off entirely, so their heads are as smooth and shiny as pumpkins.

"Their eyes are also unlike ours: round . . . quite round . . . like the eyes of the raccoons . . . and blue like the color of blueberries."

There was more laughter, but by now the men, women, and children were nursing aching bellies and painful sides.

"And their dress is as quaint as their appearance. For one thing, they cover their bodies completely, day and night, summer and winter; only their faces are visible. On their heads are head-winders that they wear indoors and outdoors, in sunshine and in rain. The men and boys wear a peculiar garment, which is a loincloth and leggings made of one piece to cover their hams, but the garment is so tight that the men walk like mud hens. Each time they go to the toilet, even to drain their bladders, they must unfurl these rump binders down to their ankles. And the women's garments are not much better. The women wear a robe that covers them from their wrists down to their ankles. Underneath these sagging dresses, the women wear tit flatteners and belly compressors. Their moccasins are made of a hard substance, almost like wood, and cover their legs up to their kneecaps. It is only at night that the white people remove some of these garments."

"Are they ashamed of their hair? Of their organs?" an old woman quipped, rousing tired laughter.

Daebaudjimoot resumed his narrative. Hours later he predicted, "When they come, they will come from the east across a great body of salt water, and they will arrive on board great wooden canoes five times the length of one of our own canoes. At either end of these long canoes are tall timbers. From the limbs of these timbers are suspended blankets for catching the wind to drive the canoes without the aide of paddles."

"Are they ash or maple? Fresh wood or dead? They go against the wind?" voices asked and made remarks ridiculing the idea of an oversized canoe with trees at either end.

"You laugh because you cannot picture men and women with white skins or hair upon their faces, and you think it is funny that a canoe would be moved by the wind across great open seas. But it won't be funny to our grandchildren and their great-grandchildren.

"In the beginning the first few to arrive will appear to be weak by virtue of their numbers, and they will look as if they are no more than harmless passersby, on their way to visit another people in another land, who need a little rest and direction before they resume their journey. But in reality they will be spies for those in quest of land. After them will come countless others, like flocks of geese in their migratory flights. Flock after flock will arrive. There will be no turning them back.

"Some of our grandchildren will stand up to these strangers, but when they do, it will be too late, and their bows and arrows, war clubs, and medicines will be as nothing against the weapons of these white people, whose warriors will be armed with sticks that burst like thunderclaps. A warrior has to do no more than point a fire stick at another warrior, and that man will fall dead the instant the bolt strikes him.

"It is with weapons such as these that the white people will drive our people from their homes and hunting grounds to desolate territories where game can scarcely find food for their own needs and where corn can barely take root. The white people will take possession of all the rest and they will build immense villages upon them. Over the years the white people will prosper, and though the Anishinaubaek may forsake their own traditions to adopt the ways of the white people, it will do them little good. It will not be until out grandchildren and their grandchildren return to the ways of their ancestors that they will regain strength of spirit and heart.

"There! I have told you my dream in its entirety. I have nothing more to say."

"Daebaudjimoot! Are these white people manitous, or are they beings like us?"

"I don't know."

As the men, women, and children went out, a young man who had lingered behind remarked, "It's good to listen to you, but I don't believe you."

The Fulfillment: "Don't You Remember?!"

Just as the old storyteller had foretold, strangers with light complexions landed on the brown men's land. They arrived on board quaint vessels driven by the wind. Some brown people at first regarded them as manitous; others were suspicious and were for killing them or driving them away. But many more bade the strangers welcome and helped them until they were ready to resume their odyssey for the passage that would bear them to the Orient, spices, and gold.

One traveler, a white man, related to his host, a brown man, that he and his companions had enlisted in their leader's expeditions to escape conditions at home and to break free from their bondage as peasants and serfs, for that is what they were in their homeland. Now they were bound for the Orient in quest of silk, spices, precious stones, silver, and gold. This man and his companions could then return to their own country no longer embedded in poverty or indentured to the nobility.

The white man described the life where he and his companions came from, its customs, laws, practices, traditions, and habits. He said that the king and the nobles owned everything: the land, lakes, deer, boar and foxes, the man's labor and his produce, and even his life. If it pleased or suited the king, he could order a person beheaded. If a man was caught killing one of the king's deer to feed his family, the king or queen could order the hunter executed. Despite the king's power, men still took risks because after the king, the nobility, and the clergy were done collecting taxes and tribute from the peasants and serfs, there was little left for their families.

Try as he might to comprehend the life on the far side of the ocean that the white man described, the brown man was unable. Such a life was almost beyond belief. He could not envision one man or a small group of men and women owning all the land, all the animals who dwelt upon it, all the produce, man's labor and his harvest, and men's lives. But he felt sorry for his friend.

His friend went on. He said that while the king and nobles owned and governed men's lives and destinies, the clergy (cardinals, bishops, priests, and nuns) presided over people's souls and their spirits, now and in the hereafter.

The clergy dictated a person's thoughts, prayers, and laws, and they could sanctify and canonize those they deemed worthy and condemn to everlasting fire those they adjudged to be deserving of damnation.

Had he not seen what his friend had told him, the brown man would not have believed a word of his account. He saw the man's commander order men to perform work and watched the men discharge the orders as if they were slaves. "Fall in! Attention! Forward march! Halt!" He further saw the commanders slap, whip, imprison, and even execute men who failed to comply with the commands. It was true, the nobility did own the men. And what the traveler told him about the clergy was equally true. The black robes acted as if they owned people.

The brown man had never seen another person exercise such control over human beings, nor had he seen men and women allow themselves to be subject to a single person. It was unheard of, inconceivable, yet it was true.

Observing that the brown man came and went without asking permission, the white man inquired, "How is it with you, my friend? Do you have royalty and clergy, people of rank and power who own everything and have precedence over you and your freedom? Do your chiefs and headmen own the land? Do they have the power to seize your goods? Conscript your labor?

Have they authority to command you? Are your holy men and women vested with the authority to prescribe what you may believe and how, when, and where you may worship? How is it with you, my friend? Have you anything to compare?"

"No! Nothing like that!" the brown man replied.

Wistfully, the white man answered, "I envy you, my friend. You are a free man."

"Yet despite your hardship and your servitude," the brown man added, "you have accomplished much, turning metal into vessels and weapons, ornaments, and implements. These I covet. I will trade my bow and arrow for your gun, my birch-bark bowl for your cauldron, my scraper for your knife, and my shells for your beads."

After a while the white man and his companions grew rest-less. They had to go on; they had to find a passage to the Orient and to silks and spices that would make them wealthy, con-tented, and free.

Some of the brown man's kin and friends offered to show the travelers the way and indeed guided and accompanied them westward. But not all the white men accompanied their leader.

When he saw that his friend and a few of his companions meant to remain to make a tent camp, the brown man pressed his friend to construct warm dwellings for the winter months ahead. Under the direction of their commanders and holy men, the white men built houses.

Before long, winds tore from the north, driving snow against lodges and buildings and holding the land in an icy grip. The white men were chilled to the very marrow of their bones. They shivered and longed to return to their own homes. They fully expected to die in the snow. But the brown man had kept an eye on his friend. He brought the man his coat, mittens, and moc-casins to wear. His friend's garments were fit only for summer. Moreover, he showed the white man how to make garments and blankets from furs.

Not only was the white man cold, he was famished and fac-ing starvation. Though the white man possessed a deadly weapon, he could not venture into the forests to use it on game and birds. The snow was too deep. Besides, there were few animals to be hunted and killed in the winter. In the meantime, the brown man shared the food with his friend that he had set aside for his own family for the winter; he and his kin brought fish and meat, smoked and dried, and corn, squashes, melons— whatever he could spare. He gave him snowshoes to bear him over deep snows and a toboggan to transport his goods and his kill. Moreover, he taught the stranger how to trap and set snares and prepare meat and what birds were suitable and which were not. Once the white men, who were quick to learn, learned to hunt, fish, and trap, they were able to look after their own wants; they no longer needed to look to the brown man for meat or a helping hand. From that time on, they kept their storehouses stocked with meat and fish.

The brown man's friend should have been fat and strong, but he and his countrymen fell ill, bleeding from the mouths and noses, without strength or spirit. Seeing his friend's condition, as well as that of the other white men, the brown man brought a medicine man to learn the cause of the men's ill health and to see if he could restore them to health. The medicine man knew at once what afflicted the white men. He brought remedies, and the patients recovered. Afterward he taught them the brown men's medicine.

With the brown men's goodwill, medicine, and alms, the white men survived until spring.

For the welcome and reception that he had received on his arrival in the brown people's land, and for the food, clothing, shelter, guidance, and land that he had usurped on which he had built his home and his village, the white man was deeply grateful. For having been brought back from the edge of starvation and infirmity or death from illness, the white man felt that he owed something to the brown man and that he ought to do something in return. His clergy rendered thanks to God.

"How can I repay you, my friend?" he asked. "What can I do in return for the many favors that you've bestowed upon me and my companions? I'm forever indebted."

The brown man thought about his friend's goodwill. But he

could not imagine what amount to place on the favors that he had done for his friend and his companions or what favors he might ask his friend to perform in return. He had never given requital any thought, and now, pressed for an answer, he didn't know what to say. But his friend pressed him again for an answer, "Tell me, let me know," and he meant what he said. The brown man had to say something to please his friend. At last he said, "If ever I should be so unfortunate as to find myself in need, may I come to you?"

"Why! . . . Of course," the white man said. And he assured the brown man, "We can do no less for you than what you and your people have done for me in our time of need." He would regard and value the brown people as friends and allies, worthy of standing by his side; he promised that if the brown man needed or wanted food, drink, medicine, clothing, or anything else, he had only to ask, and the friend would give him meat and tea and a bed and blanket in his own house and would lend him his coat and garments if he was cold or damp. And just as the brown man had freely imparted his knowledge of the climate; routes; geography; the ways of the animals, birds, and fish; and his beliefs and almost everything that he knew, so, too, would the white man open his books and pass on his skills and arts. All that the brown man needed to do was to ask or call on the friend and he would receive whatever he needed.

The friend meant every word that he uttered. To show that he was sincere, the white man shook his brown friend's hand. As if this act was not binding enough, he sat down and wrote all his promises on paper, affixing his signature to the document next to the mark of the brown man.

In the summers that followed, the foreigners built houses and founded a village. Around this village the brown people's white friends erected a wall and posted sentries at the gates and at intervals all around the barricade within. The brown man could not see within, and although he often went to visit his friend and his companions, he was seldom admitted into the enclosure. When he was allowed entry, he was granted only a short audience and . . . always under the watchful eye of the sentries who were armed with drawn weapons.

Just as the old prophecy had foretold, the white man's kin from the other side of the ocean arrived in great numbers, like flocks of geese in the migratory season. Shipload after shipload came.

The newcomers multiplied and prospered. They felled trees and laid waste to the forests. They drove the deer, bear, beaver, their kin and kind, from their haunts. They drove the brown man from his land and made war on the brown man's neighbors and on any other nation that resisted or stood in the way of their vision of Manifest Destiny. Nothing could stop the migrants; nothing would appease or fulfill them.

While the migrants prospered, the brown man's circumstances declined. He could not feed his family as well as he had done in the past; they were now in constant hunger. He, his family and kin, and their neighbors suffered new and alien maladies that his medicine people could not heal. Dispossessed of lands given him and his wife and their children by Kitchi-Manitou, he and his family now dwelt on lands where corn could not take root and where animals could find little nourishment.

In his adversity, the brown man hoped that his friend would notice his condition and come with provisions. He was loathe to ask his friend, lest he appear like a beggar. But his friend was entrenched behind walls and could not see what was taking place beyond them. The brown man had to go see his friend, to ask for food and clothing and medicine; he had to remind his friend of the agreements that they had made and the promises that his friend had undertaken and written. The brown man and his family, along with several companions, went to his friend's village.

He knocked at the portals until someone drew back a small panel in the wall, looked out, and asked, "Who are you?"

"I am the brown man, your friend," the cold brown man answered.

"What do you want?" the man inside inquired.

"I should like to see my friend. I have a favor to ask of him."

"Wait," the man inside growled, closing the panel without opening the portals. The brown man, his family, and his companions huddled outside and tried to keep warm by stamping their feet and blowing on their hands. And they tried to comfort their children with assurances that "soon you'll be warm. Don't worry. Our friends will invite us into their homes. Set a table for us, and lend us warm coats until spring returns and the geese and the deer and the fish have multiplied."

But no one came to open the portals; after some time had passed, the brown man knocked again.

Again the panel opened. This time there was a different face behind the frame. "Who is it? What do you want?" he demanded.

For a second time the brown man explained that he had come to see his friend, that he was there by his friend's invitation. He meant to ask his friend only one or two small favors. The brown man added that his friend had once promised to look after him, should he ever meet hardship.

"Wait!" the man said, and he closed the panel. Secretly the brown man hoped that the watchman would open the door and allow him and his companions into the warmth of the interior, but the man did not invite them inside.

Inside were men and women demanding in loud voices, "Who in hell's knocking? What t'hell does he want?"

"Some brown men and women and their kids. Say they want to see their friend about meat, and clothes, and medicine and shells. Say they've fallen on hard times," the watchman explained.

"Well! Who in hell do they think we are? Their keepers? Send them off. Tell 'em it's not our fault that they are facing hard times. They're not our responsibility. Tell 'em to get t'hell to work and quit disturbing us. Tell 'em we're busy. Tell 'em if they don't wanna live like us, they deserve all the damned hardship that they can get."

The watchman returned to the portal and relayed the message to the brown man.

Though he was dismayed by the rebuff, the brown man refused to leave. He insisted on seeing his friend. "I want to see my friend . . . , and I won't leave until I see him." If only he could see him, everything would be all right. He told the watchman again, "My friend invited me. He said that if ever I had need, he would help me. I can prove it. He put it in writing. He said that he would live by his word forever and that I could trust him. You just ask him. He'll bear out what I'm telling you now."

"Wait," the watchman said, and he slammed the panel shut. And though it was cold and the brown man's children were crying, the watchman did not invite them in or offer them broth or a crust of bread.

The brown man did not wait quite as long as he did on the previous occasion before knocking again. Almost at once the panel was opened and a face appeared. "Who are you? What do you want?" the watchman demanded. The brown man told his story once again.

"Wait," the watchman said, as if he meant he would return presently.

The brown man knocked. Another watchman appeared, listened to the brown man's story, and said, "Wait." After him came another watchman, who was followed by another and yet another, each asking the self-same questions and each stating, "Wait! Wait! Your friend will be here presently. If only you would be patient. He is busy; he cannot see you right now, but he will be with you soon. In the meantime, will you cease your knocking, you are disturbing the people within, and can you not keep your children from coughing and crying? Can you not see that they are blighting the neighborhood?" And the panel closed.

No sooner was the panel shut in his face than the brown man resumed knocking once more, with greater force than before. At the same time he raised his voice, demanding to see his friend. "I know he's inside. Let me talk to him. Let him know that I'm here. I need to see him."

While he was beating on the wall, the panel opened. As yet

another face appeared; though it was different from those of the others, it had the same hard, unfeeling eyes and tone.

"I want you to tell my friend that I'm here. I want to see him. It is urgent," the brown man said in a loud voice.

"Who is it that dares to force his way in and make demands on us?" a voice bellowed in indignation.

"A brown man. A delegation of brown men and women and their progeny."

"Tell them to get t'hell away from the walls and go back where they belong, and if they don't leave, we'll use lead," a voice boomed. Other voices resounded in · support, "Here! Here! Shoot 'em."

Points of rifle barrels were thrust out every peephole and window, aimed at the brown people.

"Fire!"

Pow! Pow! Pow! Before the shots had echoed away, some brown men, women, and their children immediately fell to the ground, their blood staining the snow. Others who were struck by bullets bled and moaned in pain as they retreated from the walls.

While the brown people were ministering to their sick and injured, soldiers and police came out of the building and clubbed several men and women with truncheons, binding their hands and feet before dragging them inside, where they cast them into prison.

But not all the brown men and women withdrew from the walls. Many remained where they were, caring for the wounded and comforting the bereaved. They were both sad and angry.

"Don't you remember?" the brown people shouted and shook their fists at the retreating soldiers and policemen. The portals clanged shut.

Angrily the brown men and women picked up sticks and stones. The men beat upon the walls with their makeshift clubs, while the women pitched stones at the barricade.

The sliding panel was drawn once more. A face came into view.

Before the face could utter a word, the brown man snarled, "Who in hell are you?"

The man blinked. "I'm new here. My name is Waffle. What do you want?"

"What do you mean, '"What do I want?'" the brown man almost barked. "You know damn well what I want. Why should I repeat it? Can you not read? Can you not see? Can you not feel? I'm just asking for what you promised."

"What's all the commotion out there? several voices cried out.

"It's a brown man," Waffle shouted. He had to shout.

"They're still here? Haven't they gone yet?"

Waffle's companions inside were wrangling and bickering, their exchange getting louder and sharper. It was hard to hear and be heard. But way in the background, a long way back, their voices almost smothered by the clamor in the foreground, were the brown people's friends. "Waffle!" they said. "For God's sake listen to them! We've ignored them for too long. It's about time we paid off a little of what we owe them and fulfilled our promises, isn't it? Let's do what's right and honest."

Other voices, sharp and angry, broke through the boisterous unrest. "Waffle! Leave them alone. We don't owe them a G—— D—— thing."

"I don't know what to do! My hands are tied," Waffle wailed. "I must ask the governor, Warren B. Guile," and he closed the panel, pleading, "Wait!"

The brown men picked up stones and began pitching them against the barricade. They now started to yell, "We will wait no longer."

Within moments the panel was drawn back, framing a man's visage. It was the governor himself. The Right Honorable Warren B. Guile's jaw twitched, and his lips curled back.

Before the governor had a chance to speak, the brown men and women vented their demands.

"We are the people who befriended your ancestors, your kin, and your friends when they had need." Mr. Guile looked at his watch. "We are the people who brought them food and clothing and medicine when they were cold and hungry and sick." Mr. Guile again looked at his watch and then away. "We are the people who gave a portion of our blankets when you had none in your ancestral home." Mr. Guile looked at his watch still again, his lips curled back some more, and fire lit in his eyes. "Your kin and neighbors promised to do no less for us than what my kin and friends had done for them. We are demanding justice, nothing else; we are demanding that you live up to your promises." All Mr. Guile did was look down at his watch.

Behind the walls there was more quarreling. Angry young brown men continued to pitch stones and began to point pistols at the walls.

The governor turned around to glance at the disturbance behind him. He looked at his watch again and said, "Wait!"; then he vanished into the interior.

The brown men did not stop heaving rocks and curses at the wall. Those who had pistols polished and brandished them.

Almost immediately Mr. Warren B. Guile reappeared. He pursed his lips, thrust out his jaw, and knit his brow into lines.

"How dare you?" he demanded. "I will not be intimidated. Did I not ask you to wait? Why did you not suspend your assault?" He looked at his watch and then glared at the brown people. "We have been most patient," he pontificated. "You are pushing me. I will not back off another step."

"What t'hell do you know about waiting, about patience!" an anonymous brown voice spat out.

"That's it!" Mr. Guile barked. He snapped his fingers, and at once rifle barrels and cannon muzzles bristled from every window and slit in the wall.

"I need say one word," Mr. Guile declared, with iron in his voice. "I need not describe the results that will follow. You well know what they will be. Therefore, it's up to you! The choice is in your hands. Leave at once. Stay away from our walls. We have more pressing matters to attend to than your grievances. I cannot understand how you can believe that your concerns are of vital importance."

"What t'hell would you know about priorities?" one of the brown men retorted.

Above the clamor within were heard voices. "My Lord! Most respected! Sir! In the name of all that's fair and equitable, why can you not sit down with all these people?"

But Mr. Warren B. Guile was set; no one could move him, nothing could touch his heart or soul. He thrust out his jaw still further. "No!" he declared forcefully and shook his head at the same time.

Someone yelled, "Fire."

The guns roared and barked and rattled. Brown men, women, and children slumped to the ground. They writhed and groaned, staining the snow with their blood. Above the moans of agony were cries of grief and sorrow. Those who were not hurt ran to the sides of the fallen to render what aid they could, if aid could be given. They picked up the fallen and carried them away from the walls to the woods, where they buried the dead and tried to nurse the wounded back to health.

But Mr. Warren B. Guile turned his back and walked away. There were more urgent matters that needed his attention— other wars, other blood.

The few brown people who remained near the walls shook their fists and raged, "Don't you care? . . . Don't you remember?"

CHAPTER TWELVE

PAUGUK

"Are you awake?" Meemee (Dove) whispered as low as she could so as not to awaken or alarm the children.

Receiving no answer, she nudged her husband, Waub-kookoo (White Owl). "Wake up!"

"What is it?" he asked sleepily.

"Listen!" she said.

With the wind whining through the trees and the breakers battering the rocky shore, it was difficult to hear. Still, they made out a melancholy, thin voice, an eerie voice, calling, "Help me! Someone! I can't get out!"

Meemee pressed closer to her husband and began to shiver. "I'm afraid . . . it doesn't sound like a man or a woman."

"Shshshsh! . . . I can't hear!" Waub-kookoo hushed his wife.

Meemee lay still. In the dark she felt her husband prop himself on one elbow and suspend his breathing.

"Help me . . ." and the rest of the words were muffled by a fresh burst of wind.

"Someone's down at the shore," Waub-kookoo ventured after some moments. "I'm going down to see what the matter is and to give what help I can." He cast the blankets aside and fumbled for his leggings and his moccasins.

"Wait for me! I'm coming with you," Meemee hissed at her husband, and she fumbled in the dim light cast by the red embers of the fire to find her dress, moccasins, and wrap while Waub-kookoo waited.

"Where are you two going?" Meemee's mother asked.

Waub-kookoo explained that he was going down to the shore to see who was calling for help. "Didn't you hear anyone calling?" he asked.

"Yes, I did! But it didn't sound like a human being to me. Leave it. Don't go down there."

"Don't worry. We'll be right back," Waub-kookoo assured his mother-in-law as he followed his wife out of the lodge.

Though the wind blew with gale force, it was not cold. Nor was it as dark as might be expected of a blustery night. Driven by the whipping wind, clouds raced across the sky, shrouding the moon and casting the earth into darkness, then blowing by and brightening up the land.

"Help! . . . before it's too late . . . this way . . . Needjee! [Friend]"

"This way," Waub-kookoo directed his wife toward the shore over boulders and shrubs. "Watch your step!"

Waub-kookoo and Meemee were near the shore, looking up and down the length of the lakeside, when the clouds unshrouded the moon. Sprays of water fell on them as waves broke over boulders.

"Needjee! . . . Help me," came the call, directly in front of them. Waub-kookoo looked.

"Eeeeeeeeyoooh-aaaah!" Meemee screamed as her knees buckled and she slumped to the ground.

An instant later Waub-kookoo saw it, too, a skull wedged between boulders, rolling to and fro according to the motion of the water. His knees gave way and he sat, quaking, on his haunches beside his wife's form. He rested his hand on her shoulder.

"Needjee!" the skull said. "I can't hurt you. Don't be afraid of me. I can't even touch you, as you can see. Help me!"

Waub-kookoo opened his mouth; his jaw went slack, and he couldn't utter a word, not a sound. He could only gape in repugnance at the skull.

"Needjee!" the skull spoke again. "Why look at me in

loathing as if I was something abominable? You ought to know that I was once like you and that you will someday look like me. Instead of shrinking from me, you should bear me some sympathy and tolerance and understanding."

"W'w'what do you w'w'want?" Waub-kookoo stammered.

"My bones are scattered, as you can see. I am Pauguk. I am broken . . . dismembered . . . now just a skull. Put my bones together in their natural order. Make me an entity, complete . . . and I shall nevermore disturb beings of flesh."

"But . . . I am not a m-m-medicine person. Only they are warranted to commune with the dead . . . and why are you still here? . . . Why are you not in the Land of Souls with your kin and ancestors?"

"Dearly would I like to be with them, but I cannot. They will not have me. Nor will the Underworld have me. Neither do I belong here in your world, but here must I dwell, pleading with your kind until someone incorporates my bones and sets me free."

"Why? How is it that you are dismembered? Why will they not have you in the Land of Souls?"

"If I tell you, will you collect my bones and restore them to their proper configuration? I've never told anyone my story, for thus far, no one has remained in my presence as long as you have. It is a story that I am ashamed to tell, for it is a sordid story. But I must confess it if I am to surmount the pain of being unwhole, a skull detached from its frame that is disjointed and scattered along the shore and at the bottom of the sea . . . to be devoured into oblivion by turtles, crayfish, and who knows who else, or else to be worn away into dissolution by the winds, the waves, and the currents. Will you listen? Will you tell my story?"

Waub-kookoo nodded without saying a word. He felt sorry for the skull and less afraid of it now than he had been at the beginning. He drew Meemee, who had come to, closer to his side.

"My name is Pauguk," the skull began, and the following is the story that he told.

"Five years before, my younger brother, Waub-oozoo, came home with a wife whom he had met in his travels. Our parents, everyone for that matter, considered my brother exceedingly lucky to have such a woman as a wife. And indeed he was, and I envied him, not in a covetous way, but in a selfish manner when I ought to have been glad and complimentary. It was easy to see from the way that Beewun [Down] looked at Waub-oozoo that her love went beyond mere love and bordered on adulation. Some of the women in the village were critical and talked about Beewun, saying that she behaved more like a servant than a wife, the way she waited on Waub-oozoo and brought him whatever he needed without being asked or directed.

"Waub-oozoo was as contented as any man that I had ever known or heard about. Whereas once it had taken no more than the mention of the words 'hunt, fish, trip' to persuade him to leave home and not return for days, it now became almost necessary, the hunters said, to kidnap him to detach him from his wife. If he was not the leading hunter in the village, it would not have mattered, but Waub-oozoo was next to indispensable. And the men jested that they when they were on a trip with him, they had to watch him to keep him from making off and going home. 'Oh! He'll get over it,' they said.

"Ever since I could remember, my brother had regarded me as someone special. As boys, Waub-oozoo followed me as a child clings to his mother or a fawn to the doe. Even in our later years, he preferred my companionship to that of other boys his own age. And even when he got married, Waub-oozoo still sought my companionship, inviting me to visit anytime and to stay as long as I pleased. And I accepted my brother's invitation, dining with him and his wife, sleeping in their lodge, and listening to them consummate their marriage and love.

"Yes, the manitous had indeed been kind to Waub-oozoo, and deservedly, for he was a good-natured, generous, trusting man who had never shown a mean bone to anyone. I hoped that the manitous would bestow similar favors on me.

"I had noticed Beewun's eyes from the moment that I first saw her; never had I seen such soulful, sultry eyes. Soon after I began to visit Waub-oozoo and Beewun, I thought that she looked at me with a longing that women cast only on men they love and desire. And her glances, sultry and full of want and promise, impassioned me. Though they aroused me, those eyes and their lure and magic disturbed me.

"And her touches were as electric as her glances were provocative. If Beewun had to put her hand on my shoulder for momentary support, I would be aroused; a fleeting accidental brush of her hand or garment would set my flesh tingling. Up to this time no woman had moved me so. But it was my brother's wife, who custom and decency had committed beyond my reach.

"What was I to do? How would I get her out of my mind? What ought I to do to avoid hurting my brother's feelings, shaming my parents, or breaking the Anishinaubae code? I knew of only one recourse, and that was to leave for a while, for six months, a year, or however long it took to get over this infatuation.

"Before I left, I told my parents, my brother, my kin, and my neighbors that I was going out to see the world and that I didn't know when I would come back home, but I reassured everyone that I would return when my wanderlust had been quenched. In the meantime, they were not to worry; I was well able to look after myself. Besides, my guardian would keep me from harm. With their good wishes for a safe journey and my family's mis-givings that were mingled with my mother's tears, I set out.

"But it was easier said than done. No sooner had I gone around the most distant point and beyond sight of the village than I was choked by an oppressive loneliness and heartache. I felt an overpowering urge to turn back. In fact, I suspended my paddling for some moments and turned my canoe about, ready to abandon flight. I wanted to gaze upon Beewun once more, to hear her laughter again, and to feel her caress upon my shoulder just one more time. But if I was to turn back, the men, my friends, would laugh at me to my face and behind my back. That I couldn't bear. I brought my canoe around.

"Over the next few days Beewun stole into my mind unin-vited or came as summoned and lingered, almost real, taunting and tormenting me until I dismissed her reluctantly by force of will. During these moments, I wavered and was ready to face the ridicule of my friends. I didn't care whether I hurt my brother's feelings. I was quite prepared to violate tribal practice. Only the mortification that my parents and grandmother would have to face prevented me from returning home.

"The nights were torture. I had no one to talk to, no face to look upon, no voice to hear except the faces and voices of the past and the distant. Even these visions gave way to one face, one voice. And the eyes, the beautiful black eyes, asked, 'Why did you leave? When are you coming back?' But as the days and nights passed, the luster of the eyes faded, and the enchantment of the voice grew fainter.

"Half a month later, I came to a village whose people spoke the same language, which made it a little easier for me to gain welcome. But some of the elders were skeptical of my explanation that I had left my family, kin, and village to see the world. No one traveled simply for the sake of travel or for seeing the sights; men traveled to seek out new hunting grounds, to deliver messages, to pursue enemies . . . or to run away. My hosts didn't put their doubts and questions to me directly in words, but I could see it in their eyes and hear it in the tone of their voices.

"Like other people, this village didn't want troublemakers or fugitives seeking shelter among them and embroiling them in unwelcome feuds or vendettas. But because it was their custom and nature to make guests, kin or strangers, welcome, they invited me to pitch my wigwam in their village and to stay until I was ready to resume my world tour.

"To relieve my hosts of the burden of providing me with meat, as they had done on my arrival the previous day, I accompanied a party of hunters to their hunting grounds. I brought down two deer. For the hunters of the village, my success was a challenge. To see whether my success was luck or skill, the hunters invited me to accompany them again. Once more we came back the same day with venison to feed the entire village for a week.

"Almost immediately, some of the hunters, convinced that I was an exceptional hunter, hinted that I should suspend my plans to see the world and remain there as a member of the community. And to dissuade me from going any farther, they described the hostile nations that occupied the territories through which I proposed to pass. Besides, travel was restricted to foot, and the weather was hard as flint in winter. It would be better for me to remain as their guest among friends in a land that had been given to them by Kitchi-Manitou. And who knows, 'One of the young widows may want you as a husband,' one of my companions suggested.

"I decided to stay another few days. If I left, it would appear that I had rejected their invitation to remain and would surely be construed as a slight on their hospitality. The few days extended into a week, the week into a month. It was then late summer, too late to resume my odyssey.

"As long as I was with people, I found that I suffered less heartache, and I deliberately sought company and conversation. Even though the chief topic of discussion among the men was hunting, and often repetitious, I and the others never tired of hearing or telling of marksmanship or how they missed their quarry at point-blank range. Over and over the hunters described their skills with pride or their ineptitude without embarrassment. If I wasn't listening to the hunters' tales, I was giving all my attention to the tribal storytellers who were instructing and entertaining the audience with their accounts. Children, too, alleviated my hurt. To see them tumble and hear them laugh or to listen to them cry as they nursed their bruises or vented their feelings helped me forget and loosen the bond with the past.

"Little by little the bond that held my mind, spirit, soul, and heart to the memory of Beewun was slowly released.

"But while I was gradually severing my memories of and yearning for Beewun, I longed to see my parents and grand-mother and, kind and generous as were the people in my tem-porary adoptive village, I wanted to go home to my village, to my place of birth. I wondered if my grandmother was still alive, how my father managed alone, and if Waub-oozoo was able to assist our father, and I recalled my mother with affection—brooded when I remembered how she used to stay awake at nights worrying until my father or I and my brother came home. She always worried; she would never change. I must be constantly in her mind, pausing now and then in her work to try to find an explanation of why I left and to worry about my safety and well-being. Yes, she must offer tobacco frequently to the manitous for my sake.

"How long had I been away? Five months. Long enough? Had the bond of infatuation, love, been so dissolved as to preclude regeneration and enable me to look upon Beewun with the same detachment and indifference with which I regarded most women? But when I thought of Beewun, my heart's pace quickened. It was too soon. I would not be able to withstand my urges. I decided to remain where I was until the following spring, when I would again reconsider my feelings. By then it should be enough time.

"When I decided not to return home, I asked my hosts if I could remain in their village until spring. 'Of course,' they said. 'We were hoping that you would stay. Of course. As long as you want.'

"Soon after I had asked permission to winter in their village, an older woman, one of the elders, accosted me alone and inquired whether I disliked women. I guessed what she meant and assured her that I was indeed fond of women, but that I had not as yet turned any woman's head enough to inspire her to put up with me for life. Within days of my conversation with the old woman, a young widow invited me to her lodge, not only for the winter but permanently.

"I told the young woman that I was not yet ready for marriage, but it didn't matter too much. Such relationships were not uncommon. She hoped that I would stay.

"The following spring when the trees began to blossom, I, feeling in command of self, bade adieu to my companion and friends and left to visit my parents and kin. How long I would be gone or when I would return, I dared not say. But already, even as I plied my paddle and sent my canoe forward, I felt an excitement as the image of Beewun appeared and seemed to beckon me to hurry.

"When I felt a tremor course through my hands and arms, I realized that I had not yet got over this feeling, this obsession, and that it would be better for me and for everyone if I waited for at least another year. But I went on, drawn home by love and duty to my parents and lured by Beewun; I half hoped that something would intervene to prevent me from doing anything rash or even from fanning old sparks.

"Half a month later I was in sight of my old village. While I was still some distance away from the landing area, the dogs began to bark as if I were a stranger, which, of course, I was to many of them. Their barks and howls naturally aroused the villagers, who suspended their labors to look up to see what was disturbing the dogs. 'Someone's coming!' the children shrilled, pointing to the approaching canoe. 'Who is it? Recognize him?' Men and women shielded their eyes from the sun to make their vision keener and thus to determine whether the oncoming paddler was a friend, enemy, or neighbor coming home. The dogs continued to bark despite the people's efforts to silence them.

"Most of the villagers went down to the shore to see who was arriving, asking one another, 'Who is it? Can you recognize him?' Only the very old remained where they were when the commotion began.

"'Looks like Pauguk!' one of the onlookers ventured, as he strained his eyes. Soon after, another voice supported this statement. 'For sure. No doubt, it's Pauguk.'

"'It's Pauguk! Pauguk's coming home! Someone tell his parents. It's Pauguk. He's here! He's not dead!'

"As if it was necessary, some boys and girls ran up the incline to deliver the good news to my parents. Then, without waiting for an answer, they ran back down to the shore to look on and greet the prodigal from his world tour and to listen to my accounts and stories.

"No sooner did I beach my canoe and disembark then a dozen hands lifted my craft out of the water and set it gently on an unoccupied frame. And even before they did so, the questions began. 'Where did you go? What did you see? What was the land like? The people? The animals? Were you afraid?' I was too busy greeting friends, kin, youths whom I had not seen in a year, to answer all the questions. 'Ahneen! How are you? My, you've grown! Later! I'll tell you later, but there's not much to tell. How's your mother? your father?'

"With children, friends, and dogs pressing in on me from every side, I made headway only at a snail's pace; I wanted to see my parents and grandmother.

"My father and mother then came down to meet me. The crowd of boys and girls in front gave way to allow them to come through.

"'Ahneen!' My father greeted me cheerfully and took my hand in his. 'It's about time. I thought I'd have to go in search of you,' he said.

"My father had not changed, as far as I could tell.

"I quickly disengaged my hand from my father's clasp to put my arms around my mother.

"'Son! I'm so glad you're home. I'm so glad that you're all right!' she said, as she put her arms around my waist and squeezed affectionately. 'Didn't you bring her home?' she teased.

"'Who?' I asked, momentarily taken aback by the question. Then I realized the substance of her hint and chuckled, 'There was no one to bring home. . . . And how's grandmother?'

"'She'll be so glad to see you. She's talked about you often since you left last spring. Why, she was calling your name only yesterday. Son! I'm so glad that you're home. I hope you'll stay. This is where you belong.'

"I looked down at my mother. I saw in her eyes the same love and affection that she had always expressed ever since I could remember. Nothing would ever change that.

"'Where's Waub-oozoo?' I asked, suddenly realizing that my brother was not there to greet me.

"'He went down the end of the bay early this morning. He should be back by now,' father explained.

"As I walked up the slope with my father and mother and the crowd that formed a reception committee, I saw Beewun push through the crowd to welcome me. She drew herself to my side opposite my mother. Just as my mother had done, Beewun now put her arms around my waist and her head upon my shoulder. 'I'm so glad that you've come back. . . . I've missed you.'

"I inclined my head slightly and met her eyes. Had they been able to speak words, they would have said, 'Come to me this day. Come into my arms. Let me hold you now and forever. . . . I am yours.' But her eyes spoke their own language. And had we been alone, I would have swept Beewun into my arms and unclothed her, joined my body to hers there on the ground where we now stood. Then and everyday . . . forever. My skin broke out in goose bumps, and my heart beat hard and fast. I wanted to sit down to get control of myself.

"'Waub-oozoo will be so glad to see you,' Beewun said, looking away and disengaging her arms from my waist. I wished that she had not removed her arms, but her touch lingered like a hot brand where her arm had rested.

"In the excitement of seeing Beewun, I was almost oblivious to everyone beside me and indifferent to the snail's pace of their walk home. 'How far did you travel? What's it like?' The questions continued to besiege me.

"I glanced up to take in the family lodge and to note what changes, if any, had been made to it since I left.

"There was grandmother sitting to one side of the entrance, just as she had always done, as if she had not moved, bent over slightly, searching for something on the ground and then, having retrieved whatever it was that she had been looking for, affixing her glance to another object that she held in her left hand. From where I observed her, it appeared to me that she still looked the same. Certainly, her manner did not seem any different from what it had been. Nothing could distract her from her work or disturb her equanimity—not thunder, earthquakes, or visitors. And now she did not bother to look up.

"'N'okomiss!' I hailed grandmother. 'N'okomiss! I'm home,' and I broke away from mother and the crowd to rush forward to greet her. 'Grandson!' she said as she embraced me. 'Welcome home. Sit down.'

"As invited, I sat down beside my grandmother, and the crowd that had come settled down on the ground, with the children in front, all eager to hear of my adventures; encounters with giant animals, manitous, and enemy warriors; descriptions of other lands and other peoples; and explanations of alien customs and dress. When I explained that I had gone no farther than half a month's travel westward by canoe and had lived with people akin in language, customs, and beliefs, some of the adults left to return to their lodges to resume the work that they had suspended on my arrival. Even Beewun left with the adults, waving her hand and casting a parting glance on me before she walked away. Only the children stayed on, moored to their places by curiosity and a conviction that if they left they would miss something important.

"I was attempting to explain, without much success, why I had gone. 'I just wanted to see the world. I wanted to see how others lived, how others' customs compared to ours. I left not because I was unhappy here, though life tends to be changeless, monotonous . . .' when excited shouts came from the shore, disrupting my account. 'It's Waub-oozoo!' and then louder, 'WAUB-OOZOO! YOUR BROTHER IS HOME!'

"I stood up, waved my arms, and then went down to the shore to meet my brother and to escort him back. Beewun was there, too, and it made me uncomfortable. After greetings and handshakes and backslaps, Waub-oozoo, Beewun, and I went up to our parents' lodge, where we traded news of our experiences and our affairs during the past year, each eager to learn how the other had fared.

"It was an exercise in catching up. Not until we had assimilated as much news from each other to give us a sense of the direction and spirit of the others, could any one of us resume life and work as if little or nothing had occurred to disrupt the continuity of our relationships. We now shared the same knowledge of who had died, who had become parents, who had received many favors from the manitous, and who had remained unchanged. Only after we had become reacquainted could we turn to the more immediate business of fishing and hunting.

"After Waub-oozoo told me where he and our father and some of the men had been fishing and what they would be doing tomorrow, he issued a brotherly challenge, 'See if you've still got the touch.'

"For me, the next day went as if I'd never been away. Neither my father nor my brother referred to my absence or asked me for explanations. The fishing was as good as it ever was. With the number of trout and whitefish harvested, the coming winter would be good.

"'Tau-hau! Needjee,' Waub-oozoo exclaimed in admiration when we were done. 'It looks like the fish still come to you.' And after making a few observations about luck and the prospects for the coming summer, he added, 'Beewun and I would be glad to have you stay with us . . . What . . .'

"'That's kind of you,' I broke in, 'and as much as I would like to accept your invitation, I really feel that I should stay with Mother, Father, and Grandmother. It wouldn't be quite right and proper after having been away a winter not to stay at home as expected, at least for a while.' I was forced against the horns of a dilemma. Considering the family circumstances and the origin of the invitation, I had no choice. Sooner or later I would have to accept my brother's invitation. In the meantime, I could only delay. And I was afraid. One glance, one word, one touch from Beewun was all that it took to impress on me that I had not overcome my obsession.

"But it was difficult to refuse my brother without giving offense; it was difficult to offer an excuse that Waub-oozoo would accept. 'Surely Mother and Father would not want to keep you for themselves alone. . . . Perhaps they'd be relieved to be rid of you for a few more days,' Waub-oozoo teased.

"'Not right away. Give me a few more days with them,' I pleaded.

"It was by begging that I managed to put off accepting my brother's invitation, but I could not well refuse the next request, that I eat with them, delivered on the basis that a meal had been prepared especially for me, at considerable trouble, and that I should bring my pallet with me.

"Indeed, the meal was as good as was promised. But throughout our dinner of venison and beaver with maple-syrup sauce, smoked trout, and blueberries, which absorbed Waub-oozoo and ought to have held my attention, I was distracted by Beewun's presence, her voice, and her eyes. I found it difficult to put my whole heart, mind, and spirit into the meal and into the plans for the autumn hunt that Waub-oozoo unfolded.

"It was only when Beewun removed her top and began to unbraid her hair in preparation for bed that we realized that it was later than we realized. Seeing a woman without a blouse was nothing new or out of the ordinary, but seeing Beewun bare down to her waist for the first time excited me. I did not want to remove my gaze from her breasts, which were partly draped by her hair and at other moments fully bared and vibrant and flushed in the flickering flashes of flame. Yet I had to look away; I did not want either my brother or Beewun to notice that I was staring at her body as if I had never before beheld a woman's body. As best I could, I tried to be casual.

"I considered returning to my parents' home, manufacturing some excuse, such as that I did not feel well, but I knew that no story, no matter how sound, would gull my brother. I had to stay, or so I convinced myself.

"When we went to bed for the night, I on my own pallet and they on theirs, I did not fall asleep at once as was my habit; visions of Beewun's breasts appeared and reappeared. What made it worse for me was that she was there, naked, only an arm's length away. And I could hear her breathe and sigh and move. 'If only my brother were not here . . . if only it was I lying by Beewun's side . . . if only. . . .' My envy and desire turned into jealousy and hatred.

"There was only one way to gain Beewun, to gain access to her side on the pallet. The very thought appalled me and kept me awake for most of the night.

"In the morning I caught a glimpse of Beewun fully naked, even though it was only for a moment, as she stood up to slip a full-length dress over her head. In that moment Beewun was never lovelier; no woman was as lovely as she. My desire was refueled. Beewun would be mine.

"In the days that followed, I considered going to a sorcerer to obtain poison and a love potion, but I dismissed the idea. No one except me should know of my motive and my deed. I would have to do it alone.

"Having decided to murder my brother, I considered how. Under the circumstances, it would be best to drown Waub-oozoo, a poor swimmer. If I drowned him, people would be more inclined to accept that Waub-oozoo's death was accidental.

"The next question was where. I could think of no better place than the narrows that I had come across in my travels, four days' paddling from the village. There the current was swift and treacherous.

"While we were fishing the next day, I casually mentioned that in preparation for the forthcoming fall hunting season we ought to explore this particular area that I had passed on my homeward journey. From the tracks and marks, the place deserved closer investigation than I had given it when I had come by, I hinted. If I was correct in supposing that the place was a deer crossing and that the surrounding area was replete with deer, then the fall hunt would be easier and more rewarding and productive. The area certainly deserved a thorough study, and there was not a better time than the present to go there. With food abundant, the men could be spared a few days without hardship to their families or the community. Waub-oozoo was all for the idea; we could set out anytime, as early as the next morning, when Beewun would have everything ready. I had to pause to consider my brother's intention to bring his wife. The idea had its appealing features, but I knew that Beewun's presence would serve only to abort my plans. It would be better to leave her home. It was a delicate matter, but I managed to dissuade my brother from bringing his wife. 'It'll be only for ten days or so, she won't waste away in heartache. Don't worry; she'll be all right with her mother and father.'

"That afternoon we set out.

"Five days later, during which I frequently suffered second thoughts, depression, and repugnance about what I was about to do, we came to the place that I had referred to. My brother trusted, loved, and admired me; he would do almost anything I would ask. The image of Beewun appeared in my mind to reanimate my resolve. I had to have her.

"Waub-oozoo noticed these changes in my moods, these moments of preoccupation. Though it was none of his business to inquire into the innermost thoughts of his fellow human beings, Waub-oozoo felt constrained to remark, 'Tau-hau! Needjee! You look as if you're lost in another world. Better pay attention, or else we'll run aground some place and sink. I don't want to have to try to swim.'

"'Don't worry.' I replied. 'I was just thinking.'

"And Waub-oozoo accepted the explanation.

"'This is the place that I was telling you about,' I said as we were approaching the narrows. We drifted along for a while in the middle of the channel, studying, our paddles at rest atop the gunwales of the canoe.

"The narrows resembled a gorge that has neither bank nor shore to speak of. The south side was solid rock, perpendicular from the waterline to the brow of the escarpment, a height of two hundred feet or more; the north side was also of solid rock, but not half the height or half as rough or craggy. The surface was quite smooth, as if some giant had polished it with a scraper. Bisecting these two masses of primordial rock was a well-wooded valley, a half mile or so in width, that bore north and south.

"After taking stock of the contour and character of the chan-

nel, the valley, and the mainland from the water, Waub-oozoo
and I went ashore on the north side to study the land more
closely. We saw countless tracks, all recently made, bearing
inland and northward. We both agreed that this was a fording
passage, and all that remained to do was to establish on which
side the herd wintered and when it was they likely that they
made their crossing.

"As we stood on the north side, Waub-oozoo pointed to an
overhanging rock on the brow of the south cliffs and remarked,
'Wouldn't that be a wonderful place for a lookout? One would
be able to see a long way off.'

"'It would also serve as a fine retreat for dreams, visions,' I
added. 'There is something sacred about that rock.'

"'Let's go up there,' Waub-oozoo proposed. 'We'll have a
much better idea of the land from up there. We may even see a
herd; who knows. . . . That place reminds me of the story of the
ambush of Kwaessind [the Feared One] by the little people. Do
you remember, Pauguk? Do you remember how the little people, armed with stones, waited on top a cliff for Kwaessind to
arrive, and when that bully drove his canoe directly below their
ambush, they released their missiles and sunk the canoe of their
enemy? Nobody's bothered the little people since. Do you
remember that story, brother?'

"'Yes! Very clearly,' I answered, looking at the promontory,
but I was looking at the cliff from an entirely different point of
view. It was not a sacred place for the conduct of spiritual exercises. Rather, it was to be the rock of doom, a thought that
made my blood and heart race. What I was about to do would
be easier and less risky than overturning a canoe.

"An hour later we were standing at the edge of the precipice,
taking in the vista all around to the very horizon. Although we
had often wondered what the eagle and the hawk beheld from on
high, we had never imagined that we would one day, as we now
did, look upon their world from their vantage point. And like
eagles and hawks, we looked down in silent awe at the lakes and
streams, valleys and heights, meadows and muskegs and listened

to the murmur of the wind and the ripple of the waves below.

"Finally, after some moments, Waub-oozoo broke the silence with an observation, 'So this is what hawks and eagles see.' And he stepped closer to the edge and looked down.

"As Waub-oozoo stood precariously near the edge, I put my hand forward directly in the small of my brother's back and thrust forward, hard.

"Waub-oozoo pitched outward, arms waving wildly. 'Eeeeeeyoooooh!' he screamed. Then there was a splash . . . silence.

"I backed away from the brink. My hands were shaking, my palms were damp and clammy, and my heart pounded as much in my descent as it had in my ascent. I frequently cast nervous glances to my right and to my left and then behind me, as if expecting to see someone who had witnessed what I had done, who now could incriminate me or hold me in bondage. No one was in sight. But my ears, keener than ever before, heard foot-steps, knocks, taps, raps, slaps, a rustle that made me start and throw my head around to catch sight of my pursuers. As before, there was no one except a chipmunk or a flicker on the side of a tree that darted out of sight in fear of me. I descended quickly lest someone see or take hold of me.

"Down at the shore I wasted no time boarding and launching my canoe. I made my way directly to the foot of the cliff. There my brother's body was stretched, broken and bloody, on a rocky shoal that extended the length of two canoes from the base of the cliff, a hand's width just below the surface of the water. I vomited as I levered the mangled corpse with my paddle away from the shoal into the deep.

"As I paddled away, I again looked all around to see if there was someone watching me. There was no one, as far as I could see, except the animals and the birds, the eagle, the sparrow, and the mole, which now shrilled in horror in their language to tell each other, 'Did you see! He killed his brother!'

"During the next five days, I constantly looked behind me, expecting someone to come in pursuit. At night I slept fitfully, awakening to every crackle, creak, and scratch. All sorts of thoughts assailed me. Was it my brother now stealthily creeping up on me in the dark to plunge his knife into my chest in revenge? No, it couldn't be. That was just a mole venturing out in his own dark world. Was it possible that my brother had recovered and would sooner or later make his way home? Was it him, just then . . . or was it a spirit, far worse than human, I had heard. I should have made certain that Waub-oozoo was dead before I left him and the scene. But how could anyone survive such a fall? How could Waub-oozoo survive the ordeal of water?

"I thought of Beewun. As my brother's survivor, I could now claim the young widow. I could now hold her and feel her softness. I thought of her until the next clash or screech set my hair on end and my nerves taut to the point of snapping.

"In the morning when I set out, I felt no more rested than I had been the night before.

"As I drove my canoe forward, neither too slowly or too leisurely, I rehearsed the answers that I would give to the questions that everyone would surely ask. 'Where is your brother? What happened? What did you do?' I prepared myself mentally and emotionally to face the questioners as calmly as the circumstances would allow. And I blackened my face as evidence of my mourning.

"Ten days to the day after Waub-oozoo and I had cast off together, I was within sight of home. On shore was a small crowd, made up mostly of curious children who were often gathered near the beach, playing at some game or waiting for the hunters and fishermen to come home. There were some men and women as well, performing tasks that always needed doing, such as the repair or construction of a canoe or the mending of fishing equipment. Then there were the ever-present seagulls and dogs.

"When I was still some distance away, the children began their game of guessing who the lone paddler might be from his style of paddling. As I drew closer, enabling the children to recognize me, the children asked, 'Wonder where he left Waub-oozoo?' But the adults were filled with presentiments and bade the children say no more. Their presentiments were confirmed the moment they discerned my blackened face.

"To be met without greeting, not even 'Ahneen!' disturbed me. And though my neighbors helped me draw my canoe out of the water in an act of neighborliness, I saw, in the brief moment that their eyes met mine, that they were filled with distrust and fear, as if they could see the guilt impressed in my soul-spirit through my eyes. They need not ask what was plain.

"One boy, who had just run down to the shore, did ask what the others had not dared. 'What happened? Where's Waub-oozoo?'

"I hesitated, groping for breath and words as if what had been asked was too horrible to recount. 'We . . . we . . . capsized . . . in rapids . . . and Waub-oozoo did not come back up . . . I . . . I . . . searched and waited . . . oh!' and here I faltered.

"Children detached themselves from the crowd to run home to deliver the news of the tragedy. Within a short time the entire community, except my parents and grandmother, knew of the accident. The messengers did not break the news to them; they did not want to. That was my burden.

"Of the people, young and old, who listened to my explanation of the accident, none uttered a word of condolence or offered to accompany me as I plodded unwillingly and unhappily up the grade.

"Some men and women remained at the beach to finish their tasks before going to the lodge of the bereaved to attend the vigil. They watched me with pity, but not with half the pity that they felt for my parents and grandmother. It was bad enough to be the bearer of sorrowful news, but it was worse still to be the recipient.

"One of the men who had helped draw the canoe out of the water asked his companions if they felt that my story was consistent with the condition of the canoe. After inspecting the canoe fore and aft, one declared that if the canoe had undergone an accident, then it ought to bear some evidence of wear and tear, but another person denied the assumption, saying that it wasn't necessarily so.

"For me, the last few steps before I came face-to-face with my parents were the worst ordeal. I wavered, but I went on.

"My grandmother saw me first. She gasped when she saw my mask of death and then began to keen. My mother, hearing the cry, came out of the lodge to see what had alarmed her mother. One look at me set off her wailing. Within moments my father was drawn from the other side of the lodge to the front.

"'Mother! . . . Grandmother! . . . Father! . . . Waub-oozoo,' I said, and then I choked and shook. I cried; I cried to hear and see my mother and grandmother desolated. When I recovered my voice and regained a measure of control over myself, I resumed, halting frequently to stifle a sob. Amid tears and broken words, I described how Waub-oozoo had become unnerved as we passed through some narrows and that his sudden movement capsized the canoe, how he had been sucked under in the whirlpools as if he were drawn or pulled down into the Underworld by the manitous. And I told of my struggles to save my brother and of my own close call.

"I attempted to console my mother and grandmother by drawing them into my arms, but they pushed me away. Unable to bear the sound of my mother's and grandmother's soul-piercing lamentations or to endure the pained and misty eyes of my father, I withdrew and stumbled my way toward Beewun's home to deliver the news.

"But Beewun was already on her knees, rocking back and forth, keening in grief, calling for Waub-oozoo. She already knew; someone had told her.

"My voice quivered as I expressed my sorrow for her loss. Over and over I repeated how sorry I was, how much my brother had meant to me, and how I had almost lost my own life in my efforts to save him. As I unfolded the tragedy, Beewun's ululations and her calls for Waub-oozoo grew louder and more heartrending. Touched by Beewun's grief and longing to comfort her and myself as well, I knelt down by her side and put my arm around her shoulders and drew her to me. I whispered, 'I will look after you from now on.'

"'Noooo! Noooo! Nooo! . . . Never,' Beewun wailed even louder. At the same time she twisted her shoulders violently to throw off my arm. 'Noooo!' Beewun hissed as in anger.

"Startled by Beewun's vehemence, I withdrew my arm and, hurt, I slowly got to my feet and retreated, leaving Beewun alone as she wished. As for myself, I went home to console my parents, but they would not be comforted. I sat with them well into the night until exhaustion felled me into a deep, troubled sleep that was disturbed by images of my brother and the reflection of questions in the eyes of my kin and neighbors. 'What did you do to your brother?'

"'Wake up! Wake up!' A voice that sounded as if it issued from the stars commanded me to rouse myself. I tried to raise my head, but the effort was next to impossible; I dropped off or floated into the space of unconsciousness. 'Wake up! Wake up! It's Beewun! She's dead!'

"At the mention of Beewun, I was on my feet, rubbing my eyes, which refused to open of themselves. 'What?' I asked in disbelief. 'What did you say?'

"'Beewun! She's dead!' my father repeated.

"'How? Where?' I asked.

"'Down at the shore. They found her just now.'

"I didn't wait. I raced down to the shore where a crowd was gathered. I pushed my way through the ring and knelt down beside Beewun. I reached out to caress her hands and her garments, which were wet, and I began to cry softly.

"'Kegoh [Don't],' a medicine woman rasped. 'You're not the husband.'

"I withdrew my hand. At the same time I looked up into the eyes of the woman, which bore into my own like rays, deep into and to the ends of my soul and inner being. I saw, or imagined that I saw, the image of my mangled brother etched in her eyes. And I looked away. Did she know? Then I looked down at Beewun's lifeless form, and I shook and heaved as I fought back my sobs.

"I ought not have cried for a woman who was my brother's wife, but I couldn't help myself. Beewun would have been my wife. Those who were present would, of course, be curious to know why I was shedding tears without shame.

"'Ahow,' the medicine woman said, and the bearers lifted their burden and carried the dead Beewun to her lodge, where the wake would be held. The crowd moved, forming a procession behind the bearers. I remained rooted where I was, shoulders heaving, head cast down, my arms hanging limp by my side, a vision of abject misery. No one in the crowd invited me to go. It was as if I didn't exist.

"With the entire village preoccupied with Beewun's death, I launched and boarded my canoe. Some instinct guided me into my boat. The same feeling gave motion to my arms to take up the paddle and to drive my canoe forward. I had but one object at that moment—to get away. Where I was going I knew not. How long I would be absent, a day, a year, forever, did not enter my thoughts. My mind was clouded, and my vision was unclear, distorted by the mist in my eyes.

"I paddled all day at the same pace, like something that had been set into motion to go at the same rate. I paddled onward until dusk. It was only when the sun was beginning to sink that I realized that the day was ending and that I must make camp for the night. The moment that I suspended my paddling and rested my paddle on the gunwales, I was overcome by an overpowering weariness and remorse, guilt, and sorrow.

"As I looked over the shorelines for a suitable place to camp, my mind now took over from instinct or whatever it was that had directed me since morning.

"But what was the purpose of making camp? Why sleep? What good would it serve, except to go on. And what did the morrow promise? What did the land beyond the horizon have to offer? Nothing. There was no hope, no purpose, no meaning to be gained by enduring—nothing except the slap of waves upon the rocky shore.

"There was suddenly a scream. Real or imagined, it shook me.

"'Aaaaaaaaah!'. . . splash!

"I let the paddle slip from my grasp without being conscious of having lost it. Wildly I looked about, shoreward, upward, and outward to the horizon. There was no one, but I was shaking.

"Only when I went into the motion of dipping my paddle into the water did I realize that I did not have it. I glanced beside the canoe. There, looking up at me from an arm's length below the surface, was Beewun.

"I gasped in terror. At the same time I shrank back abruptly from the apparition, too far back. The canoe rolled over. I was upside down in the water. I struggled to free my legs from under the bar, but they were caught fast. I struggled to keep from breathing, but could not. I lost consciousness.

"When I came to, I was across the Bridge of Death, about to set foot in the Land of Souls, when the Guardian took hold of the log that made the bridge and pitched it to and fro until I lost my balance. 'You don't belong here. Killers of their own brothers don't belong here!' The Guardian shrilled the words, assailing my ears as I fell into the rapids below.

"In the Underworld the manitous shrank from me and hid. 'He killed his brother. . . . He coveted his brother's wife. . . . He killed his brother. He doesn't belong here. He belongs with his own kind,' they shrilled.

"And the turtles and the crayfish destroyed my flesh and sinews until the bones fell away and sank. But the manitous and the residents of the Underworld, not wanting my bones to desecrate their world, asked the manitous that presided over the winds and those that governed the currents to cast my bones out of the sea.

"The manitous unleashed the winds that stirred the waters to boil and churn until they had cast out my bones and scattered them on the rocky shore.

"That's my story," Pauguk said. "That's how I came to be here. . . . I don't belong here. . . . I do not know where the likes of me belong. All that I know is that I must leave the Land of the

Living. I must go as I was born and as I lived, with body and limbs, with frame and shape. My friend! Set my bones in their proper, natural order; give me form, and I will leave and go to that place where I belong, wherever that may be; otherwise I must remain where I am, unsettling men and women with my harping. My friend, brother! Do me this small favor; set me free from my bondage, and I shall never frighten your kin or your neighbors again. . . . Do not be afraid. . . . I cannot hurt you."

Waub-kookoo did not answer the skull. Instead he asked his wife, "Do you think I should do what Pauguk asks?"

"No! Leave him! . . . Oh! Do what you want, but I'm not staying," Meemee cried, and she stood up uncertainly and returned to the lodge.

Waub-kookoo gathered the bones that were flung over a large area on the shore and, by the light of the moon, assembled them in their rightful places according to their natural order. When the final bone was set and the skeleton composed, Pauguk was lifted and was airborne into the skies.

Waub-kookoo stood and watched the night sky and then he heard Pauguk address him from somewhere in the sea of stars, "My friend. I am between the sun and the Realm of Ice. Too close to the sun and I burn; too far and I freeze. I'm an outcast even in the afterlife." As he continued to look upward, Waub-kookoo thought he heard the hiss and rattle of burning bone.

Finally, when he heard nothing further, Waub-kookoo returned to his home and his wife.

"Did you do as Pauguk asked?" Meemee inquired.

"Yes!"

"And what did you do with them? Where are they now?"

"The skeleton ascended into the sky like a bird, and I heard someone speak, the voice of the skull. He was alternately near afire and then near frozen in his dwelling place in the afterlife."

CHAPTER THIRTEEN

WEENDIGO

Of the evil beings who dwelt on the periphery of the world of the Anishinaubae peoples, none was more terrifying than the Weendigo. It was a creature loathsome to behold and as loathsome in its habits, conduct, and manners.

The Weendigo was a giant manitou in the form of a man or a woman, who towered five to eight times above the height of a tall man. But the Weendigo was a giant in height only; in girth and strength, it was not. Because it was afflicted with never-ending hunger and could never get enough to eat, it was always on the verge of starvation. The Weendigo was gaunt to the point of emaciation, its desiccated skin pulled tautly over its bones. With its bones pushing out against its skin, its complexion the ash gray of death, and its eyes pushed back deep into their sockets, the Weendigo looked like a gaunt skeleton recently disinterred from the grave. What lips it had were tattered and bloody from its constant chewing with jagged teeth.

Unclean and suffering from suppurations of the flesh, the Weendigo gave off a strange and eerie odor of decay and decomposition, of death and corruption.

When the Weendigo set to attack a human being, a dark snow cloud would shroud its upper body from the waist up. The air would turn cold, so the trees crackled. Then a wind would rise, no more than a breath at first, but in moments whining and driving, transformed into a blizzard.

Behind the odor and chill of death and the killing blizzard came the Weendigo.

Even before the Weendigo laid hands on them, many people died in their tracks from fright; just to see the Weendigo's sepulchral face was enough to induce heart failure and death. For others, the monster's shriek was more than they could bear.

Those who died of fright were lucky; their death was merciful and painless. But for those who had the misfortune to live through their terror, death was slow and agonizing.

The Weendigo seized its victim and tore him or her limb from limb with its hands and teeth, eating the flesh and bones and drinking the blood while its victim screamed and struggled. The pain of others meant nothing to the Weendigo; all that mattered was its survival.

The Weendigo gorged itself and glutted its belly as if it would never eat again. But a remarkable thing always occurred. As the Weendigo ate, it grew, and as it grew so did its hunger, so that no matter how much it ate, its hunger always remained in proportion to its size. The Weendigo could never requite either its unnatural lust for human flesh or its unnatural appetite. It could never stop as animals do when bloated, unable to ingest another morsel, or sense as humans sense that enough is enough for the present. For the unfortunate Weendigo, the more it ate, the bigger it grew; and the bigger it grew, the more it wanted and needed.

The Anishinaubae people had every reason to fear and abhor the Weendigo. It was a giant cannibal that fed only on human flesh, bones, blood. But the Weendigo represented not only the worst that a human can do to another human being and ultimately to himself or herself, but exemplified other despicable traits. Even the term "Weendigo" evokes images of offensive traits. It may be derived from *ween dagoh,* which means "solely for self," or from *weenin n'd'igooh,* which means "fat" or excess.

The Weendigo inspired fear. There was no human sanction or punishment to compare to death at the hands of the Weendigo, no threats more certain to bring about the exercise of moderation. The old people repeatedly warned, "Not too much. Think of tomorrow, next winter. *Kegoh zaum! Baenuk!* [Think of others! Balance, moderation, self-control]"

As long as men and women put the well-being of their families and communities ahead of their own self-interests by respecting the rights of animals who dwelt as their cotenants on Mother Earth, offering tobacco and chants to Mother Earth and Kitchi-Manitou as signs of gratitude and goodwill, and attempting to fulfill and live out their dreams and visions, they would instinctively know how to live in harmony and balance and have nothing to fear of the Weendigo. If all men and women lived in moderation, the Weendigo and his brothers and sisters would starve and die out.

But such is not the case. Human beings are just a little too inclined to self-indulgence, at times a shade too intemperate, for even the specter of the Weendigo to frighten them into deference. At root is selfishness, regarded by the Anishinaubae peoples as the worst human shortcoming.

In the meantime, the Weendigo waited in the shadows, hungry to the point of collapse and tormented by an unrelenting ache that was worse than any ache known to humans.

Sooner or later a man or woman would have to leave his or her camp or village and come within reach. Of this the Weendigo was certain, given the weakness and unchangeableness of human nature. But to suspend one's labor to rest and renew oneself or to take up another interest for self-growth is not in and of itself bad. As Western Europeans say, "All work and no play makes Jack or Jill dull." There is nothing harmful in humankind's inclination to rest, play, celebrate, feast, and pursue hobbies. The trouble is that some people don't know when to stop and appear not to care, because nature, or Kitchi-manitou, has endowed them with slightly more than is good for them: appetites, passions, and desires that dilute their talents, common sense, and judgment. It doesn't take much. A fraction too much or too little of anger, envy, or lust is enough to create an imbalance in a person's character to impair his or her judgment and weaken his or her resolution. Is it any wonder, then, given humankind's inherent selfishness and imbalance, that men and women, when put to the test, would prefer safety to risk, ease to toil, and certainty to uncertainty, which makes them so conservative that when the opportunity arises they tend to indulge their self-interests?

In this and other respects, the Weendigoes are men and women except on a grander, exaggerated scale. Nature has done them a disservice by endowing them with an abnormal craving, creating an internal imbalance to such a degree as to create a physical disorder. The Weendigo has no other object in life but to satisfy this lust and hunger, expending all its energy on this one purpose. As long as its lust and hunger are satisfied, nothing else matters—not compassion, sorrow, reason, or judgment. Although the Weendigo is an exaggeration, it exemplifies human nature's tendency to indulge its self-interests, which, once indulged, demand even greater indulgence and ultimately result in the extreme—the erosion of principles and values.

It is ironic that the Weendigo preys upon and can only overcome ordinary human beings who, like itself, have indulged themselves to excess, and hence illustrates the lesson that excess preys and thrives on excess.

The Weendigo was born out of human susceptibility. It was also born out of the conditions that men and women had to live through in winter when it was sometimes doubtful that the little food they had would carry them through until spring. From the moment their supplies began to thin, the people faced starvation and death . . . and the Weendigo. What they feared most in their desperation and the delirium induced by famine and freezing to death was to kill and eat human flesh to survive. Nothing was more reprehensible than cannibalism.

In the following stories, humans must kill the Weendigo to betoken that they must put an end to certain self-serving indulgences or be destroyed. Every community had its catalog of stories of Weendigoes, of men and women becoming Weendigoes, of the carnage perpetrated by these giant cannibals that ends in the people's destruction. In the end, David slays Goliath; moderation triumphs over excess. The Nipissing Weendigo story exemplifies this moral.

There was once a man, as reasonably successful as any other hunter, whose family fell upon hard times during an unusually hot and dry summer, when the berries burned before they ripened. The birds and animals had enough sense to leave to find some other place, but the humans didn't have such an instinct to let them know what was forthcoming and to take measures to protect themselves. All the humans had was a kind of optimism, a conviction and hope that conditions could not long remain the way they were. And so, men and women remained anchored where they were, hoping for a change in the weather.

That winter the man and his family, like their neighbors, were reduced to eating roots and bark and snowbirds before the winter was half over. Everyone was desperate, but only this one man went to a sorcerer for a talisman that would enable him to find food and allay his hunger. The sorcerer gave him a powder made of roots, with instructions for him to brew it and drink it as a tea in the morning.

In the morning, before anyone was awake, the man woke up and made a tea, which he drank. Almost at once he began to grow in height until he was six times the height of an ordinary man.

For the moment the man was so absorbed by his growth and height that he forgot his hunger and his family's situation. He went forward to try his pace and the length of his stride. The pace of his motion pleased and excited him. He could go faster and cover greater distances than any human being alive. He would be able to outrun most large animals. In his flush of ecstasy, with the advantages and benefits now available to him, the man overlooked the disadvantages and forgot other things.

He ran until he was gasping for breath and tired; then he sat down to rest. It was only then that he became conscious of his hunger, a reality that he had temporarily forgotten. His hunger was now greater than before, and having had little sustenance before his hard run, the man weakened himself to the point of shaking. He thought of food, but the thought of animal flesh sickened him. Yet he was still hungry. He needed food to allay not only his hunger but his peculiar indescribable craving. He needed something at once, or he would collapse and waste away, providing fodder for the ravens, lynxes, and wolves. After a short rest the giant wobbled to his feet and went on.

Soon, from atop a hill, the giant saw a village in the distance. It was such a welcome sight. He put his hands to his mouth and hailed the residents before he waved at them in greeting. His voice so boomed and crackled like thunder that it startled him and so frightened the people in the camp that many dropped in their tracks and died. The giant had meant no harm. All he meant to do was to let them know that he was in their land and was there on friendly business. But he had killed many of them, though he didn't know it then, without even laying a hand on them. The rest fled.

The giant did not break his stride as he went forward. He forgot his hunger for a few moments as he listened to the echoes of his thunderous voice and saw the stricken human beings keel over. But his hunger restored him to reality, the reality made sensible by the aroma of human flesh.

In a few moments the giant was in the encampment. He took a corpse and ate it whole. He grew, but he didn't know it. He ate another corpse. He grew some more. His hunger should have diminished, but it didn't. Instead, it was as demanding as before. And he ate until he had eaten all the inhabitants who had died of fright. And he was no less hungry—no better satisfied at the end of his ravenous meal, despite all he had eaten.

Without so much as touching any of the meat that had been stored by his victims for their future needs, the giant, formerly a man, now became a Weendigo.

A man of the village survived the carnage only because he had been away when the Weendigo attacked his people and their homes. Without family or home, the man now had only one thing to live for: revenge. He set out at once, following the trail left by the Weendigo. Toward the end of winter, hundreds of miles away, the man overtook the Weendigo, now shrunk in size to the normal stature of an ordinary Weendigo. The man slew the Weendigo in the same way the monster killed his victims— unmercifully. With utter indifference to his cries for mercy or of fear and pain, he clubbed the Weendigo to death, leaving its remains to the ravens or whoever craved even the flesh of a cannibal.

A human being could become a Weendigo by his or her own excesses. That was the usual way. But one human being could also transform another into a Weendigo.

One man asked another man and wife for the hand of their daughter in marriage. The father refused, pointing out that the petitioner had already had several wives, more wives than most men, and should not take on yet another lest one of the wives be neglected. The father suggested that the man should think of other men who did not yet have wives.

The man took the refusal as an insult, as humiliating as a slap in the face in public. He didn't say anything to the father, but he was cut to the quick. As soon as he got home, he made an effigy of the girl with snow and then immersed it in water before setting it outside in the cold, where it froze solid. Afterward he buried the effigy in ashes, performing a ritual and chanting arcane psalms as he did so.

Around the same time, while the girl and her family were camped on their trapline some distance from the main village, she complained of being cold, although she did not have a fever and was not shivering. She was cold within and without. It was more than a physical cold that chilled the flesh; this cold chilled the blood, the spirit, and the soul as well. It was a chill that numbed her entire being and made her unbelievably hungry, which was strange because she and her family had just eaten a short time earlier.

The family made her a hot broth and a hot meal and wrapped her in blankets, but the girl didn't even touch the food, complaining that the smell alone made her ill and that the extra blankets and heat added to her discomfort. She was hungry and wanted food, but not the kind that she had been accustomed to eating . . . something different.

At last, unable to stand her hunger, she turned on her own family, and with great strength born of desperation, overcame and bludgeoned her family and then ate them.

When the family was overdue to return to the village by several days, the suitor-sorcerer volunteered to go in search of them. He found what he had hoped to find. As the creator of the "new" girl and her rescuer, custom allowed that he could claim the girl as his wife if he wanted to.

The girl was in a daze, unable to recall what had become of her family, of whom other than their few possessions there was no trace. But her hunger had subsided, and she went meekly with her rescuer.

Her introduction into the family not only as one of the wives but as the favorite caused a great deal more friction and unhappiness in the household than already existed. The other women resented the girl and wouldn't talk to her, but they talked about her, about her survival while her family had died. The only one who seemed to be happy with the arrangement was the sorcerer, certain that the women in the household would eventually come to terms with the situation and that their lives would become stabilized.

But the relationships in the household did not warm up as the sorcerer had hoped, and he blamed his newest wife for not making enough of an effort to fit in. The accusation only made matters worse, hurting the girl even more than she was already hurt and intensifying her loneliness and sense of isolation, even in the company of people.

The other women had families to visit and talk with, but she had none, not even the remembrance of a single one. She had only this vague sense that there was a family, that she must have had someone to love and someone to love her in return. She longed for affection and to care for someone, to belong some place where she wanted to be. Every chance she had, whenever they were alone, she asked her husband who she was, where she came from, and whether she had kin, but all he would tell her was that he had come upon her in the woods and that she was probably abandoned.

Finally, she overcame her fear and asked one of the other women in the sorcerer's household if the woman knew who she was or if she knew how she might find out. The other woman didn't know what to make of such a question—didn't know if the younger woman was putting her on or actually had lost her senses. She retorted sarcastically, "Why ask me! Why don't you ask him? What's the matter with you? Don't you know that he'd do anything for you?" The other woman hissed. "ASK HIM!"

The young woman persisted, explaining that she had already asked and had not received any satisfactory answer. Now she pleaded for help.

But the older woman remained adamant. "Ask him again!" she barked, intimating in her tone that their husband knew more about her than he let on.

Following the older woman's advice, the younger woman badgered their husband to tell her what she wanted to know. She asked him several times a day until her questions drove him to such exasperation that he told her that she had murdered and then eaten her own family. He said he had kept this fact from her to save her from guilt and that if it wasn't for his care and protection, other Weendigoes and manitous would have killed her by now.

The girl was horrified, but she didn't believe the sorcerer's story. She went to the oldest woman in the household and told her what their husband had said. The older woman explained that someone had indeed killed her family and that people suspected she had done it. People were afraid of her.

The younger woman went into a depression. She had killed the people who had loved her and whom she had loved. She no longer had anything, no memories or hopes, nothing but guilt and remorse, loneliness, and self-revulsion.

Then an awful hunger settled on her, making her feel as if she had not eaten in several days and that if she did not eat she would collapse and die that night. And as the hunger mounted, she forgot everything else. There was nothing else, only hunger.

She thought of food, meat, but such thoughts made her nauseous. She wanted nourishment, not ordinary food but human flesh.

Along with this hunger, she was enveloped by a chill akin to one brought on by fear and the onslaught of a sickness. As it settled in, the cold went deep into her soul and spirit, hard and brittle as flint.

She had to get warm or else turn into ice and die. She bundled up and gathered wood with which she made a fire and then continued to cast firewood into the blaze until it was an inferno. She stood near the blaze, but it didn't do her any good, and her hunger grew sharper. Finally, she hurled herself into the flames.

Those present were horrified. They screamed; they tried to remove her body from the flames, but the heat drove them back and they were driven away from the crematorium by the sight and stench of death. There was no outcry from the girl as she was consumed by the fire, only a hiss and vapor of steam issuing from her body as it was transformed into carbon, black.

In the morning, when the sorcerer and his wives sifted through the cold ashes in search of the girl's remains so they could give her a proper funeral, they uncovered a figurine of a woman in ice and next to it a figurine of an infant, the unborn child that she had been carrying. In the end the girl had her revenge.

As far as is known, this is the only case in which a Weendigo killed itself to turn on its creator. All other Weendigoes who were slain were slain not so much as a result of the heroism and ingenuity of humans, but as a result of the Weendigo's own personal foibles, indulging their self-interests much like humans eat hors d'oeuvres or drink a toast before the main course or engage in a period of gloating after victory before they put the enemy away. They must relish and savor the aroma of the forthcoming meal to enjoy the flavor and savor victory to an even greater degree. Weendigoes were no different from human beings in this respect.

A Weendigo residing in the Mille Lacs, Minnesota, region ambushed Nana'b'oozoo, who was in the course of hunting it. The Weendigo caught its pursuer and, though desperately hungry, put off eating Nana'b'oozoo for a while to relish the sight of this so-called human champion crying and shaking in despair. Any other time this Weendigo wouldn't have considered such a thing. Besides its physical hunger, the Weendigo had another hunger that it didn't know about, to relish the spectacle of a champion stripped of his pretensions.

The pleasure that the Weendigo derived from watching Nana'b'oozoo was worth putting off satisfying its hunger a while longer. The Weendigo had never experienced such pleasure before. It watched and listened as Nana'b'oozoo quaked, wondering what people saw in him and how he could continue to assume the role of people's champion when he was not what people thought he was.

At first the Weendigo believed that its victim was putting on an act to deceive it, but after observing him for a while, it became convinced that the tears and the trembles were real. The Weendigo decided to prolong its victim's discomfiture and its own pleasure.

Weendigo commanded Nana'b'oozoo to gather firewood for his own barbecue, and the captive complied more readily than he had ever undertaken any work. Nana'b'oozoo sweated and groaned as he went to and fro, carrying stumps and dried poles to the site of his own funeral pyre. Even when he had amassed a huge pile of wood and was at the point of dropping from exhaustion, he didn't think to rest. Nor did it occur to Nana'b'oozoo to make a break for it, to escape while he was in the forest out of sight.

To the Weendigo, Nana'b'oozoo lacked the fiber to attempt to escape, as shown by his refusal to run away despite numerous opportunities to do so. Besides, the Weendigo would have no trouble overtaking such a weakling. And to think that some Anishinaubaek looked on Nana'b'oozoo as a hero, a manitou. So sure and contemptuous of Nana'b'oozoo was the Weendigo that it decided to take a nap. Nana'b'oozoo would still be there drawing wood until he was told to stop.

Before going to sleep, the Weendigo warned Nana'b'oozoo not to try to run away and to have the fireplace, spit, and a blaze ready by the time it woke up, or else it was going to eat him alive.

Many animals saw Nana'b'oozoo work as they had never seen him work before and heard him whimper as a beaten cur, but none felt the least bit sorry for him, except one. A curious mouse wondered why the people's champion was chanting a death song when he should have been singing a joyful, cheerful tune and why he was amassing such a huge pile of wood on such a happy day.

Nana'b'oozoo stuttered between sobs that the Weendigo was going to barbecue and then eat him later on that day and that he was forced to gather firewood for his own cremation.

Asked why he did not hide or run, Nana'b'oozoo answered that if he could outrun the Weendigo or knew where he could disappear to, he would make off at once, but alas, he was not capable of outrunning the monster and knew of no place that was beyond the Weendigo's reach. He had no choice but to accept his fate and do the Weendigo's bidding.

"Why not kill the Weendigo," the mouse asked Nana'b'oo-zoo, "and be done with it."

"Ah, yes," Nana'b'oozoo sighed bitterly, he would if he knew how. The mouse told him what to do.

As instructed, Nana'b'oozoo found a long, dry stave, hard and stiff with age, and thrust one end into the white-hot coals as a blacksmith does when he tempers metal. He kept the stave in the coals until the point, which was as long as a man's forearm, was as white and red as were the coals and sent off sparks. The stave was ready. Nana'b'oozoo withdrew it from the forgelike fire and retreated a little from where the Weendigo was sleeping on his stomach with his rump upraised like a hillock.

At one hundred paces from the sleeping monster, wielding the stave like a fish spear above his head, Nana'b'oozoo turned and ran forward like a javelin thrower, running as fast as he could to give his thrust maximum force. His target was the very middle of the Weendigo's rump, and his aim was dead on. He drove the stave deep and as far forward as he could.

The Weendigo's mighty shriek of pain nearly burst Nana'b'oozoo's eardrum and sent ripples scurrying along the top of waters as the shriek echoed in every direction around Mille Lacs. The next moment, the Weendigo shot up over the trees, screaming and shrieking in agony. Its legs were already in motion the instant its feet touched the ground. Within a short while, the Weendigo was out of sight, and soon after its screams faded away.

The Mille Lacs Anishinaubaek were never again molested by a Weendigo, for the Weendigoes were afraid of Nana'b'oozoo.

Weendigoes were alike regardless of where they came from. They all had their predilections and personal fancies, preferences, and quirks that led to their downfall.

The Nipissing Weendigoes were no different. For years, they had been terrorizing the Nipissing Anishinaubaek, killing and killing until the people, hearing about the champion Nana'-b'oozoo, sent for him to get rid of the monster on their behalf.

Nana'b'oozoo, as befits a true champion avenger, left his work, family, home—everything—to go to the aid of the oppressed. Nothing else mattered, not his chances or his safety or the odds.

Nana'b'oozoo and his guides went directly to Nipissing. Not once during the course of their travel, which took several days, did Nana'b'oozoo speak other than to ask his companions to stop to eat or to allow him to go to the toilet. Nor did his companions dare interrupt him, so angry and formidable did he appear. They were afraid to cross him and be bludgeoned themselves. The man they were conducting didn't waste time in talk; he was a man of action who asked questions afterward.

At Nipissing, where a crowd had gathered at their summer village, the champion asked only one question: "Where is the Weendigo?"

From the foothills of the highlands, Nana'b'oozoo hailed the Weendigo, hurling the worst insults that he could think of upward toward the hilltops.

But instead of one monster, as he had expected, more than three dozen emerged from their dens and into Nana'b'oozoo's sight.

One look, and Nana'b'oozoo turned and fled.

To the Weendigoes, to have the champion of the Anishinaubaek come to their very door was beyond belief—it was good luck. The archenemy, the impostor, the pretender . . . there was no one they would rather have as the prize of prizes. The Weendigoes forgot everything in their eagerness to lay their hands on their archenemy.

They roared as they thundered down the hillside and stampeded toward the fleeing figure, who ran directly into the lake. Instead of sinking, he ran on top of the water, leaping from one stone to another, which had thrust to the surface as if by a miracle. The Weendigoes ran on, using the same stepping-stones as did Nana'b'oozoo, not even questioning the phenomenon of walking on water. Had they taken a moment to think about the improbability, they might have lived. They couldn't even swim. That alone ought to have stopped them from rushing headlong into the lake.

Everyone profited, as was to be expected, by the destruction of the Weendigoes, but none more so than Nana'b'oozoo. He led forty Weendigoes to their destruction in Lake Nipissing and received a hero's credit for their destruction. Actually, the Weendigoes destroyed themselves in their single-minded, blind pursuit of Nana'b'oozoo to satisfy their insatiable appetites.

▼   ▼   ▼

Over the years, the belief in and fear of Weendigoes has diminished. There is no longer the sense, as there once was, that
malevolent beings are nearby, just out of sight, ever present,
waiting to turn humans into Weendigoes. The Weendigoes may
or may not roam the north in winter any longer as they were
once believed to do, but their spirit and the ideas they embody
live on in the modern world.

The Modern Weendigoes

Once woods and forests mantled most of the North American
continent. It was the home of the Anishinaubaek (Ojibway,
Ottawa, Pottawatomi, and Algonquin), their kin, and their neighbors; it was also the home of all the animals of the land, water,
and air. Furthermore, this land was the wellspring from which all
drew their sustenance, medicine, and knowledge.

Also dwelling in the woods and forests were Weendigoes that
stalked villages and camps, waiting for foolish humans to venture
alone beyond the environs of their homes in winter. Even
though a Weendigo is a mythical figure, it represents real human
cupidity. However, as time went by, more and more learned
people declared that such monsters were a product of superstitious minds and imaginations.

As a result, the Weendigoes were driven from their place in
Anishinaubae traditions and culture and ostracized by disbelief
and skepticism. It was assumed, and indeed it appeared, as if
the Weendigoes had passed into the Great Beyond, like many
North American Indian beliefs and practices and traditions.

Actually, the Weendigoes did not die out or disappear; they
have only been assimilated and reincarnated as corporations,
conglomerates, and multinationals. They've even taken on new
names, acquired polished manners, and renounced their crav-
ings for raw human flesh in return for more refined viands. But
their cupidity is no less insatiable than that of their ancestors.

One breed subsists entirely on forests. When this particular breed beheld forests, its collective cupidity was bestirred as it looked on an endless, boundless sea of green. These modern Weendigoes looked into the future and saw money—cash, bank accounts, interest from investments, profits, in short, wealth beyond belief. Never again would they be in need.

They recruited woodsmen with axes, cross-cut saws, shovels, chains, and ropes and sent them into the forests to fell the trees.

The forests resounded with the clash of axes and the whine of saws as blades bit into the flesh of spruce, pine, and cedar to fulfill the demands of the Weendigoes in Toronto, Montreal, Vancouver, New York, Chicago, Boston, and wherever else they now dwelt. Cries of "Timber!" echoed and reechoed across the treetops, followed by the rip and tear of splintering trees. Then, finally, the crashes thundered throughout the bush.

As fast as woodsmen felled the trees, teamsters delivered sleighload after sleighload to railway sidings and to riverbanks. Train after train, shipload after shipload of timber, logs, and pulp were delivered to mills. Yet, as fast as they cut and as much as they hewed, it was never enough; quantities always fell short of the demands of the Weendigoes.

"Is that all? Should there not be more? We demand a bigger return for our risks and our investments."

The demands for more speed and more pulp, more timber, and more logs were met. Axes, saws, and woodsmen, sleighs, horses, and teamsters were replaced, and their calls no longer rang in the forest. Instead, chain saws whined, and Caterpillar tractors with jagged blades bulled and battered their way through the forest, uprooting trees to clear the way for auto-matic shearers that topped limbs and sheared the trunks. These mechanical Weendigoes gutted and desolated the forest, leaving death, destruction, and ugliness where once there was life, abundance, and beauty.

Trucks and transports, faster and bigger than horses and sleds, operated day and night delivering quantities of cargoes that their predecessors, horses and sleighs, could never match.

Still, the Weendigoes wanted more. It didn't matter if their policies of clear-cutting to harvest timber and pulp resulted in violations of the rights of North American Indians or in the further impairment of their lives—just as it didn't matter to them that their modus operandi resulted in the permanent defilement of hillside and mountainside by erosion. They are indifferent to the carnage inflicted on bears, wolves, rabbits, and warblers. Who cares if they are displaced? What possible harm has been done? Nor does it seem as if these modern Weendigoes have any regard for the rights of future generations to the yield of Mother Earth.

Profit, wealth, and power are the ends of business. Anything that detracts from or diminishes the anticipated return, whether it is taking pains not to violate the rights of others or taking measures to ensure that the land remain fertile and productive for future generations, must, it seems, be circumvented.

And what has been the result of this self-serving, gluttonous disposition? In ten short decades these modern Weendigoes have accomplished what once seemed impossible. They have laid waste to immense tracts of forest that were seen as beyond limit as well as self-propagating, ample enough to serve this generation and many more to come. Now, as the forests are in decline, the Weendigoes are looking at a future that offers scarcity, while many people are assessing the damage done, not in terms of dollars, but in terms of the damage inflicted on the environment, the climate, and botanical and zoological life. These new Weendigoes are no different from their forebears. In fact, they are even more omnivorous than their old ancestors. The only difference is that the modern Weendigoes wear elegant clothes and comport themselves with an air of cultured and dignified respectability. But still the Weendigoes bring disaster, fueled by the unquenchable greed inherent in human nature. Perhaps, as in the past, some champion, some manitou, will fell them, as Nana'b'oozoo did in the past.

GLOSSARY

Abeewi-dae The expected and anticipated guest or visitor.

Ae-pungishimook The West. A manitou who represents old age and death—the destiny and end of everything. He is lured by the youth and beauty of Winonah into possessing her, as age must ravish youth. He fathers Maudjee-kawiss, Pukawiss, Cheeby-aub-oozoo, and Nana'b'oozoo.

Algonquin A term whose origin is uncertain, it is used by anthropologists to refer to a group of first nations speaking a common language. There is no such word in the Anishinaubae language. Our word for the Anishinaubae people dwelling around the most eastern large lakes, Temagami and Nipissing, is *D'ishkwaugummeek,* a term descriptive of the location of their lands. These people call themselves Anishinaubaek.

Anamiewin A chant accompanied by drumbeats, comparable to a psalm in content, form, and style.

Anishinaubae (Anishinaubaek or Anishinaubaewuk) The good good being or beings. The word is to be understood as meaning that human beings derive their goodness from their intent. Generally, men and women intend to do what ought to be done and what is of benefit.

Anishinaubae-aki   The Anishinaubae land territory, mother land. *Aki* means earth, land, soil.

"Aupitehih igoh nauh w'gageebaudizih"   He (or she) is exceedingly foolish, foolish beyond words.

Auttissookaun (Auttissookaunuk)   The muses that dwell at the Earth's four cardinal points: North, South, East, and West. They assist storytellers in the creation of stories. *Auttissookaun* also means "story" when used in lower-case; the plural form is auttissookaunun.

Awaetchigun, awaetchigunun   A story akin to a parable.

Beboonikae   The manitou who resides at the northern cardinal point and creates winter and its hardships. The name may derive from *abi,* meaning "here," "now," and *boonikae,* meaning "to put an end to growth and life (temporarily)."

Beewun   Down, fur; a woman's name.

Cheeby (cheebyuk)   A ghost or ghosts; souls of the dead. The principle of life of a human being is known as *cheechauk.* When it leaves the human body at death, the cheechauk is transformed in form and substance and continues to exist as cheeby in the Land of Souls.

Cheeby-aub-oozoo   Born after Pukawiss to Ae-pungishmook and Winonah. Throughout his life Cheeby-aub-oozoo was preoccupied with the manitous, the supernatural, and humankind's kinship with them and their world. They revealed to him through dreams that he and humankind were to communicate with the manitous in dreams, vision quests, and purification ceremonies by means of chants and drums. Although he was considered sensible and prudent, Cheeby-aub-oozoo could not ignore Maudjee-kawiss's taunts and rashly accepted a dare that resulted in the loss of his life. Cheeby-aub-oozoo became a ghost, as his name implies, Chief of the Underworld. Just as in life Cheeby-aub-oozoo reached out to the manitous and the other world, he began the tradition of visions and dream quests and purification ceremonies; he bequeathed the spirit of music, chants, and poetry to the Anishinaubae people.

Chekaubaewiss or Chekaubishin   Terms meaning "poked in the eye." A dwarf who overcame Mishi-naubae, the Huge Being, defeating the giant as David did Goliath in biblical history. Che-kaubaewiss himself was slain by the manitous for his rashness.

Chippewas (Ojibway) To the Cree, who speak a sister language, the Anishinaubae people are unintelligible owing to their habit of speaking with machine-gun rapidity and abridging their words in the process. They coined the term "Chippewae," meaning "he or she who mumbles, stammers, or slurs," to express this perceived trait. In the plural it is *chippawaek*.

Dae'b'wae He (or she) tells the truth, is right, accurate. In its most fundamental sense, however, it means "he (or she) explains or describes perceptions according to his (or her) command of language." In other words, there is no absolute truth, only the highest degree of accuracy of which a person is capable.

Daebaudjimoot A storyteller or raconteur (man or woman) who told stories throughout the winter to entertain and teach the people about their heritage.

Daebaussigae Far-reaching light. A man's name, now a surname.

Gawaunduk The spruce; the word means guardian. According to one story, the spruce and the evergreens sheltered a chickadee when he could not accompany his kin and flock in the autumn migration to the south owing to a broken wing. From that time on, chickadees have made spruces and evergreens their shelter.

Geezhigo-Quae Sky Woman, a manitou who dwelt in the heavens. She is the mother of the Anishinaubae people and nation. She re-created the Earth from a moiety of soil that was obtained from the bottom of the sea. In doing what she did, Geezhigo-Quae exemplified what men and women are to do to fulfill themselves and to create their own worlds and beings. That is, they must go deep within themselves to retrieve the substance for creation.

"K'zaug-in" I love you.

Kawaesind The Feared One. This figure was a bully who abused and victimized the little manitous to the point where they rose up and assassinated him.

Kikinoomaukae-assin or kikinoomaukae-waubik The teaching rock. A number of these teaching rocks were situated in remote parts throughout the territory occupied by the Anishinaubae people.

Symbols were engraved on these rocks with some kind of instrument. Select youths, who were designated to be teaching elders when they grew older, were brought to these sites and tutored by elders in the meaning of the symbols. Two of the better- known sites are in the Agawa Canyon, north of Sault Ste. Marie, Ontario, and near Peterborough, Ontario.

Kitchi   Grand, immense, huge, vast, preeminent ancient, foremost. Kitchi is predicated not only of the concrete but of the abstract, whereas *mishi,* which also means big, grand, and so forth, refers only to the concrete.

Maemaegawaehnse (maemaegawaehnssiwuk)   Little people. The word means stranger who speaks a strange language. These little people are regarded as special guardians of children.

Maemaegawauhnse (maemaegawauhnssiwuk)   Butterfly (butterflies). From *meegawauhnse*—a feather, down. Anishinaubae people compared butterflies to feathers in their weight and texture.

Manitou   Mystery, essence, substance, matter, supernatural spirit, anima, quiddity, attribute, property, God, deity, godlike, mystical, incorporeal, transcendental, invisible reality.

Manitoussiwuk   Little manitous, sprites, such as maemaegawaehnssiwuk, pau-eehnssiwuk, mizauwabeekummoowuk, chekaubaewiss.

Mattawa   The name of a river in northern Ontario. It may mean either a shallow river or, more likely, a river flowing into another body of water.

Maudjee-kawiss   The first son of Ae-pungishimook and Winonah. A warrior and hunter, he led his brothers and the nation into the world and through life, exemplifying care, diligence, and courage. Maudjee-kawiss and men and women such as he perform deeds that inspire emulation and pride and are worthy of commemoration in records like the waumpum belts.

Maundau-meen   From *maundau,* meaning "wonderful," "marvelous," "extraordinary," and *meen,* meaning "seed," "berry." It denotes that the plant is foreign to the land, both in origin and in structure. The story of the origin of maize exemplifies, among other things, an unwillingness to accept agriculture as an alternative to hunting and fishing. Mandau-meen, pronounced "mandau-min," also refers to the Spirit of Maize.

Medaewaewin The sound resonance. It refers to a society of medicine men and women that was formed to preserve and advance the knowledge of plants and healing and to establish the relationship between health and upright living, known as walking in balance.

Medawaewae-igun A drum; that which produces a resonance.

Meemee A pigeon; a women's name.

Mino-idjiwun Fair current.

Mishi-bizheu The Great Lynx, which dwelt at the bottom of the sea. As the foremost inhabitant of the deep, the Great Lynx draws people down to their deaths. It has also caused floods.

Mishi-naubae A name given to any man abnormally large—a giant.

Mizauwabeekum (mizauwabeekummoowuk), or zauwabee-kum (zauwabeekummook) The little manitous that dwell in mountainous regions and escarpments, deriving their name from the gold, copper, and pyrite imbedded in the rock.

Muzzu-Kummik-Quae Earth Mother or Mother Earth. The earth nourishes, clothes, shelters, heals, teaches, and instills a sense of beauty and good, as does a human mother.

Myeengun A wolf. A child, once left untended for a few moments by his guardians, wandered away. He was found by and cared for by wolves. Eventually he became one of them. Thereafter he and the wolves shrank from human beings.

"N'gah auttissookae" I call on the muses to be with me, inspire me, guide me. . . ; I invite you to come with me on the odyssey that I'm about to embark on. . . .

N'okomiss or N'oko A grandmother. Traditionally, grandmothers were the principal teachers, the guardians of knowledge. In this text, Nana'b'oozoo's grandmother is the only person to understand his character. He always returns to her for comfort, guidance, and love.

Nana'b'oozoo The youngest son of Ae-pungishimook and Winonah. Some Anishinaubae people regard him as a manitou;

others see him as the all-man, all-woman archetypal human being. Nana'b'oozoo means well, but all too often he is prevented from fulfilling his intentions by the coarser side of his human nature—his passions, drives, whims, and emotions—just as many human beings are often prevented from attaining their purposes and discharging their responsibilities. Like many human beings, Nana'b'oozoo blunders along and sometimes is successful.

Nana'b'oozoo represents a caricatured understanding of human nature. He is not what he appears to be; his real character is hidden. Nana'b'oozoo himself does not see things as they really are.

Despite his misdeeds and violations, perpetrated on his own family and on the world of birds, animals, insects, and fish, and his profanation of ceremonies, Nana'b'oozoo has retained the affection of the Anishinaubae people, who have told hundreds of stories of his misadventures. The name derives from the prefix *Naning,* which means trembling, shaking, or quivering, combined with *oozoo,* which is the abbreviated form of *oozoowaunuk,* meaning tail. Trembling tail reflects the character of many people, timid and unwilling to take risks.

Nana'b'oozoo represents that portion of humanity that often gives in to inner weaknesses and exemplifies what ought and what ought not be done.

Nawautin Calm, peaceful, tranquil, serene; a man's name.

Nebaunaubae (nebaunaubaewuk) Merman. A manitou that lives at the bottom of the sea, lakes, or rivers and that attempts to lure women to their lairs, where they are changed into mermaids.

Nebaunaubaequae (nebaunaubaequaewuk) Mermaid. Also a manitou that serves the same purpose as a merman.

Needjee "My friend"; a companion.

Nipissing A lake in northern Ontario. It may mean "near the waters," "among the leaves," or "by the elms."

Ogimauh The foremost leader. The term is derived from *Ogindaussoowin,* which means to count or calculate. In referring to a leader, the term means he (or she) who counts a number of followers and, conversely, he (or she) who many count. Leaders did not seek followers; followers sought them. It was common for a community to have more than one leader, just as there are many flocks of geese, each with its own leader.

Ottawa Commonly believed to mean trader or traders. This meaning is doubtful because the Anishinaubae words for trade are unrelated to *ottauwauh* or *w'odauwae,* which is supposed to mean "sell," a practice that did not begin until after the Anishinaubae came into contact with white people. It is more likely that the term came from *ottauwuhnshk,* a river reed that this branch of the Anishinaubaek used as matting, bedding, and partitions.

Ozauw-amik A man's name, now a surname.

Pau-eehnse (pau-eehnssiwuk) A little manitou or manitous that dwelled on shores and beaches and emerged at night to warn humans of mermen and mermaids. Little waker-uppers.

Pauguk The Flying Skeleton; the term means the emaciated one. Pauguk, under the mistaken impression that his sister-in-law loved him, killed his brother to possess her. She killed herself in her grief. Overcome by guilt, Pauguk heard the voice of and saw the visage of his sister-in-law in the water, which caused him to overturn his canoe and drown. But the manitous and the beings of the Under-world, so horrified and incensed by Pauguk's crime, did not want him in their midst, nor did the beings in the Land of Souls. He became an outcast who was welcome nowhere.

Pawaugun A pipe; a man's name.

Pottawatomi Keepers of the Sacred Fire. The term refers to a group of men and women who were appointed to safeguard coals and to tend the fires of sacred societies.

Pukawiss Second son of Ae-pungishimook and Winonah. Whereas Maudjee-kawiss represented the serious and practical side of life, Pukawiss stood for the lighter side. From childhood, Pukawiss found meaning in the conduct of birds, animals, insects, and human beings that he enacted in dance for the entertainment and instruction of people. His father saw no point in his perfor-mances and turned from his son, prompting people to name him "the Disowned." It is from Pukawiss that the Anishinaubae people inherited their love of dance, theater, and fine dress.

Saemauh Tobacco. Used as an incense, the most suitable and fit-ting substance to immolate as an offering to the manitous. Petition-ers of favors would offer tobacco to other men and women to obtain their goodwill. The offer of tobacco was tantamount to an expression, "May Kitchi-Manitou [or another manitou] grant you your own request and petition."

Tau-hau   From *Weeshitau-tau-hau,* meaning, "Unbelievable! Beyond words! Extraordinary, astonishing."

Tissauwaesheehn   The cicada; the little painter, artist.

Totems   Symbols of birds, animals, small creatures, and fish that serve as family heralds. Originally there were only five of each, representing the five basic functions of humankind: leading, defending, providing, healing, and teaching. The word comes from *dodaem,* meaning action, heart, and nourishment.

"W'zaum-audjimoh"   He (or she) exaggerates.

Waemetik   Heart of an oak or swaying tree; a man's name.

Waub-meegwun   A man's name. The name of a mythological war chief, White Feather.

Waub-ooz or waub-oozoo   The rabbit, the white- tailed one.

Waub-kookoo   A white owl; a man's name.

Waubigun   Clay.

Waubizee-quae   Swan Woman; a woman's name.

Waubun-anung   Morning Star; a woman's name.

Waubunowin   A society of men and women dedicated to the study of medicine and healing. From their habit of convening at night and terminating their meetings in the morning, they were known as the Society of the Dawn.

Waugizih   A discolored, disfigured kernel of corn. It also refers to a form of marriage lottery in which single women took part during the corn harvest; the woman who drew the cob that bore the discolored, disfigured kernel was destined to marry an old widower.

Waumpum or wampum   A quilled or beaded sash with symbols woven into it, that served as a historical record to speakers in their references to past events, ideas, and beliefs, and to many aspects of the cultural heritage.

Ween'b'oozoo   A Menominee and a western Anishinaubae name for Nana'b'oozoo. Dirty tail or soiled. Though the name is different, the basic understanding of the figure is the same.

Wigwam A lodge (dwelling) constructed of birch bark.

Weegwauss A birch tree.

Weendigo (Weendigook or Weendigoes) A giant cannibal (or cannibals). These manitous came into being in winter and stalked villagers and beset wanderers. Ever hungry, they craved human flesh, which is the only substance that could sustain them. The irony is that having eaten human flesh, the Weendigoes grew in size, so their hunger and craving remained in proportion to their size; thus they were eternally starving. They could kill only the foolish and the improvident.

Winonah Daughter of a woman known only as N'okomiss, grandmother, Winonah means "to nourish." She was ravished four times by Ae-pungishimook and gave birth to a son after each ravishment over a period of generations, but no daughters. Through sexual union with a manitou, Winonah, a human, acquired the supernatural, mythical attributes of fertility and long life.

Zhauwuno The South. A manitou that dwells in the south and presides over growth and abundance.